JAMAICA IN MAPS

to Aidan and Veronica

JAMAICA IN MAPS: Graphic Perspectives of a Developing Country

Colin G. Clarke, M.A., D.Phil.
Senior Lecturer in the Department of Geography and
Centre for Latin-American Studies,
University of Liverpool

Cartography by Alan G. Hodgkiss
Senior Technical Officer,
Department of Geography,
University of Liverpool

AFRICANA PUBLISHING CO · NEW YORK
A division of Holmes & Meier Publishers, Inc.

Published in the United States of America 1974
by Africana Publishing Company
A division of Holmes & Meier Publishers, Inc.
101 Fifth Avenue, New York, N.Y. 10003

Library of Congress Catalog Card No. 74 – 84659
ISBN 0 8419 0175 9

Printed in Great Britain

CONTENTS

ACKNOWLEDGEMENTS

For permission to redraw maps and diagrams in the following sections I am indebted to:

Section 9: Director, University of Florida Press, for Figure 12 in L. Alan Eyre, *Population Dynamics in Jamaica*, Florida Atlantic University Press, Boca Raton, 1972, p. 32;

Section 3: Department of Defense Aerial Photographic Library, Washington, for the vertical air photographs of Central Jamaica, Air Photographic and Charting Service (MATS), US Air Force;

Section 28: Editor, *Area*, for Figure 2 in Barry N. Floyd, 'Rural land development in Jamaica', *Area*, 1970, no. 1, p. 9;

Section 22: Editor, *Geographical Review*, for Figure 6 in L. Alan Eyre, 'The shantytowns of Montego Bay, Jamaica', *Geographical Review*, vol. 62, 1972, p. 405;

Section 16: Editor, *Social and Economic Studies*, for Diagram 1 in E. Ahiram, 'Distribution of income in Trinidad and Tobago and comparison with distribution of income in Jamaica', *Social and Economic Studies*, vol. 15, 1966, p. 107;

Section 8: Barry W. Higman, for 'Holdings of more than 100 slaves, 1832' and 'Town Slaves 1832', in 'Slave population and economy in Jamaica at the time of emancipation', unpublished Ph.D. thesis, University of the West Indies, 1970;

Section 29: Donald Q. Innis, for Figure 1 in 'The efficiency of Jamaican peasant land use', *Canadian Geographer*, vol. V, no. 2, 1961, p. 20;

Section 29: Jamaica Agricultural Society, for maps of soil erosion and slope categories in T. F. Finch, 'Soil survey of the area administered by the Yallahs Valley Land Authority' and 'A land-capability classification for the Yallahs Valley Area' in *The Farmer's Guide*, Kingston, no date;

Sections 20, 28, 29, 30, 31, 32, 33, 34: Ministry of Mining and Natural Resources, Government of Jamaica, for maps of small farming, sugar, grassland, bananas, citrus, coconuts, coffee, cocoa, markets, forests and land settlements in the *National Atlas of Jamaica*, vol. II, Kingston, Government Printing Office, 1971.

Sections 3, 4, 19, 22: The relief map of Jamaica and the maps of geology and drainage are based on the Directorate of Overseas Surveys' 1:250,000 series; the maps of Hampden, Christiana, Port Antonio, Spanish Town and Falmouth are based on Directorate of Overseas Surveys' 1:50,000 series, DOS 410, and the map of Montego Bay on the 1:25,000 series DOS 310, by permission of HM Stationery Office.

INTRODUCTION

This volume contains 42 sheets of maps of Jamaica, each accompanied by a text. The aim is to provide the reader with a wide range of geographical material, though only certain aspects of each topic are, of course, amenable to cartographic or diagrammatic treatment. The text aims at more than a simple analysis of the line-drawings; each sheet is accompanied by a brief essay. A drawback with this type of book is that it suggests linkages between topics but does not explore them. This deficiency has been partly remedied by including separate introductions to the social and economic geography of the island. The role of these sections is to synthesize patterns and processes which are isolated by the format.

The sequence of maps and text has been arranged so that the book can be read straight through. However, many people will want to consult only a few maps at a time. Each page of text is self-contained, but readers are reminded that some of the topics are closely related, and that to examine one sheet of maps without looking at its neighbours will result in missing much that is important. A word of apology is also appropriate. As the text is fragmented, a certain amount of repetition is unavoidable.

It is a geographical platitude to speak of 'unity in diversity'. But Jamaicans of all walks of life must eventually come to the realization that the island consists of many ill-co-ordinated spatial elements, and that a coherent functional unity can be achieved only by a system of regional planning which takes areal differentiation into account. There are already signs of a growing awareness in Jamaica of the importance of regional variations. The Jamaica Town Planning Department and the United Nations Development Programme have produced an atlas to accompany their National Physical Plan. There is less excuse now for government economists to depict the island as a homogeneous plain. These observations seem to run counter to the current trend in geography, which is towards an emphasis on the general at the expense of the unique. But these two approaches represent different sides of the same coin; this book stresses the diversity of Jamaica largely because it has so often been denied.

Jamaica developed as a slave society, and its early history has produced a variety of institutions, structures, attitudes and geographical patterns which are still of considerable moment. No part of the book is devoted to historical geography, but several maps incorporate an historical dimension, while graphs depict more recent time-series. The sections dealing with sugar, population, race and religion contain a certain amount of information on the eighteenth and nineteenth centuries. Much of it provides an underpinning to contemporary problems.

Jamaica is relatively well-endowed with statistical compendia and the map coverage is good. Topographic sheets are available at 1 : 50,000 and some of the towns have been mapped at larger scales. The principal sources used when compiling the maps and diagrams for this book were the *Reports of the 1960 Census*, the *Annual Digest of Statistics*, the *Economic Survey of Jamaica*, various departmental reports, the *Reports of the Agricultural Census, 1960-61*, and the *Handbook of Jamaica*. At this time each decade social scientists are confronted with a major dilemma: previous census material is old, but the results of the most recent enumeration have yet to be fully tabulated. In the case of Jamaica this decennial problem is compound by the temporary shortage of alternative sources of data. The excellent *Handbook of Jamaica* has not been published for several years. The *Annual Digest of Statistics* has not appeared since 1967, and the *Economic Survey of Jamaica* for 1970 arrived only in the middle of 1972, just as the maps were being completed. Economy drives in government departments have resulted in the stencilling of annual reports, and the latter are not easily obtainable. Paradoxically, as the island has developed, so the sources needed to trace its progress have dried up. However, these quantitative deficiencies have been partly remedied by the spate of publications on Jamaica by West Indian scholars. Their writings on geography, politics, sociology and economics enable the text to deal in some detail with the decade since independence.

This study is the outcome of more than a decade's research on Jamaica – much of it devoted to Kingston, the capital. During this time I have visited the island four times and accumulated numerous debts to institutions and individuals. The Institute of Social and Economic Research and the Department of Geography at the University of the West Indies have provided me with accommodation and facilities; the Central Planning Unit, Government Town Planning Department, the United Nations Development Programme, and the Department of Statistics have generously supplied me with information and insights. I owe a special word of thanks to Dr Barry Higman and Mrs Phyllis Mensah for the trouble they have taken to send me up-to-date information about Jamaica, and to Professor R. W. Steel for his advice and encouragement, especially in the early days of the project. My greatest debt of gratitude, however, is to my cartographer, Alan Hodgkiss. The book has been a truly co-operative venture, and I have derived both pleasure and profit from our association. His cartographic skill speaks for itself.

1 JAMAICA IN THE AMERICAS

Jamaica is situated in the zone which extends southwards from the United States border with Mexico to the Caribbean coastlands of Colombia and Venezuela. This entire region is frequently known as Middle America. Located in the north-western sector of the Caribbean archipelago, the island lies between latitudes 17° 43' and 18° 32' North and longitudes 76° 11' and 78° 21' West. Its closest neighbours are the republics of Cuba and Haiti, 145 km (90 mls) to the north and 160 km (100 mls) to the east, respectively. The physical fragmentation of the Caribbean facilitated the establishment of colonies by the European powers during the sixteenth, seventeenth, and eighteenth centuries. Cuba was Spanish, Haiti (Saint Domingue) belonged to France, and Jamaica for a time became one of the most prosperous of the British colonies. The metropolitan dominance of Britain from 1655, when the island was captured from Spain, until its independence in 1962, had an inhibiting influence on Jamaica's contact with adjacent territories – including the other British islands. Although both Canada and the United States have been among Jamaica's trading partners for scores of years, the island's links with its closest neighbours have been tenuous and temporary. At the beginning of this century Jamaicans helped to build the Panama Canal, emigrated as plantation labourers to the 'banana republics' of Central America, and worked on the sugar estates in Cuba; but formal contacts through trade and diplomacy were minimal.

Since independence Jamaica has exchanged political representatives with a number of Latin American countries, and agreed with Venezuela to study ways and means of effecting technical co-operation in a variety of fields. Nevertheless, trade between Jamaica and the republics of Central and South America still accounts for less than two per cent of the value of the island's imports and exports, and this proportion is unlikely to expand in the near future. The mainland territories peripheral to the Caribbean are already involved in two major economic groupings, the Latin American Free Trade Association (LAFTA) and the Central American Common Market (CACOM). LAFTA embraces Mexico and all the South American units with the exception of the Guianas. CACOM incorporates the Central American countries but omits Panama. It has developed rapidly since 1951, and has proceeded through a series of stages which involved the setting up of a free trade area, its transformation into a custom's union, and finally, in 1960, the creation of a common market characterized by the free internal circulation of people, goods and capital.

Jamaica is a member of the newest economic grouping in Middle America – the Caribbean Free Trade Association (CARIFTA). CARIFTA was inspired by economists at the University of the West Indies, and established in 1968 through the initiative of Barbados, Guyana and Antigua, located 1,600 km (1,000 mls) away from Jamaica in the south-eastern Caribbean. All the Commonwealth Caribbean units have joined, including the two mainland enclaves. It is hoped to foster inter-territory trade, ameliorate the constraints of small scale economies, embark upon regional economic planning, and encourage integration. According to one West Indian leader, 'Our aims and aspirations are set towards a common external tariff and a full customs union.' Jamaica is one of the principal industrial producers in CARIFTA and hopes to benefit from the doubling of consumers in its market. But it is unlikely that the economies of scale at this level of regionalization will be considerable, and improbable that inter-island exports will soon account for more than one-tenth of the region's total trade. All the member countries are essentially primary producers whose commodities are competitive rather than complementary. Nevertheless, CARIFTA may eventually dispel some of the mutual ignorance and suspicion which beset West Indian affairs, and could provide a framework for developing the whole region. To pursue this very policy, a Caribbean Development Bank has been set up in Barbados and a regional secretariat located in Guyana. Although they receive priority treatment from the development bank, the smallest islands have been dissatisfied with liberalization of trade, which, they claim, operates in favour of Jamaica and Trinidad. The Windwards and Leewards have created their own common market within the free trade area.

While CARIFTA brings together many of the territories omitted by CACOM and LAFTA, it is unlikely to involve either Cuba, whose trade is now almost exclusively with the Soviet bloc, or Puerto Rico, which is an 'estado associado libre', or commonwealth of the United States and lies within its tariff wall. However, both Haiti and the Dominican Republic have expressed interest in joining, and so has the mainland state of Venezuela. The membership of Haiti and the Dominican Republic would broaden the cultural basis of the grouping yet hardly strengthen it economically. But Venezuela would diversify CARIFTA's resource base, and provide a link with LAFTA. There is nothing to suggest that Jamaica would welcome such a move, and the island's leaders seem more attracted to an association with the European Common Market now that Britain has joined.

Paradoxically, since independence Jamaica's international horizons have contracted in certain respects. The island has become more American in orientation. While remaining in the British Commonwealth, it has secured admittance to the Organization of American States (OAS), and access to the institutions, expertise and funds established by this regional grouping. British influence is now counterweighted by that of the United States, the wealthiest and most powerful country in the hemisphere, and the self-appointed defender of the political integrity of the Americas as expressed by the Monroe Doctrine. Jamaica is comforted that the United States has filled the geopolitical vacuum created by the British withdrawal from the Caribbean since 1962, and indebted to the United States and Canada for inflows of capital and aid. The island subscribes to the anti-communist stance of the 'free world', but has renewed trade and diplomatic links with Cuba.

JAMAICA IN THE AMERICAS

110° 100° 90°W

U. S. A.

- Baltimore
- Washington

-30°

MEXICO

- Houston
- New Orleans
- Tampico

Gulf of Mexico

- Mexico City
- Vera Cruz

-23½°

-20°

- Miami
- Key West
- Havana

BAHAMA
ISLANDS

GUATEMALA
Belize
BRITISH
HONDURAS

HONDURAS

SALVADOR

NICARAGUA

PACIFIC OCEAN

COSTA
RICA

Canal Zone
Colon

PANAMA

-10°N

JAMAICA Kingston

CUBA

GREATER

DOMINICAN
REPUBLIC

HAITI

ANTILLES

PUERTO
RICO

Caribbean Sea

Leeward Islands

LESSER

ANTILLES

Windward
BARBADOS
Islands

TOBAGO
TRINIDAD

ATLANTIC OCEAN

10°N

Caracas

VENEZUELA

GUYANA
Georgetown

Paramaribo

SURINAM

Cayenne

FRENCH
GUIANA

COLOMBIA

- Bogota

-0°

ECUADOR

- Quito

PERU

B R A Z I L

0°

- Belem

Organisation of American
States (O.A.S.)

0 Miles 500
0 Kilometres 800

0 Miles 500
0 Kilometres 800

Latin American Free Trade
Association (L.A.F.T.A.)

Caribbean Free Trade Association
(C.A.R.I.F.T.A.)

Central American Common Market
(C.A.C.O.M.)

100° 80° 70° 60° 50°

2 JAMAICA IN THE WEST INDIES

Jamaica covers an area of 11,396 sq. km (4,400 sq. mls) and is scarcely equal in size to the English county of Yorkshire. It experiences problems common to many small islands. Insularity entails a small-scale economy and high transport costs caused by the break of bulk at the sea-ports; it breeds isolation and parochialism. Jamaica's isolation in the Caribbean is exacerbated by two factors. From the point of view of its history, society, politics, economics and language it is closer to the small Commonwealth islands of the Lesser Antilles than to either Cuba or Haiti. But more than 1,600 km (1,000 mls) of sea separate Jamaica from the Windwards and Leewards, and it is largely excluded from the pattern of close inter-island contacts which characterize the south-eastern Caribbean.

At the end of the second world war only Jamaica's neighbours in the Greater Antilles – Cuba, Haiti and the Dominican Republic – were independent. However, a number of alternatives to colonialism were rapidly evolved. France and Holland proceeded to incorporate their West Indian territories. Guadeloupe, Martinique and French Guiana became *départements* of France, sending representatives to the Chamber of Deputies in Paris. Holland transformed itself and its Caribbean possessions into the Tripartite Kingdom of the Netherlands, and granted the Antilles and Surinam separate legislatures with powers of internal self-government. But Britain was determined to shed its impoverished West Indian territories, and in 1947 the Secretary of State for the Colonies convened a conference at Montego Bay to discuss the creation of a Federation of the West Indies.

Negotiations about the constitution, political representation, finance, taxation, migration and the location of the capital dragged on throughout the 1950s, and several important issues had been only partially resolved when the federation was finally inaugurated in 1958. The union embraced the 'big three' islands, Jamaica, Trinidad and Barbados, together with all the British Leewards and Windwards; the peripheral colonies of the Bahamas, British Virgin Islands, British Honduras and British Guiana chose to remain outside the federation. Tensions were soon created between Jamaica and the federal government, which was located in the distant and little-known island of Trinidad. The situation was aggravated by the refusal of federal leadership by Jamaica's most prominent politicians. Furthermore, in 1959 Jamaica was granted full internal self-government, and thus possessed a constitution more advanced than that of the federation itself.

Many Jamaicans opposed the creation of a strong federal centre because they feared it would undermine the island's right of self-determination. They anticipated federal interference in taxation and tariffs and suspected this would undermine Jamaica's attempts to industrialize its economy using incentives and protection; and they claimed that although they accounted for half the population and area of the federation, they were under-represented in the legislature yet bore a disproportionately large percentage of the costs of government. The Jamaican premier, Norman Manley, eventually secured the various amendments to the federal constitution required by his own party, but the political opposition maintained that Jamaica should withdraw from the federation. Although an ardent West Indian himself, Manley felt constrained to put Jamaica's membership to the test of a referendum. In September 1961 the island, by a small majority, rejected federation. Jamaica became independent in August 1962 and was followed by Trinidad (September 1962), and by Barbados and Guyana (1966). Most of the other islands have subsequently become self-governing states associated with Britain – rather on the lines of Puerto Rico's relationship to the United States.

Although the federation collapsed in 1962, Jamaica still co-operates with the other units through a variety of organizations and institutions. Outstanding among the latter is the University of the West Indies which was founded in Jamaica in 1946. The university now maintains campuses in Jamaica, Trinidad and Barbados, and frequently gives students their first awareness of a West Indian identity. Some of the common services set up under the auspices of the federation survive. The Caribbean Meteorological Service is supported by all the former federal units, together with British Honduras, the Bahamas, Venezuela, the USA and the French and Dutch territories. If co-operation in meteorology is essential in an area beset by the danger of hurricanes, a West Indian Shipping Service has been vital to inter-island contact and trade. Two boats, the Federal Maple and the Federal Palm, were presented by Canada to the West Indies Federation. In 1962 they were placed under the control of the Regional Shipping Service, and one of them still plies a regular trade between Jamaica and the south-eastern Caribbean. An important inter-territory service is provided by British West Indian Airways, originally a subsidiary of BOAC, and now owned by the Trinidad Government. There are several professional societies that cater for Jamaica and the other English-speaking territories – the West Indies Bar Association, the Guyana and West Indies Teachers Association, and the Federation of Civil Servants of the West Indies. Jamaica also co-operates with a number of other territories in finding markets and fixing prices for certain exports: outstanding examples are the banana trade and the West Indies Sugar Agreement.

Although these modest arrangements have been consolidated by the Heads of Government Conference and the establishment of the Caribbean Free Trade Association (CARIFTA), Jamaica has not been a major advocate of post-colonial integration. Incipient chauvinism characterized Jamaica's relations with the other islands during the 1960s. It joined CARIFTA late, and only after its attempt to secure the regional bank had failed; and it eschewed the abortive Declaration of Granada published in November 1971, which set 1974 as the target for the creation of a new federation. However, in July 1973 Jamaica agreed to form a Caribbean Community with Trinidad and Tobago, Barbados, and Guyana. It is hoped that the small Commonwealth islands of the Lesser Antilles will eventually become members.

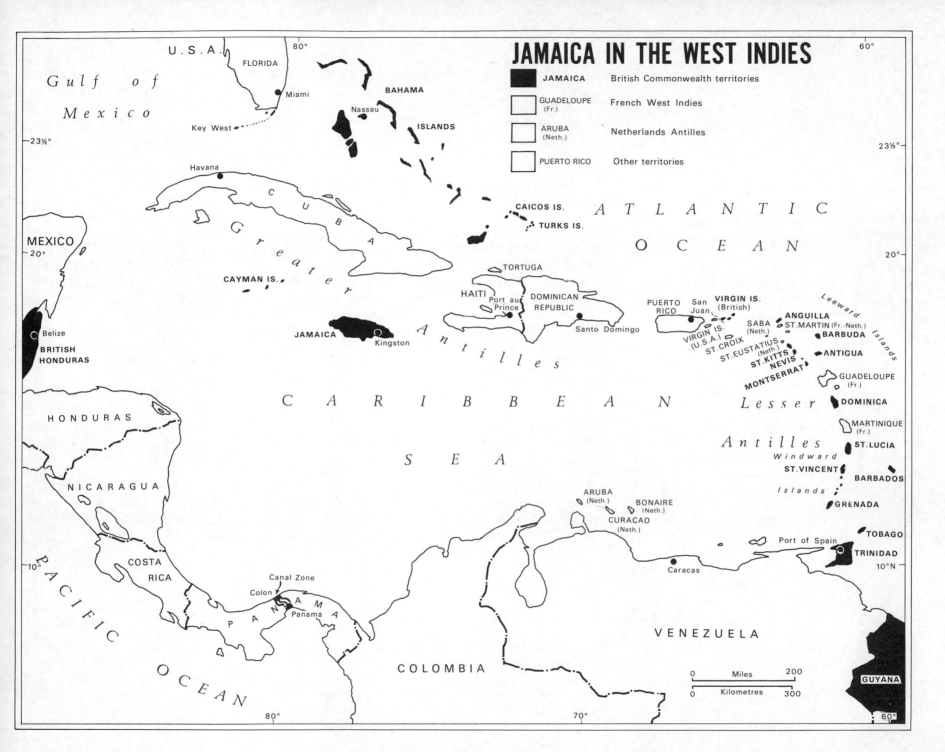

JAMAICA IN THE WEST INDIES

■	**JAMAICA**	British Commonwealth territories
□	**GUADELOUPE** (Fr.)	French West Indies
□	**ARUBA** (Neth.)	Netherlands Antilles
□	**PUERTO RICO**	Other territories

Gulf of Mexico

U.S.A.

FLORIDA

Miami

Key West

23½°

20°

MEXICO

Greater

C U B A

Havana

CAYMAN IS.

Antilles

JAMAICA

Kingston

Belize

BRITISH HONDURAS

BAHAMA

ISLANDS

Nassau

CAICOS IS.

TURKS IS.

A T L A N T I C

O C E A N

23½°

20°

TORTUGA

HAITI

Port au Prince

DOMINICAN REPUBLIC

Santo Domingo

PUERTO RICO

San Juan

VIRGIN IS. (British)

VIRGIN IS. (U.S.A.)

SABA (Neth.)

ST.CROIX

ST.EUSTATIUS (Neth.)

ANGUILLA

ST.MARTIN (Fr.-Neth.)

BARBUDA

ANTIGUA

ST.KITTS

NEVIS

MONTSERRAT

GUADELOUPE (Fr.)

Leeward

Islands

HONDURAS

NICARAGUA

COSTA RICA

C A R I B B E A N

S E A

Lesser

Antilles

DOMINICA

MARTINIQUE (Fr.)

ST.LUCIA

Windward

ST.VINCENT

Islands

BARBADOS

GRENADA

ARUBA (Neth.)

BONAIRE (Neth.)

CURAÇAO (Neth.)

Canal Zone

Colon

P A N A M A

Panama

10°

P A C I F I C

O C E A N

COLOMBIA

Caracas

V E N E Z U E L A

Port of Spain

TOBAGO

TRINIDAD

10°N

GUYANA

0	Miles	200
0	Kilometres	300

80°

70°

60°

3 RELIEF

Shaped planimetrically like a swimming turtle, Jamaica's maximum dimensions are 235 km (146 mls) from east to west, and 80 km (50 mls) from north to south. Jamaica is a mountainous island; half of it stands above 300 m (1,000 ft) and the highest point, 2,256 m (7,402 ft), is achieved in Blue Mountain Peak. From the physiographical point of view there are two Jamaicas: a highland interior, which forms the backbone of the island, and a flat, coastal periphery. The shape, long axis, and elevation of the island reflect the influence of a mountain system which once probably linked the Greater Antilles and Central America.

As the evidence of the map and cross-profiles indicate, the highlands may be divided into peaks and plateaux. The former characterize the Blue Mountains which make up the eastern end of the island. The Blue Mountains consist of a series of peaks, each more than 900 m (3,000 ft) high, joined together by the Grand Ridge. To the north and south of this ridge the land drops steeply to a narrow coastal plain. Subsidiary ridges lead down from the centre of the mountain complex and divide the flanks into a fretwork of spurs and deep, steep-sided valleys. The high plateaux occupy large tracts throughout the remainder of the island and occur at two main levels; between 300 and 600 m (1,000 and 2,000 ft) and between 600 and 900 m (2,000 and 3,000 ft). The higher of the two levels is best-developed in the Dry Harbour Mountains, though a similar height is also recorded in the Santa Cruz Mountains, the May Day Mountains, and in several isolated uplands scattered throughout the interior. The 300–600 m (1,000–2,000 ft) surface covers a much wider area, and at its edge drops down to the coastal plains. There is, however, a certain amount of land between the 150 m and 300 m (500 ft and 1,000 ft) contours. A col at this elevation lying to the north of St Thomas in Ye Vale leads eastwards into the Blue Mountains; the upper reaches of the broad Rio Minho valley have been etched into the plateau

surface just below the 300 m (1,000 ft) contour; and detached outliers with summits in the 150–300 m (500–1,000 ft) range occur in the coastal plain. However, in some places the plateaux drop precipitously to the lowlands; for example, near St Ann's Bay on the north coast, at Long Bay on the south, and at Spur Tree Hill where the high plateau edge overhangs Horse Savannah.

The plain is no more than two miles wide along the north coast of the island, and is equally restricted on the south side immediately to the east of Kingston and in the area adjacent to Long Bay. Elsewhere the coastal strip has expanded to form broad embayments, the most extensive being at the eastern and western ends of the island, and on the south coast between the Liguanea Plain and the mouth of the Milk River. Partially enclosed embayments are located at Horse Savannah on the south coast and the Queen of Spain's Valley on the north, the latter opening up the narrow plain behind Falmouth. Two features on the south coast deserve passing attention; the swamps, and the Palisadoes spit which protects Kingston harbour from the open sea. Lowlands are not confined to the periphery of the island. Two major interior valleys are depicted on the map, and there are many smaller examples. One is located along the course of the Great River to the south of Montego Bay; the other forms St Thomas in Ye Vale, which occupies part of the narrow neck of land between the high plateaux in the west and the Blue Mountains in the east. St Thomas in Ye Vale is almost oblong in shape and surrounded on all four sides by a steep plateau edge. In the south, an exit is provided by a narrow defile or gorge which leads down to Spanish Town and the Plain of St Catherine.

With the exception of the Blue Mountains, the general impression presented by the map is of an island characterized by flats rather than slopes; of plateaux, coastal plains, coastal embayments, and interior valleys. However, nothing could be further from the truth, as the vertical air-photographs clearly indicate. Photograph A* shows the dissected nature of the high plateau in the Dry Harbour Mountains. Landforms

comprise rounded, conical or elongated hummocks, with depressions between them. In some areas the depressions lose their cockpit shape and the upper slopes are steeper and less convex: here the dominant suite of landforms comprises upstanding towers of rock. Cockpits, often of a degraded type, cover about two-thirds of Jamaica. This landform achieves its optimum development in the Dry Harbour Mountains, the Cockpit Country and the John Crow Mountains, but also occurs on the fringe of the Blue Mountains and penetrates some of the coastal plains. On the edge of the lower plateau the haystack hills are often laid out in linear formations; but in the Hellshire Hills the hummocks are few and the surface is almost flat. The scale of the local relief in the cockpit country varies from a few metres to as much as 150 m (500 ft) on the most mature interior plateaux. Only rarely is the pimpled surface organized into clear-cut ridges and valleys, and the herring-bone pattern which typifies the topography of the Blue Mountains occurs in relatively few locations in the central and western districts. Photograph B, however, taken just north of Christiana, contains both cockpit country and a finely fretted landscape of ridges and valleys. Furthermore, the north-eastern corner of the photograph represents a degraded district where the surface is pitted with depressions. The contrast between cockpit country and ridge and valley on the microscale, and between mountain peaks, plateaux and lowlands on the macroscale, can be fully understood only in the light of the island's geology.

* The two plates set out in photograph A may be viewed together under a hand stereoscope to produce a three-dimensional effect.

RELIEF
After D.O.S.

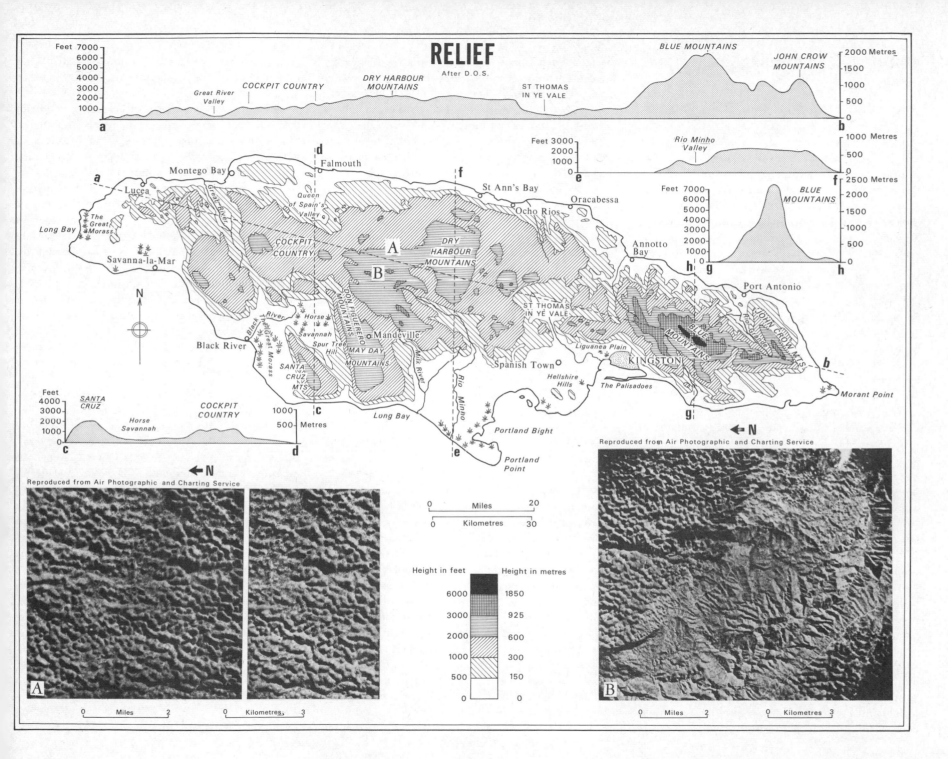

Feet 7000 6000 5000 4000 3000 2000 1000 — 2000 Metres / 1500 / 500

BLUE MOUNTAINS

JOHN CROW MOUNTAINS

Great River Valley   COCKPIT COUNTRY   DRY HARBOUR MOUNTAINS   ST THOMAS IN YE VALE

a ——————————————————————— b

Feet 3000 2000 1000 — 1000 Metres / 500

Rio Minho Valley

e ——————————————————————— f   2500 Metres

Feet 7000 6000 5000 4000 3000 2000 1000 — 1500 1000 500

BLUE MOUNTAINS

h ——————————————————————— g

Montego Bay
Falmouth
St Ann's Bay
Ocho Rios
Oracabessa

Lucea
The Great Morass
Long Bay

Great River
Queen of Spain's Valley

COCKPIT COUNTRY

A
B
DRY HARBOUR MOUNTAINS

Annotto Bay
Port Antonio

Savanna-la-Mar

N

Black River
The Great Morass

DON FIGUEREO MOUNTAINS
Horse Savannah
Spur Tree Hill
SANTA CRUZ MTS
MAY DAY MOUNTAINS
Mandeville

ST THOMAS IN YE VALE

BLUE MOUNTAINS
Rio Grande
JOHN CROW MTS

b

Liguanea Plain
Spanish Town
KINGSTON

Hellshire Hills
The Palisadoes

Morant Point

Feet 4000 3000 2000 1000 — 1000 500 Metres

SANTA CRUZ   Horse Savannah   COCKPIT COUNTRY

c ——————————————————————— d

Long Bay
Portland Bight
Portland Point

Rio Minho

g

e

A

← N

0 — Miles — 2   0 — Kilometres — 3

B

← N

0 — Miles — 2   0 — Kilometres — 3

0 — Miles — 20
0 — Kilometres — 30

Height in feet		Height in metres
6000	■	1850
3000		925
2000		600
1000		300
500		150
0		0

4 GEOLOGY AND DRAINAGE

Jamaica comprises two distinct geological zones. Its eastern extremity is composed principally of igneous and metamorphic rocks, while the remaining two-thirds of the island is formed by limestones which lie unconformably on the older material. The island has an anticlinal structure, its axis running from east to west. The basal complex, which outcrops in the Blue Mountains, consists of volcanic ashes and tuffs, intruded granodiorites, and metamorphosed rocks of Cretaceous and possibly Jurassic age: it was subject to two cycles of Laramide orogenesis in late Cretaceous and early Tertiary times. The second period of mountain building severely contorted the Richmond and Wag Water formations. Submergence of the land beneath mid-Tertiary seas resulted in the sedimentation of the Yellow and White Limestone Formations. Elevation and block-faulting of the white limestone occurred in the late Tertiary; faults run north-south and east-west, the latter reflecting structural trends in the Cretaceous basement. The embayments on the south coast have been down-faulted and floored with loose alluvial and deltaic deposits of Pleistocene age. In most of these plains alluvial deposition is still in progress. A broad, shallow shelf extends for several miles off the south coast, and is studded with coral and algal reefs and cays of coralline detritus and sand. The Caribbean is almost tideless, and the Palisadoes spit which is underlain by a series of karstic knolls, has been extended across Kingston harbour by westward-moving material supplied by the Hope, Cane and Bull Bay Rivers. Both on the north coast and in the vicinity of Morant Bay, Quaternary uplift has raised a wave-cut platform and coral reefs above sea level. The north coast is faulted, and a steep scarp leads down to the Bartlett Trough. Fringing reefs and barriers are confined to a narrow coastal belt and are absent wherever river mouths reduce the salinity.

Substantial erosion has occurred in the Blue Mountains where recent uplift has entrenched the river valleys to depths of several hundred metres. Moreover, in central and western districts, the capping of white and yellow limestone has been breached, and inliers of Cretaceous materials, especially shales, conglomerates, limestones and tuffs, have been revealed. The central inlier is an outstanding geological feature; it outcrops at heights above 600 m (2,000 ft), and produces a distinctive landscape of ridges and valleys. The system of faults, too, has direct topographic effects. Fault scarps set a limit to coastal plains and interior basins, as exemplified by Spur Tree Hill and St Thomas in Ye Vale. The southwest coast follows the alignment of faults, and so do the valleys of the Milk, Great and Plantain Garden Rivers. The Wag Water and Yallahs Faults in the Blue Mountains are loci for the epicentres of earthquakes. Jamaica has experienced two major shocks: in 1692 Port Royal on the Palisadoes was destroyed; in 1907 Kingston was severely damaged and the city centre gutted. The most recent earthquake occurred in 1957 and was centred on the sea-floor eight kilometres west of Montego Bay. Tremors were relayed throughout the island by the system of faults.

The broad geological divisions are clearly expressed in relief and elevation. Furthermore, the hard, crystalline white limestone is responsible for the cockpit karst which characterizes the wet interior plateaux. The limestone is well-jointed and permeable, and there is virtually no surface run-off. The dual processes of solution and collapse have created conical hills and cockpits, which contain extensive bauxite deposits. Jointing and faulting have directed the pattern and alignment of cockpits, and some depressions have been enlarged along lines of structural weakness to produce glades. On the northern edge of the Cockpit Country, where the rest-level of the water table rises to the base of the cockpits, lateral planation takes place, and landforms of cone and cockpit (*Kegel Karst*) are replaced by upstanding towers of rock (*Turm Karst*). In areas receiving less than 190 cm (75 in.) of rainfall or where the limestones contain marly facies, karst features are confined to pits or *dolines* and to interior valleys or *poljes*. These landforms are common near the north coast, the Queen of Spain's Valley providing an excellent example of a *polje* fashioned by flood water.

The main water-parting runs east-west following the long axis of the island. Jamaica's Amerindian name, *Xaymaca*, is supposed to signify an abundance of streams, but only the eastern districts deserve the Arawaks' description. The impermeable Blue Mountains are the wettest part and give rise to numerous rivers: the stream density is high and the pattern essentially dendritic. Only the Grand Ridge separates many north and south-flowing streams, and headward erosion by the Wag Water River has pushed the water-parting at one point to within 16 km (10 mls) of the south coast. The rivers which drain the Blue Mountains are permanent but highly irregular in regime. Wet seasons result in flash floods and severe erosion. Most rivers are strewn with boulders and some are interrupted by cascades: they are of little or no navigational value, and few can be harnessed for hydroelectricity.

Large areas in the central and western parts of Jamaica are virtually devoid of surface run-off. The limestone plateaux are characterized by seasonal streams, dry valleys, swallow holes, caves, caverns, and underground rivers. An outstanding example of a limestone gorge occurs south of Bog Walk, where the Rio Cobre flows through a narrow cleft, draining the *polje* of St Thomas in Ye Vale. Stream density is high only where the shale inliers outcrop or rivers cross the interior basins and coastal embayments. Some of these drainage basins are large in area, but discharge only in the wet seasons. The headwaters of the larger surface-flowing rivers rarely penetrate far into the limestone plateaux, the major exception being the Rio Minho which rises in the central shale inlier before flowing to the south coast.

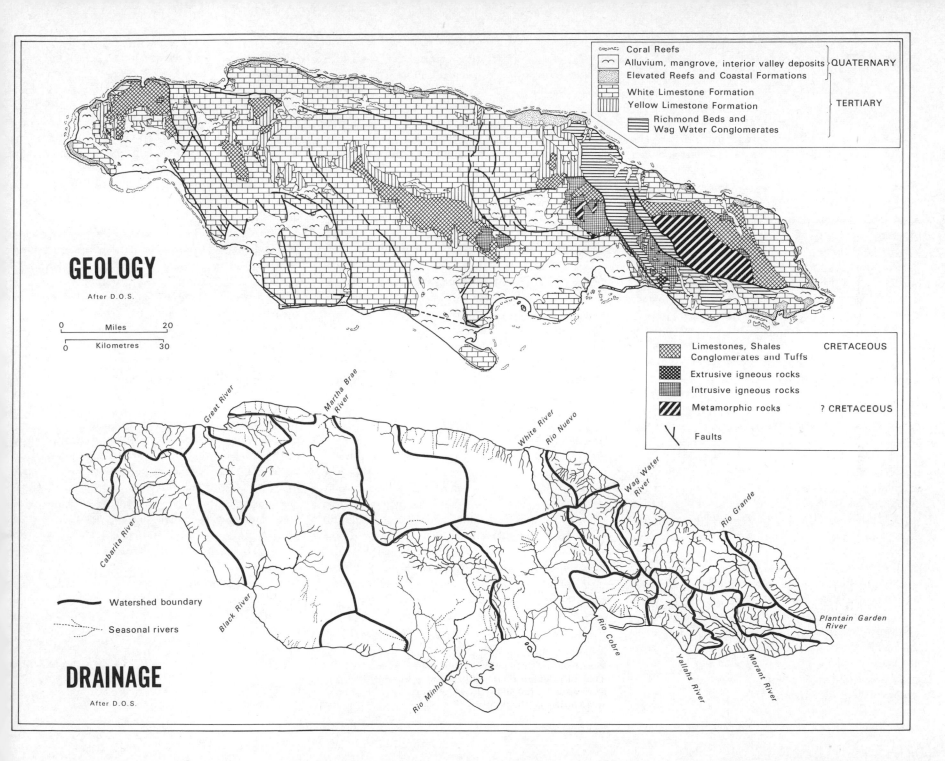

GEOLOGY

After D.O.S.

| Coral Reefs |
| Alluvium, mangrove, interior valley deposits | QUATERNARY |
| Elevated Reefs and Coastal Formations |
| White Limestone Formation |
| Yellow Limestone Formation | TERTIARY |
| Richmond Beds and Wag Water Conglomerates |

0   Miles   20
0   Kilometres   30

| Limestones, Shales Conglomerates and Tuffs | CRETACEOUS |
| Extrusive igneous rocks |
| Intrusive igneous rocks |
| Metamorphic rocks | ? CRETACEOUS |
| Faults |

Great River
Martha Brae River
White River
Rio Nuevo
Wag Water River
Rio Grande
Cabarita River
Black River
Rio Minho
Rio Cobre
Yallahs River
Morant River
Plantain Garden River

Watershed boundary
Seasonal rivers

DRAINAGE

After D.O.S.

5 CLIMATE

Jamaica lies astride the track of the north-east trade winds and enjoys a tropical maritime climate. The heaviest rainfall is orographic and concentrated on the Blue Mountains at the eastern end of the island. A marked rainshadow effect occurs in the lee of this range, and Kingston records less than 76 cm (30 in.) compared with over 500 cm (200 in.) on the Blue Mountains. Average annual precipitation exceeds 190 cm (75 in.) in some parts of the central plateau, but falls below 125 cm (50 in.) on the sheltered south coast and in the vicinity of Montego Bay. Only in the high Cockpit Country does the rainfall rise once more above 250 cm (100 in.).

The island experiences two wet seasons focussing on May and October, there being a slight lag after the passing of the equinox. The autumn months record the highest averages: much of the precipitation is convectional, and downpours usually occur in the early afternoon. The two intervening periods receive relatively little rainfall. Water-shortage is characteristic of the south coast, and many of the sugar estates employ irrigation. But the December dry spell is important for human activities; it coincides with the beginning of the sugar crop and the start of the tourist season. In addition to these regular variations, the entire island is occasionally plagued by drought. The late 1960s were years of considerable dessication, and created much hardship for the farming community. Two of the climatological stations on the north coast record December rainfall maxima. This is due to the northers which carry cold air from the North American continent and bring squalls, low temperatures, dull skies and rain. Northers rarely affect Jamaica for more than a few days each year, but are capable of destroying bananas and cocoa trees planted on exposed, north-facing slopes.

Although generally dry, the months of July and August fall within the hurricane season which extends from June to November. Hurricanes are generated in the Atlantic, and move through the Caribbean on a westerly course, their speed usually averaging about 16 km (10 mls) per hour. The winds blow in an anticlockwise direction and reach speeds of 120 km (75 mls) per hour; occasional gusts near the centre of the depression may exceed 320 km (200 mls) per hour. Gale-force winds whip up high seas and damage or destroy homes, crops and people. Since 1685 thirty-seven hurricanes have struck Jamaica. Most make their way westwards along the north coast, and Kingston has been affected only twice since 1880. In 1951, however, Hurricane Charley hit the south coast causing two million pounds-worth of destruction. Heavy rainfall is associated with the passage of hurricanes; in 1933, 200 mm (8 in.) of rainfall were recorded in 15 minutes on the Palisadoes, and intensities of 1,500 mm (60 in.) within 72 hours occur several times per century in the Blue Mountains.

Jamaica experiences high uniform temperatures consistent with its tropical location. Sea-level stations record averages of about 27°C (80°F) and ranges between January and July of less than 5°C (10°F); the north coast is exposed to the trade winds and has slightly lower figures. Temperatures vary both diurnally and with elevation. The lapse-rate averages 2°C (3°F) with each 300 metres (1,000 ft) in altitude, and the mountains are cooler than the coast. Blue Mountain Peak records a summer maximum of only just over 21°C (70°F). The range between mean monthly maxima and minima is as great as the differentiation caused by altitude and far larger than the annual variation. These high monthly ranges reflect wide differences between day and night temperatures. Night-time thermometer readings on Blue Mountain Peak drop below 5°C (40°F) in December and January, and at Kingston the diurnal range in December covers 6°C (19°F). The entire island conforms to the adage that 'night is the winter of the tropics'. The differential heating and cooling of land and sea creates a sea-breeze in the morning and a land-breeze at night. The physiological benefits of the sea-breeze have been appreciated since the eighteenth century when it was known as 'the doctor'.

The graphs of relative humidity depict conditions in the early afternoon and reflect the pattern and intensity of rainfall. Percentage values vary between stations and are largest in the mountains where temperatures are low and the rainfall high. Most stations depict two peak values in May and October separated by troughs which coincide with the dry seasons. The graphs suggest that the relative humidity increases as the year advances. Each station also records considerable diurnal changes, the values declining as the heat of the day increases.

Climate and temperament ensure that the pace of life in Jamaica is slow. But despite the enervating temperatures and high humidity, the daily round pretends to follow a British pattern, and there is no *siesta* even for manual labourers. If life-styles have not been adapted to the tropics, house-types have. In the towns, modern, single-storey houses are usually provided with deep verandahs, and louvres and jalousies are substituted for glazed windows. Flat, concrete roofs are common, though rather poor insulators. The best acclimatized dwellings are the old, wooden, shingle-roofed houses, whose sides can be opened up like Chinese lanterns. Interiors are frequently sub-divided only by wooden partitions, the top portion being of fretwork to facilitate the through-flow of air. The houses of the poor are usually more rudimentary. Windows are covered with heavy wooden panels which are wedged open in the daytime to provide light, shade and draught; at night they are battened down for security and to keep out spirits. In the town centres the streets are lined with piazzas, and shoppers discriminate between the sunny and shady side of the streets. A temperate climate is reproduced in some offices, banks, shops and supermarkets. Locals avoid the sun which is so avidly sought by the tourists.

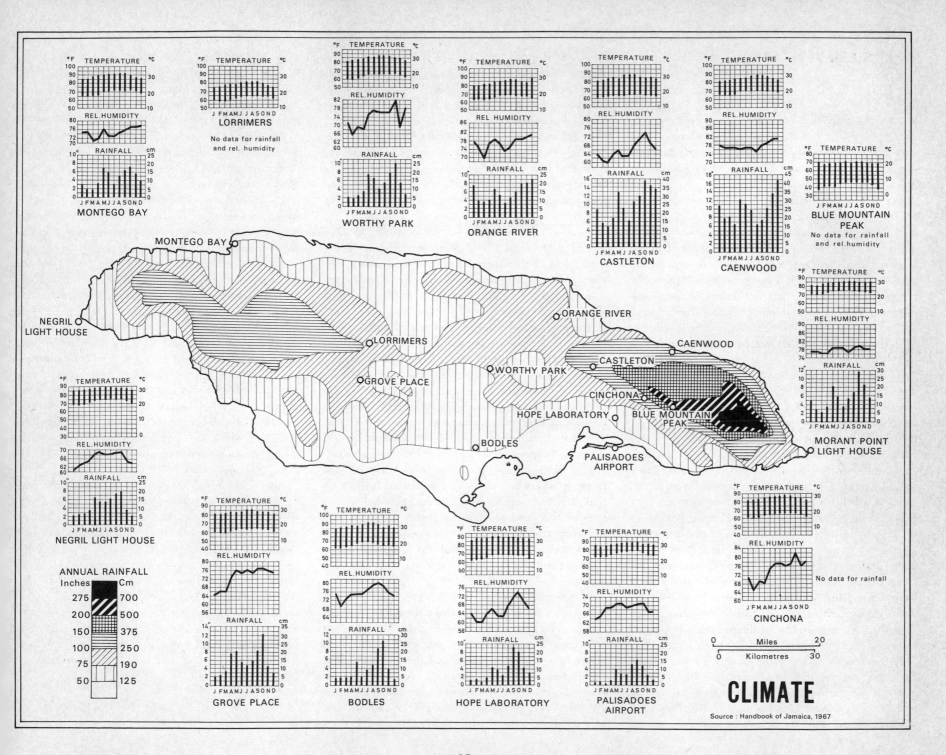

CLIMATE

Source : Handbook of Jamaica, 1967

17

6 SOILS AND VEGETATION

Five factors in soil formation are generally recognized: parent material, climate, topography, vegetation and time. Topography and geology are of outstanding importance in Jamaica, and soil and lithological boundaries tend to coincide.

In the Blue Mountains and central shale inlier, the original forest cover has supplied a high organic content to the surface layer. Where the profile remains undisturbed the first 150 mm (6 in.) consist of a dark brown gravelly loam: the lower horizon extends to a depth of 840 mm (33 in.) and contains a higher proportion of coarse material. But deforestation of the mountain slopes has led to rapid erosion, truncation of the profile, and the exposure of an infertile subsoil. This is highly porous, subject to leaching, acid, and lacking in nutrients.

Soils of the upland plateaux fall into two groups: *terra rossa*, or red limestone soils, and *rendzinas*, or black marl soils. Terra rossa is a residual bauxitic soil which occurs on the white limestone plateaux, especially in Manchester and St. Ann. This red earth has a coarse and porous texture and is usually leached, acid, well-oxidized and dehydrated. The surface layer often contains a high degree of organic matter, but there is no distinctive profile. Throughout much of the interior, terra rossa is confined to the bottom of dolines and valleys, or lines the minute pockets in the jagged limestone outcrops. Under conditions of impeded drainage, degraded versions of the soil occur; on steep slopes the mantle is thin and the soil colour brown. Rendzinas are associated with soft yellow limestones and marls, and are sporadic in occurrence. They display a mature clay profile, are rich in potash, but suffer from poor drainage.

Lowland soils occur in the coastal plains and embayments and on the floor of lacustrine basins in the interior. The most extensive area of alluvial soils is found on the southern coastal plain. Here the profile contains fluvial deposits of loam, sand and gravel, though in many districts it is overlain by heavy marine clays to a depth of 1 to 1·3 m (3 to 4 ft). The lowlands contain the most fertile soils in Jamaica, and some have been cultivated continuously for more than three hundred years without loss of quality.

Relief and climate have a direct bearing upon the pattern of natural vegetation in Jamaica. But the influence of man is also manifest. Clearing and periodic burning of the vegetation have transformed the plant geography of all but the most isolated and inhospitable regions.

Swamps, mangroves and marsh woodlands occur in several coastal localities. The largest swamp covers the flood plain of the Black River, and is known as the Great Morass. It comprises sedge marsh, scattered Royal Palms (*Roystonea Princeps*), and the four New World species of mangrove.

The paucity and seasonality of rainfall on the south coast produce an arid environment which is intensified by the porosity of the subsoil and the high insolation. Spits are covered with thorn scrub and columnar cactus (*Cereus*). Sparse, low forest occupies the dry limestone outcrops in Vere, the Hellshire Hills and to the east of Kingston; similar conditions are repeated in parts of the north coast. The red birch (*Bursera simaruba*) is widespread, and cotton trees (*Ceiba pentandra*) have become established in sheltered ravines. But even where the canopy is continuous, it is always thin; the trees are demi-deciduous, thin-boled, and branch near the ground. Epiphytes are restricted to xerophytic bromeliads, orchids and cacti. Small palms and agaves occur, and the ground layer is characterized by a few ferns, cacti or woody perennial herbs.

Wet limestone forest occurs at elevations of more than 300 m (1,000 ft), and where the rainfall exceeds 1,900 mm (75 in.). The largest area of this type of vegetation is the Cockpit Country. Trees reach a height of 15 to 18 m (50 to 60 ft) and the canopy is closed, but never dense. Trees are evergreen, and are covered with epiphytes, bromeliads and tree ferns. The limestone plateaux of Manchester and St. Ann have been cleared for tillage and grazing. Magnificent specimens of the cotton tree, West Indian cedar (*Cedrela odorata*), and the guango (*Samanea saman*) dominate the landscape. Much of the marginal and abandoned land is in ruinate and eventually forms a thorn thicket or thorn savanna dominated by *Acacia lutea*.

The original vegetation of the plains was probably a sparse forest of lignum vitae (*Guiacum officinale*), cotton trees and yokewood (*Catalpa longissima*). Most of the lowland is now cultivated or in ruinate, and supports a wide variety of naturalized species, which include the ubiquitous mango as well as the coconut palm, bougainvillea, *Poinciana regia*, *Spathodia campanulata*, and *Haemotoxylon campechiarum*.

The northern foothills of the Blue Mountains and the western slopes of the John Crow Mountains are clad in lower montane mist forest. The main canopy reaches 18 to 24 m (60 to 80 ft) and is underlain by a subsidiary tree layer and a shrub complex. All the trees are evergreen and some of the largest ones (*Psidium montanum* and *Ficus suffocans*) display buttressing. Lianes are sparse, though there are many small vines, climbing herbs and bromeliads. Ferns, bryophytes and orchids occur at the shrub level. This vegetational zone contrasts with the stunted sclerophyll belt which has been induced by burning, leaching and erosion, and covers the lower, leeward flanks of the Blue Mountains.

Above the 1,370 m (4,500 ft) contour the Blue Mountains are enveloped in montane mist forest, which is low-canopied (12–15 m: 40–50 ft) and resembles temperate forests in structure and floristics. Dominant trees include *Podocarpus urbani*, *Cyrilla racemiflora* and *Alchornea latifolia*. Palms are absent and lianes rare. Epiphytes extend up to 7·5 m (25 ft), and many are also found on fallen debris among the ground flora. At heights above 1,520 m (5,000 ft) the exposed ridges and summits are covered with an elfin woodland of gnarled and twisted trees laden with mosses, lichens, ferns and epiphytes. Open spaces support alpine grass.

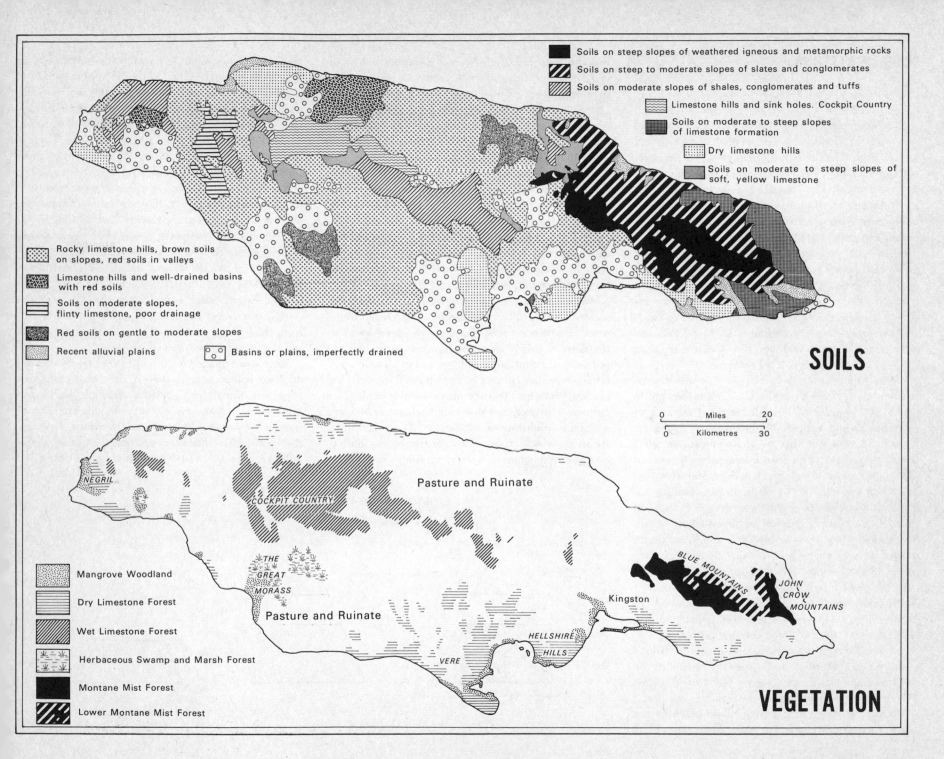

SOILS

- Soils on steep slopes of weathered igneous and metamorphic rocks
- Soils on steep to moderate slopes of slates and conglomerates
- Soils on moderate slopes of shales, conglomerates and tuffs
- Limestone hills and sink holes. Cockpit Country
- Soils on moderate to steep slopes of limestone formation
- Dry limestone hills
- Soils on moderate to steep slopes of soft, yellow limestone
- Rocky limestone hills, brown soils on slopes, red soils in valleys
- Limestone hills and well-drained basins with red soils
- Soils on moderate slopes, flinty limestone, poor drainage
- Red soils on gentle to moderate slopes
- Recent alluvial plains
- Basins or plains, imperfectly drained

VEGETATION

- Mangrove Woodland
- Dry Limestone Forest
- Wet Limestone Forest
- Herbaceous Swamp and Marsh Forest
- Montane Mist Forest
- Lower Montane Mist Forest

NEGRIL

COCKPIT COUNTRY

THE GREAT MORASS

Pasture and Ruinate

Pasture and Ruinate

Kingston

HELLSHIRE HILLS

VERE

BLUE MOUNTAINS

JOHN CROW MOUNTAINS

0 Miles 20
0 Kilometres 30

SOCIAL PATTERNS

Two sets of inter-related problems dominate the social geography of Jamaica: rapid population growth and social inequality. The island's demographic characteristics include high fertility, low mortality, substantial internal migration, urbanization and emigration. Yet all Jamaicans are immigrants or descendants of immigrants of European, African, Indian, Jewish, Syrian or Chinese descent. This multi-racial stock was largely determined by the systems of slavery and indenture established by white sugar planters during the seventeenth, eighteenth and nineteenth centuries. White servants, black slaves, Chinese and East Indian indentured labourers were imported, in turn, to cultivate the cane fields. During the First World War immigration came to an end, and labour deficiency soon gave way to conditions of labour surplus.

In the half century since 1921 the population has risen from 858,000 to 1,861,000. Improvements in health and hygiene have rapidly reduced the rate of mortality, while control of fertility has lagged far behind. Jamaica now has to accommodate an additional 5.5 persons per square kilometre each year, an increment seven times greater than Mexico's and twice that experienced by Haiti. Peasant farming has been unable to sustain population increases for several decades; the banana, coconut and livestock industries have taken up few new employees, and sugar has begun to shed labour, having been a major absorber of manpower in the period between 1943 and 1960. Moreover the growth industries – manufacturing, tourism and bauxite-alumina – employ small numbers of people. Rural adjustments between population and resources have been effected through migration.

Cityward migration in Jamaica results more from a push from the overcrowded, overworked land of the rural parishes than from a strong pull to the towns. The major settlements are market centres and ports, and Kingston, the capital, is the destination of the country's youth. Migrants are young adults; they flood the labour market, strain housing resources, and rapidly reproduce. Yet even in Kingston, a primate city, urbanization occurs without adequate industrialization. Unemployment soars above the national average, the tertiary refuge sector is greatly inflated, and about a quarter of the citizens live in overcrowded, poverty-stricken tenements, rent-yards or squatter camps.

Population increase, low levels of living, soil erosion, slum dwelling, inadequate schooling, and the concentration of resources in the hands of a minority represent facets of deep-seated problems which generate demands for emigration. Yet emigration involves an element of rejection. What causes Jamaicans to wish to slough off their origins? How great are the social inequalities, and on what are they based?

Although there is general agreement that Jamaican society consists of three hierarchically arranged strata, some observers contend that these are based upon distinctions of colour-class, while others stress the importance of culture in defining social boundaries. The latter argue that Jamaica is characterized by social and cultural pluralism, that the major social groupings are culturally distinct, and that each is characterized by a specific combination of institutions. The principal institutions which are involved are family and kinship, education, religion, property, economy and recreation. People who practise the same institutions and for whom they have the same values and implications form a cultural section in the society. It follows from this that the social strata in Jamaica are ranked cultures; each is internally stratified by colour and occupation.

The origins of this social system are to be found in slavery. By 1800 Jamaican society consisted of three legally defined strata – white freemen, Negro slaves, and an intermediate group of mixed descent who were no longer bondsmen, but, like the Jewish community, possessed only limited civil rights. Colour was strongly, though not perfectly, correlated with status. Nevertheless, the major social grades were usually described as white, brown and black. Institutions practised by each stratum reflected the legal differences. African traits were largely eroded under the system of slavery. Negroes adopted a plantation culture, the browns syncretized the behaviour of masters and slaves, but emphasized white norms.

Since emancipation in 1834, Jamaica has experienced no legal colour bar. However, the 'white bias' has remained important, socially, psychologically and symbolically. By the middle of the nineteenth century political power was being shared by whites, Jews and the brown elite; blacks were confined to the role of onlookers by the restricted franchise. In 1865 the

RACE AND STATUS IN JAMAICA

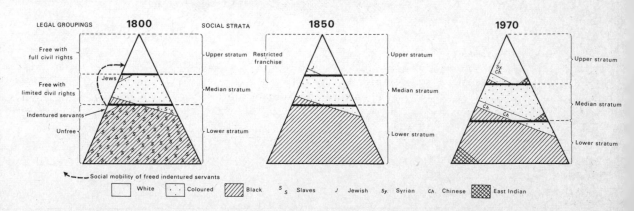

Assembly abdicated in favour of Crown Colony Government. The whites regained control over the destiny of the island; the rapid advance to power of the browns was stemmed; and the latent influence of the burgeoning group of black freeholders was swept aside. The arrival of the East Indians, Syrians and Chinese complicated the social order. Each in its way has penetrated the Creole stratification. Syrians and Chinese have used trade, education and phenotype as entrées to high social status, but the East Indians have remained largely rural and impoverished.

While each stratum or class has become increasingly multi-racial, cultural differences remain of paramount importance. Members of the upper class marry before they mate and household headship is invested in males. They are nominal members of the denominational churches, and the highest ranking ones are usually Anglican. Secondary education, often obtained overseas, is a hall-mark of this group. In the middle class marriage and extra-residential mating co-exist, though illegitimacy is despised. Fundamentalism prevails, but educational standards are moderate to high. In the lower class, illegitimacy is the norm, and household headship is invested in males or females, depending upon the composition of the household. Mating depends neither upon marriage nor upon co-residence, and there is little or no correlation between family and household. The common-law union is typical of this stratum. Most members are non-denominational Christians belonging either to sects or Afro-Christian cults. Access to secondary education is slight, absenteeism from school is high and so, too, is illiteracy. Occupational and linguistic characteristics underwrite these differences. The upper stratum speaks standard English with a Jamaican accent, and controls commerce and the professions; members of the middle class speak standard English and Creole, dominate the bureaucracy and fill subordinate white-collar positions in the private business-houses; the lower class speaks Creole, and remains tied to manual, service and agricultural pursuits.

Although all adult Jamaicans were enfranchised in 1944 and many blacks have achieved mobility through the civil service, trading, and politics, the social strata have not been disrupted. An agreement has been reached between the upper and median strata: the median stratum dominates politics and the trade unions, while the upper stratum runs the economy. Social change has been promised to the electorate, but politicians warn that it can be achieved only gradually as the capitalist system matures and economic development is achieved.

The demographic growth experienced since the Second World War has taken place in a small island with a clearly defined social stratification and grossly unequal patterns of land and income distribution. Partly because of the constraints of the existing social and economic systems, no Jamaican government has been able or willing to re-allocate land or eradicate unemployment. Moreover, it is doubtful whether the gap between the 'haves' and the 'have-nots' has been narrowed, despite the country's record of rapid economic growth. As late as 1960 the median wage for whites was almost twice that for browns and thirteen times that for blacks. Consequently, emigration has provided an avenue for advancement and a safety-valve for lower-class discontent.

Jamaica experiences problems of national identity which stem from its multi-racial and pluralistic character and from its long history as a British colony. The official version approved by upper class Jamaicans is that race is no longer socially or psychologically significant; the society practises multi-racialism. And so, up to a point, it does. Segregation is not prescribed, the upper stratum is racially mixed, and so, too, are public events. But private parties, marriages, friendships and clubbing still follow racial and colour lines. Colour in Jamaica is highly situational and attitudes to it are ambivalent. Blacks who wear white collars invariably enter the census records as brown; however hostile blacks may be to whites, white individuals are usually treated on their merit. In Kingston the subtleties of social differentiation are clearly expressed in geographical patterns; elsewhere social and spatial distance are less closely aligned. The small size of the island provides a sense of cohesion and belonging. Lineages are known in some detail, and familiarity breeds a degree of tolerance which mitigates the alienation of the poor.

Since independence, the brown middle stratum has laid claim to the leadership of the country, and has presented the outside world with an essentially Afro-Saxon image of Jamaica. However, a few black power leaders would prefer to mould a new identity based less upon British values than upon the Afro-Christian culture of the lower stratum. Other black groups stress their trans-Atlantic heritage and import West African tribal garb; for some elements, Afro haircuts and American black power slogans are adequate symbols of their would-be emancipation. The quest for a personal identity is a lifetime's preoccupation for middle class Jamaicans. Years will pass before Jamaica achieves its national motto 'Out of Many, One People'.

7 PARISHES AND CONSTITUENCIES

For the purpose of local government Jamaica is divided into fourteen parishes. Seven western parishes – Hanover, Westmoreland, St James, St Elizabeth, Trelawny, Manchester and St Ann – were created prior to emancipation. The remainder of the island was originally divided into fifteen parishes, but they were too small, and were reduced to seven in 1885 as part of the administrative reforms which followed the introduction of Crown Colony Government. Vere was merged with Clarendon, St Dorothy, St Thomas in Vale, and St John with St Catherine, and Metcalfe with St Mary. The town of Port Royal and part of St Andrew were incorporated into Kingston, and the remainder of the parish of Port Royal was added to St Andrew. St George and a part of St Thomas in the East were merged with Portland, and St David was joined to the remainder of St Thomas in the East.

The parishes of Kingston and St Andrew were amalgamated in 1921 to improve the administration of the rapidly growing capital. The Kingston and St Andrew Corporation consists of 27 elected members but the council was dissolved for a number of years in the 1960s and its affairs administered by two commissioners. Council membership in the rural parishes is also by election, and the number of seats ranges from thirteen to twenty-one. Members of the House of Representatives have seats reserved on their parish council. Local authorities are responsible only for public health and sanitation, poor relief, water supply, parochial roads, fire services, markets and civic amenities. Central government obtrudes into most aspects of local life, and controls the purse-strings even in matters nominally delegated to the parishes.

The parishes were copied from Britain during the colonial period. But the constituencies were created for electoral purposes and their introduction in 1944 marks the beginning of the process of decolonization. Originally the parishes were sub-divided to form 32 constituencies; these were increased to 45 in 1959 and to 53 in 1967. While in government, both political parties have amended constituency boundaries, and each has charged the other with gerrymandering. The 1959 constituencies are shown opposite, and display contortions which are at variance with the more linear character of the parish boundaries. The seats devised for the general elections in 1967 and 1972 are even more irregular. The constitution provides a formula defining the maximum number of electors in each constituency, but St Andrew Northern exceeded the limit in 1972.

Parishes and constituencies are the only areal units with official status, and distribution maps depend heavily upon them. The parishes are the coarsest of the units which may be used to detect and depict spatial variations in the human geography of Jamaica. They are the units for which it is easiest to obtain information, but provide the least satisfactory framework for analysis. With the exception of Kingston, the parishes run inland from the coast and are divided into north and south groups by a line which runs the length of the island. They resemble the strip parishes of medieval England and each incorporates a variety of landscapes. The distinctions between communities in upland and plain and other micro-scale variations in social and economic characteristics are obliterated in summary statistics compiled for parishes.

The constituencies are more sensitive for measuring areal differentiation. As they sub-divide the parishes into two or more units, they permit relatively small scale variations to be detected. Nevertheless, the boundaries of the constituencies are as arbitrary as those of the parishes, and much more liable to change over short periods of time. For the purpose of the decennial census of population the island is also covered by a fine network of enumeration districts. But these are simply administrative boxes set up to provide a work-load for each census enumerator. In the towns they may contain no more than a few streets, and they are variable both in size and shape.

For the geographer the problem is one of matching the scale of the analysis to the scale of the topic or phenomena in question. If the whole island is being studied, constituencies are the most suitable units for areal analysis. But in Kingston, enumeration districts are superior to the constituencies. Yet the problem of data availability looms larger still. Many statistics relating to the economy are provided only for the parishes or for the island as a whole, and solely the census of population produces material at all the spatial levels which have been discussed.

If the investigator is prepared to work with summary data for parishes or for the entire island, detailed cross-tabulations are available from the censuses of population and agriculture. Material on population is limited for the constituencies, and only a few simple tabulations were prepared for the enumeration districts after the 1960 census. Consequently, much of the map evidence for Kingston is based on sample data specially provided by the census organization.

Ideally, the spatial units employed by geographers should be comparable in size and shape, and their boundaries should be regular. But the units rarely, if ever, meet these requirements. More commonly the boundaries have been set up for purposes quite different from those of the geographer. The problem is perhaps greatest in migration studies. A migrant is defined as someone crossing a particular line – in the Jamaican case, a parish boundary. The size and shape of the parishes ensure that much mobility remains intra-parish and is therefore filtered out. Long, narrow parishes, such as Manchester, are most likely to record heavy out-migration.

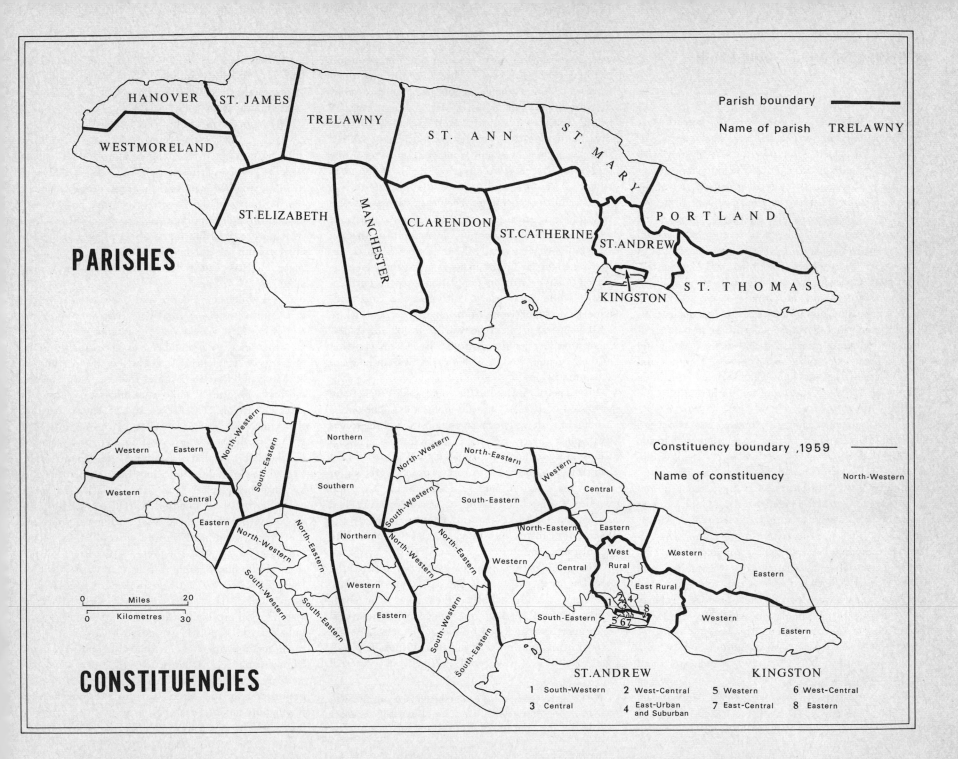

PARISHES

HANOVER
ST. JAMES
TRELAWNY
ST. ANN
ST. MARY
WESTMORELAND
ST. ELIZABETH
MANCHESTER
CLARENDON
ST. CATHERINE
ST. ANDREW
PORTLAND
KINGSTON
ST. THOMAS

Parish boundary
Name of parish TRELAWNY

CONSTITUENCIES

Constituency boundary ,1959
Name of constituency North-Western

Western
Eastern
North-Western
Northern
North-Western
North-Eastern
Western
Western
South-Eastern
Southern
South-Western
South-Eastern
Central
Central
Eastern
North-Western
North-Eastern
Northern
North-Western
North-Eastern
North-Eastern
Eastern
Western
Central
Western
West Rural
Eastern
South-Western
Western
East Rural
South-Eastern
South-Eastern
South-Western
Western
South-Eastern
Eastern

Miles 20
Kilometres 30

ST.ANDREW
1 South-Western 2 West-Central
3 Central   4 East-Urban and Suburban

KINGSTON
5 Western   6 West-Central
7 East-Central   8 Eastern

8 DISTRIBUTION OF POPULATION

The population of Jamaica resides in four distinct types of settlement: the capital city, small towns, villages and dispersed rural dwellings. Kingston with 379,600 population in 1960 is the only large community. It now contains more than one-quarter of the island's inhabitants and over 70 per cent of all urban-dwellers. Other towns are distributed around the coast or form part of an incipient zone of urbanization which runs westward from Kingston into the southern parishes of St Catherine, Clarendon, and Manchester. Rural concentrations are associated with two localities. Coastal clusters coincide with the sugar areas, each factory providing a focus for a quasi-urban nucleation. The heaviest rural densities occur in the peasant communities which dominate the central shale inlier and the narrow neck of upland lying between Kingston and Port Maria. The Cockpit Country and the Blue Mountains act as poles of repulsion for agriculture and settlement.

The initial population distribution was associated with the development of the sugar industry. During the eighteenth century plantations were established in the coastal embayments and interior valleys. The island was deficient in population, but the crop required large supplies of able-bodied adults. Manpower was supplied by the trans-Atlantic trade with West Africa, and slavery became the system of coercion. The numerical preponderance of males, coupled to the high rate of mortality associated with 'seasoning' and tropical disease, ensured a perpetual state of natural decrease. Slaves were tied to their owners' property and the pattern of population which emerged was both cellular and controlled. The heaviest densities were associated with the sugar plantations and with the coffee mountains of St Andrew, Manchester, and St Elizabeth. Slaves were held in large units on the plantations, but small groups were the norm in the coffee-growing areas.

The island's economy depended on sugar, and ports were required to export the crop and import manufactured goods and slaves. However, the growth of towns was slow. Labour was only grudgingly spared by the plantations, and industrialization was proscribed by the British government. Most of the towns were small, only the largest present-day settlements – Kingston, Spanish Town and Montego Bay – recording more than 2,500 slaves in 1832. Even at this date Kingston was more than twice the size of its two closest rivals put together. The urban slave population was different from the rural in several respects. It tended to be local-born, or creole, rather than African; slave holdings were small; the sex ratio was less severely skewed in favour of males; and natural increase played a larger part in population change. Furthermore, while rural gangs cultivated the cane-fields under the supervision of black drivers and white book-keepers, urban slaves worked as jobbing tradesmen, stevedores, and prostitutes. Slaves kept a portion of their earnings and provided their own clothing and accommodation.

Blacks predominated in the countryside: each estate possessed mulattoes – usually domestics – but only a handful of whites. The racial composition of the towns was much more heterogeneous. In 1812, when Kingston contained an estimated total of 33,000 inhabitants, 18,000 were slaves*, 10,000 were white, 2,500 free coloured, and 2,500 free black. The rural whites, fearing incitement of the slaves, expelled brown and black freemen from the plantations. By the 1830s the towns possessed substantial non-white populations.

The emancipation of the slaves in 1834 initiated the peopling of the mountains. Ex-slaves 'burrowed into the interior' and established themselves as independent cultivators, settling either unoccupied Crown land or properties abandoned by the sugar estates. As the export economy slumped, subsistence took its place; the functions of the ports declined, but internal marketing rapidly expanded. Many of the Sunday Markets originally established by the slaves for the sale of provisions developed into towns, and several were located in the centre of the island.

Although the mountains acted as a magnet for the emancipated slaves, there was evidence of a small but growing movement from the rural areas to Kingston after 1840. The attraction of high wages, however illusory, supplied a pull factor in the process. But by the beginning of the twentieth century push factors assumed greater importance. In 1910 most of the areas which were available for small farming had already been colonized, and modernization of the declining sugar industry had reduced the demand for rural labour.

These shifts in residence and occupation operated in a context of rising rural densities. Soon after the end of the First World War the ratchet effect started to bring increasing numbers to the capital. Some migrants were deflected to the coastal parishes of St Mary and Portland where the successful banana industry was located; some were drawn to Westmoreland, Clarendon, St Catherine and St Thomas, where the temporary rise in market prices stimulated a modest recovery in the sugar industry; others opened up the last tracts in the central inlier. During and after the great depression Kingston provided the sole but inadequate safety-valve for population build-up.

In the past three hundred years the population has moved inland from the coastal periphery, colonized the interior, and finally flowed downhill to the sugar estates and the towns. The present-day pattern reflects these shifts, but it rarely represents a viable distribution. Densities exceed two persons per hectare in many rural districts and are too heavy for the farming systems. Soil erosion is matched by other symptons of imbalance in population-resource relationships. Seasonal unemployment affects the sugar industry, while labour surplus is characteristic of the towns. A recent estimate considers one-fifth of the rural areas over-populated, in the sense that further increases in population cannot be absorbed without a decline in levels of living.

---

* This figure is an estimate, and should be compared with the 1832 population (shown on the map) which is lower and derived from the official slave registration.

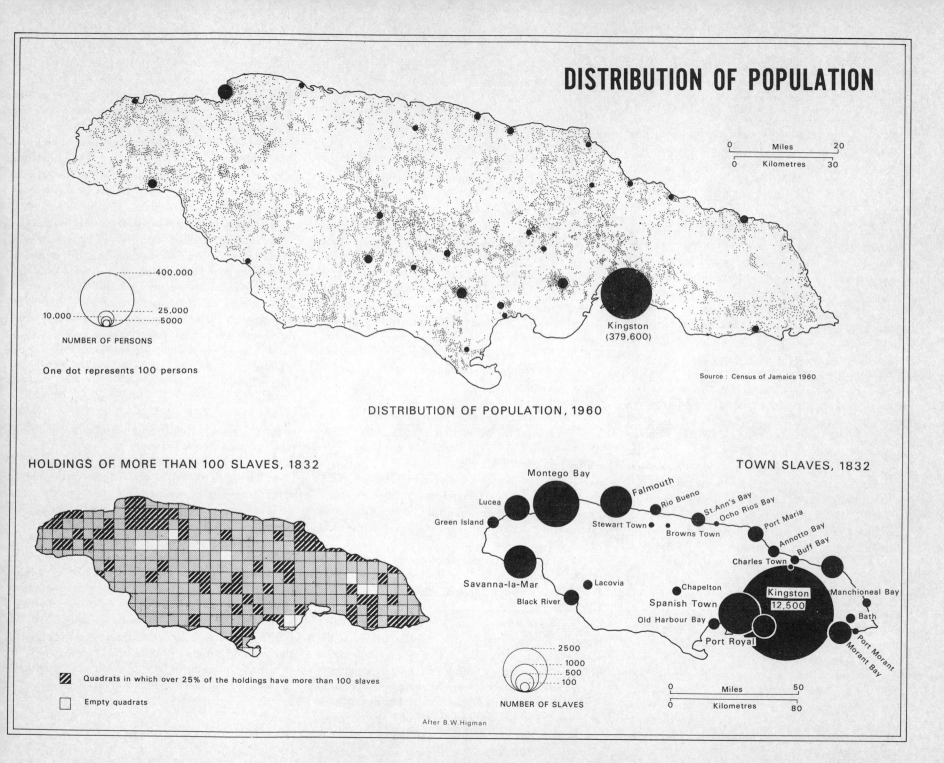

DISTRIBUTION OF POPULATION

0 Miles 20
0 Kilometres 30

400,000

25,000
10,000 5000

NUMBER OF PERSONS

One dot represents 100 persons

Kingston
(379,600)

Source : Census of Jamaica 1960

DISTRIBUTION OF POPULATION, 1960

HOLDINGS OF MORE THAN 100 SLAVES, 1832

Quadrats in which over 25% of the holdings have more than 100 slaves

Empty quadrats

TOWN SLAVES, 1832

Montego Bay
Falmouth
Lucea
Rio Bueno
Green Island
St.Ann's Bay
Ocho Rios Bay
Stewart Town
Browns Town
Port Maria
Annotto Bay
Buff Bay
Charles Town
Savanna-la-Mar
Lacovia
Chapelton
Manchioneal Bay
Black River
Spanish Town
Kingston 12,500
Bath
Old Harbour Bay
Port Royal
Port Morant
Morant Bay

2500
1000
500
100

NUMBER OF SLAVES

0 Miles 50
0 Kilometres 80

After B.W.Higman

9 POPULATION CHANGE

At the beginning of the nineteenth century the majority of Jamaica's 300,000 inhabitants were slaves. The abolition of the slave trade in 1808 forced planters to adopt a pro-natalist policy. By 1820 the sex ratio was in harmony, but the ageing population soon started to decline. Paradoxically, the cholera epidemic of 1850 provided a demographic turning point. During the following seventy years population growth was gradual but continuous, and by 1921 Jamaica had achieved a total of 858,000. Improvements in health and hygiene were rapidly implemented after the First World War. Expectation of life at birth increased from 39 years for men and 41 years for women in 1912 to just over 50 years in 1947 and to more than 60 years in 1961. The curve of natural increase turned sharply upwards, and earlier emigrants returned to the island during the depression. Jamaica recorded an annual rate of increase of 1·67 per cent during the 1920s and 1930s, and a population of 1,237,000 in 1943. Since the end of the Second World War the growth rate has decelerated, largely through the influence of emigration. A population of 1,609,000 was enumerated in 1960, rising to 1,861,000 in 1970.

Outstanding features in the re-allocation of population since emancipation have been the colonization of the interior and the growth of Kingston. By 1911 densities of more than 40 persons per km² (100 per sq. ml) prevailed throughout the central uplands; a decade later they exceeded 100 per km² (250 per sq. ml) in the shale inlier of northern Manchester and Clarendon, and they doubled again in this particular locality between 1921 and 1943. Kingston's demographic history paralleled that of the island until 1920. The city's subsequent expansion has been well above its rate of natural increase. Massive suburbs have developed around the late nineteenth-century nucleus, and since the 1930s St Andrew has exceeded Kingston parish both in total numbers and speed of growth. As early as 1943 the capital possessed 200,000 inhabitants.

Between 1943 and 1960 the population of Jamaica increased by 30 per cent. No parish experienced a decline in numbers, and the capital grew by 86 per cent, reaching 379,600 at the end of the intercensal period. Among the other areas St James, which included Montego Bay, together with the three urbanized and sugar-growing parishes immediately to the west of Kingston, recorded the highest rates of growth.

The decade 1960 to 1970 witnessed lower increases, though under-enumeration probably occurred. Jamaica's population increased by 15 per cent, and rapid growth was even more strongly associated with the urban areas. The ten largest settlements accounted for 88 per cent of the island's population growth and, by 1970, housed just over one-third of Jamaicans. St James and St Catherine were outstanding growth poles, the latter forming an incipient conurbation with Kingston. The population of the capital's built-up area rose to 506,200, expansion during the 1960s being of the order of 30 per cent. The deceleration in the rate of increase in Kingston matched the island-wide trend. Within the city two demographic patterns have merged. The population of the parish of St Andrew is now almost entirely suburban; as peripheral urban growth has occurred, so the number of inhabitants residing in the city centre in particular, and Kingston parish in general, has declined. No rural parish lost population, but the lowest intercensal gains, as in the period 1943–1960, were achieved at the eastern and western extremities of the island.

The components of population change since the end of the Second World War deserve close scrutiny. During this period natural increase rose to a peak of just over 3·0 per cent in 1960 only to fall away at a slower but fluctuating rate. One of the outstanding features of the island's vital statistics has been the secular decline in the death rate to a level achieved only by the most prosperous developed countries. Improvements in infant mortality have been spectacular, and testify to the expansion of health facilities. However, enteric complaints remain by no means uncommon among children, and protein-calorie malnutrition besets some of the most impoverished rural areas and retards infant development. The demographic transition to low fertility as well as low mortality has still to be achieved. Nevertheless, the birth-rate fell from 42·0 to 33·3 per 1,000 between 1960 and 1969, while the rate of natural increase dropped from 33·2 to 26·1 per 1,000. The cumulative influence of emigration since the 1950s has been an important factor in reducing the number of women in the reproductive age-groups. Furthermore, since 1966 the government has supported family planning.

The espousal of birth control in Jamaica has been a protracted process. Although a few family planning clinics date back to the 1930s, a bi-partisan policy in favour of contraception emerged only in the wake of independence and the imposition of British immigration controls. Jamaican leaders have gradually conceded that the island cannot sustain indefinite increases, and appreciated that unemployment, land shortage, and the general problems of social and economic development are either created or exacerbated by the rapidity of population growth. Clinics are operated by the Jamaican Family Planning Association and the National Family Planning Programme, and much of their work is funded by overseas aid. The number of clinics supported by the government increased from 94 in 1969 to 150 in 1970. By the middle of the latter year 47,000 women had sought advice, or 12 per cent of those in the groups aged 15 to 44. Almost 40 per cent of acceptors live in Kingston, and only a small proportion are aged under twenty-five. Although Jamaicans seem to prefer small families, contraceptive techniques are by no means certain to be adopted. The prevalence of visiting and consensual unions, the fact that more than 70 per cent of all live births are illegitimate, the cult of masculinity and fertility, the association of certain types of contraceptive with prostitutes, and the lack of close family life and family planning in the broadest sense, militate against the rapid success of the scheme.

POPULATION CHANGE

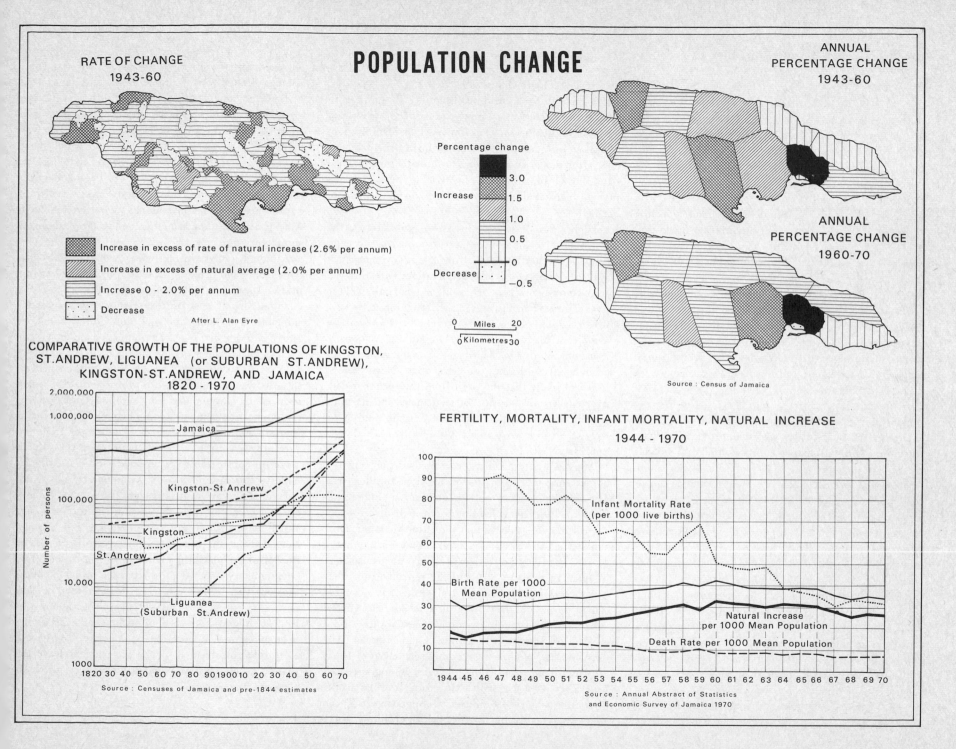

RATE OF CHANGE
1943-60

Increase in excess of rate of natural increase (2.6% per annum)

Increase in excess of natural average (2.0% per annum)

Increase 0 - 2.0% per annum

Decrease

After L. Alan Eyre

ANNUAL
PERCENTAGE CHANGE
1943-60

ANNUAL
PERCENTAGE CHANGE
1960-70

Percentage change

3.0
Increase   1.5
            1.0
            0.5
            0

Decrease   -0.5

0   Miles   20
0   Kilometres 30

Source : Census of Jamaica

COMPARATIVE GROWTH OF THE POPULATIONS OF KINGSTON, ST.ANDREW, LIGUANEA (or SUBURBAN ST.ANDREW), KINGSTON-ST.ANDREW, AND JAMAICA
1820 - 1970

Number of persons

Jamaica

Kingston-St Andrew

Kingston

St.Andrew

Liguanea
(Suburban St.Andrew)

Source : Censuses of Jamaica and pre-1844 estimates

FERTILITY, MORTALITY, INFANT MORTALITY, NATURAL INCREASE
1944 - 1970

Infant Mortality Rate
(per 1000 live births)

Birth Rate per 1000
Mean Population

Natural Increase
per 1000 Mean Population

Death Rate per 1000 Mean Population

Source : Annual Abstract of Statistics
and Economic Survey of Jamaica 1970

27

10 AGE, SEX AND MOBILITY

The age-sex structure of the Jamaican population is pyramidal in outline. Its broad base reflects the high rate of natural increase, while the narrowing upper portion of the diagram indicates mortality of the elderly. Women greatly outnumber men; in 1960 the sex ratio was 1,000:847. Among children aged under ten, boys predominate, but women account for the majority of Jamaicans over sixty. Both male emigration and female longevity influence the ratio.

The parishes deviate from the national pattern in certain important details. Some of the northern and eastern districts record small numbers of children; and most areas experience the heavy out-migration of young adults. Kingston and St Andrew are major reception areas for movers; St Catherine, Clarendon and St James lesser ones. Women have been prominent in internal migration for many decades. Kingston's sex ratio in 1960 was 1,000:820.

Jamaicans are highly mobile. In 1943 more than one-fifth were living outside their parish of birth; by 1960 the fraction had risen to one-quarter. The pace of internal migration speeded up considerably during the 1950s. In 1960 almost 60 per cent of the enumerated migrants had taken up their residence during the preceding decade. Migrants possessed two salient characteristics: they were better educated than the average Jamaican; and they were drawn primarily from the young adult age-groups. Among both men and women aged 25 to 34 movers slightly outnumbered non-movers. The upland farming areas of St Elizabeth and St Mary were outstanding suppliers of internal migrants, though all the agricultural districts provided reservoirs of some importance. The small towns and sugar estates of St Catherine, Clarendon and St James formed important reception areas, and the bauxite workings of St Elizabeth, Manchester and St Ann emerged as important foci.

The principal migratory stream is directed towards Kingston. In 1960 43 per cent of the island's movers were living in the capital. Moreover, they accounted for 57 per cent of the inhabitants of the corporate area. The flow declines with distance from Kingston, and the populous south-coast parishes contribute more than their northern counterparts. The urbanizing parishes adjacent to Kingston possibly form staging-posts in a step-wise migration ultimately centring on the capital. Parish data conceal short-distance moves, but there is some evidence for serial mobility: in 1960 18 per cent of all migrants had lived in three or more parishes.

High rates of natural increase, especially in the mountain areas, the extremes of *latifundia* and *minifundia*, together with rural under-employment, provide the context for cityward migration. Furthermore, agricultural work is poorly paid, and generally held in low repute. Jamaicans want their children to have urban, white-collar jobs. The propensity to migrate in some rural areas is more closely related to family size than to population density, and wage differentials account for the lure of the urban areas. Nevertheless, it seems likely that the push from the overcrowded, overworked uplands of Central Jamaica and the Blue Mountains is stronger than the economic pull of the towns: urban rates of unemployment far exceed rural figures.

Jamaica's natural increase exceeds 2 per cent per annum, and the population would double in less than a generation were it not for emigration. Emigration has for decades provided a means for personal advancement and a safety-valve for population-pressure. During the period 1881 to 1921 net emigration amounted to 146,000; 46,000 to the USA, 45,000 to Panama, at least 22,000 to Cuba, and the remainder to other areas. A second phase of emigration has occurred since 1953, and has been directed to the United Kingdom. Outstanding source areas are the rural parishes of Portland, St Elizabeth and Hanover. The peak outflow of almost 40,000 was achieved in 1961, the year before the Commonwealth Immigrants' Bill was enacted by the British Government. Prior to the 'beat the ban' rush the level of emigration had been dictated by fluctuations in the British economy: 1958 was a year of rising unemployment and potential emigrants were warned not to travel. Since 1963 only voucher-holders with guaranteed jobs and dependents of previous emigrants have been admitted to Britain, and the flow has been further reduced by more recent controls. Partial compensation has been received from Canada and the USA, both of which have abolished their quota systems. More than 20,000 Jamaicans emigrated in 1967, 1968, 1969 and 1970, the majority going to the United States. A further 12,000 are involved in seasonal migration to North America where they are employed as farm labourers and factory workers.

Although emigration left thousands of children as dependents and produced a shortage of skilled labour in the sugar industry during the early 1950s, the economic benefits to Jamaica seem to have been considerable. Net emigration to the United Kingdom between 1953 and 1962 amounted to about 35 per cent of the island's natural increase. If the children who would subsequently have been born are added to the young adults who left, it is probable that the island reduced its 1962 population by 200,000. Furthermore, net emigration removed 40,000 from Kingston prior to 1960 and deflected many migrants away from the overcrowded capital. Census figures for the city in 1970 are considerably below earlier forecasts, though under-enumeration as well as emigration has occurred. Emigration has brought substantial foreign exchange earnings to the island. Remittances are worth more than £6 million per annum, and long ago cancelled out the cost of the passage to Britain. The impact of emigration on unemployment is less clear cut, though it may have alleviated the problem. But if the departure of skilled workers reduced total output, per capita output was undoubtedly greater as a result. Recent emigration to the United States and Canada has been much more occupationally selective: 40 per cent of the doctors trained by the government leave the island. When emigration becomes a 'brain drain' it ceases to be a panacea.

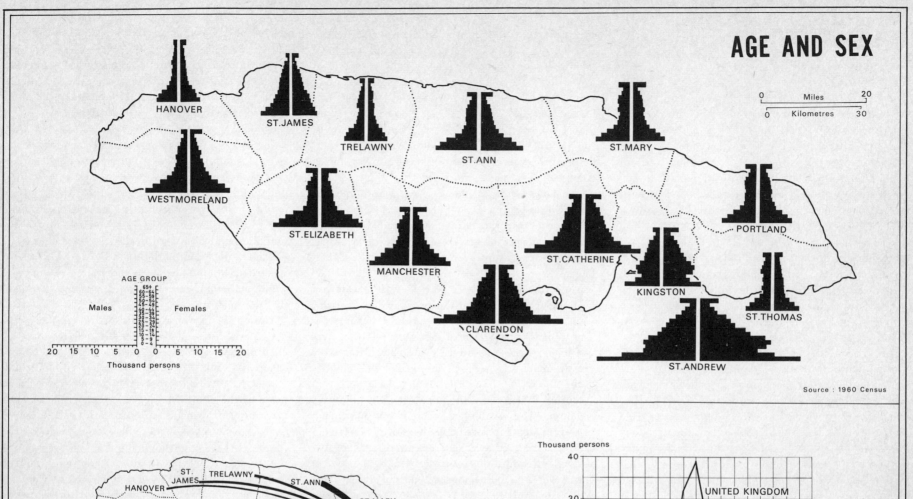

AGE AND SEX

HANOVER

ST.JAMES

TRELAWNY

ST.ANN

ST.MARY

WESTMORELAND

ST.ELIZABETH

MANCHESTER

ST.CATHERINE

PORTLAND

KINGSTON

ST.THOMAS

CLARENDON

ST.ANDREW

AGE GROUP

65+
60–64
55–59
50–54
45–49
40–44
35–39
30–34
25–29
20–24
15–19
10–14
5–9
0–4

Males   Females

20 15 10 5 0   0 5 10 15 20

Thousand persons

Source : 1960 Census

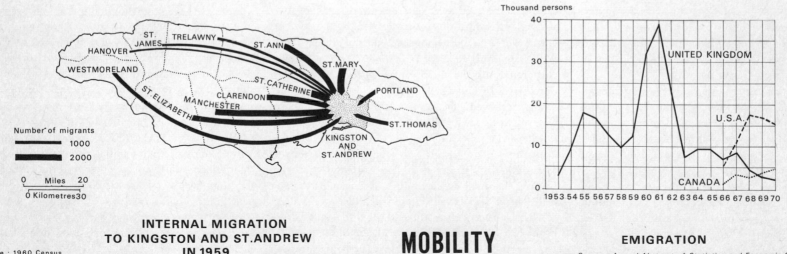

INTERNAL MIGRATION
TO KINGSTON AND ST.ANDREW
IN 1959

ST.
JAMES TRELAWNY

HANOVER   ST.ANN

WESTMORELAND   ST.MARY

ST.CATHERINE   PORTLAND

CLARENDON

ST.ELIZABETH MANCHESTER

ST.THOMAS

KINGSTON
AND
ST.ANDREW

Number of migrants
———— 1000
━━━━ 2000

0   Miles   20
0 Kilometres 30

Source : 1960 Census

MOBILITY

EMIGRATION

Thousand persons

40

30

UNITED KINGDOM

20

U.S.A.

10

CANADA

0

1953 54 55 56 57 58 59 60 61 62 63 64 65 66 67 68 69 70

Source : Annual Abstract of Statistics and Economic Survey of Jamaica

29

11 RACE AND RELIGION

Jamaica is a multi-racial society. Almost all the inhabitants are descended from immigrants. By 1800 the population comprised a free white minority, a black slave majority and an interstitial group of mixed descent.

Both the whites and blacks declined in number during the 1820s. Among the blacks this was a transitional period between the abolition of the slave trade and the establishment of a self-perpetuating population. The reduction of the whites continued into the second half of the nineteenth century, and reflected the decline of the sugar industry. This downward trend was checked, and for a time reversed, by the influx of British civil servants after the introduction of Crown Colony Government in 1865. During the twentieth century, however, the whites have experienced a renewed decline, the rate having quickened since 1943 through the departure of expatriate administrators.

Among the brown population the early nineteenth century was a period of considerable growth. They outstripped the whites by 1820, and for a short period in the 1840s looked like becoming the largest group in the island. In recent decades browns have accounted for just under one-fifth of the population, though their enumeration has been problematic. Many brown people try to pass as white, and well-to-do blacks are frequently classified as brown.

The nineteenth century witnessed a number of newcomers – Chinese, Syrians, and East Indians from the Ganges Plain. East Indians were indentured to the sugar estates before 1850, but three more decades passed before they appeared in the census. Some Chinese were indentured, but the majority entered the island as traders at the turn of the century. Only the Syrians were completely untainted with unfree labour. A small group of Syrian businessmen attended the Jamaican Exhibition in 1893, and a migratory flow was soon established. India prohibited indentured emigration in 1917, and Chinese arrivals were

eventually controlled by the Jamaican quota system. Subsequently, the Oriental population has expanded rapidly through natural increase. Since 1953 each nationality and miscegenated group has been separately enumerated by the census. In 1960 the East Indians and East Indian coloureds were the largest groups followed by the Chinese, Chinese coloureds, and Syrians. Both of the East Indian groups have outstripped the whites, the expansion of the East Indian coloureds being quite remarkable.

The 1960 census introduced new racial nomenclature: whites became Europeans, browns were termed Afro-Europeans, and blacks were called Africans. While the blacks and browns were almost ubiquitous, the minority groups were highly segregated. East Indians were largely restricted to the sugar- and banana-growing parishes where their forebears had been indentured. The majority of whites, Syrians, Chinese and miscegenated groups resided in Kingston. The capital's proportion of East Indians and browns was higher than the national figure, but blacks were grossly under-represented. The smaller the minority group, the greater its concentration in Kingston.

During slavery the white population was nominally Anglican. The established church was moribund, priests frequently possessed neither vocation nor education, and slaves were left untutored. Among the slaves the Coromantins from what is now the state of Ghana were the most important cultural group. Their pantheism and ancestor cults were gradually incorporated into the beliefs of the entire slave population. Slaves lived in fear of the spirits of the dead, and often employed obeah men to manipulate these malevolent duppies. When the island became a major mission-field soon after 1800, the Baptists, Methodists and Congregationalists were especially active. The Methodists attracted the free-coloureds, and the Baptists emerged as champions of emancipation.

The black population proved difficult to proselytize. Black class leaders channelled groups into unorthodox, if not heretical, beliefs, and often established breakaway sects. An amalgam of Christian belief and the superstition of the slaves, these Native Baptists stressed

emotional stimulation, possession, prophecy and healing. As the nineteenth century progressed and the original missionaries died, the blacks began to associate the non-conformists with the ruling class and to treat them with mistrust. Missionary hopes were raised by the Great Revival of 1860–61, only to be dashed as the religious fervour evaporated.

The period 1881–1911 was significant for the arrival of Hindus and the rapid expansion of the respectable denominations. The Anglican Church, disestablished in 1870, emerged as the largest group, followed closely by the Baptists and Methodists, and at a greater distance by the Presbyterians, Moravians, Catholics, and Congregationalists. 'Other churches', which ran the gamut of the stigmatized Afro-Christian spectrum, lost numbers. So did the Jews, many of whose ancestors were Portuguese and pre-dated the British conquest.

During this century growth in the Anglican, Baptist, Methodist, and Presbyterian Churches has levelled off, and all have recorded absolute declines in adherents since 1943. The number of Jews and Hindus has dwindled, but rapid advances have been made by the evangelical sects, especially the Seventh Day Adventists and the American-based Church of God. Furthermore, syncretic groups such as the Ras Tafari have emerged among the poor and among the educated but alienated youth, while the enthusiastic, local-led sects and cults such as Cumina, Pocomania, Convince, Revival and Revival Zion, which are subsumed by the census under the category 'other', have overtaken the Anglicans. Non-denominational groups predominate in West Kingston and many rural districts, and membership of the cults and sects probably exceeds the official figures since adherents often conceal their affiliations. Congregations of Methodists and Baptists concentrate in Trelawny and St Ann, where their missionaries were originally successful. Anglicans are fairly ubiquitous, but Roman Catholics cluster in Kingston. In the capital the elite are nominally Anglican, and the middle stratum fervently non-conformist.

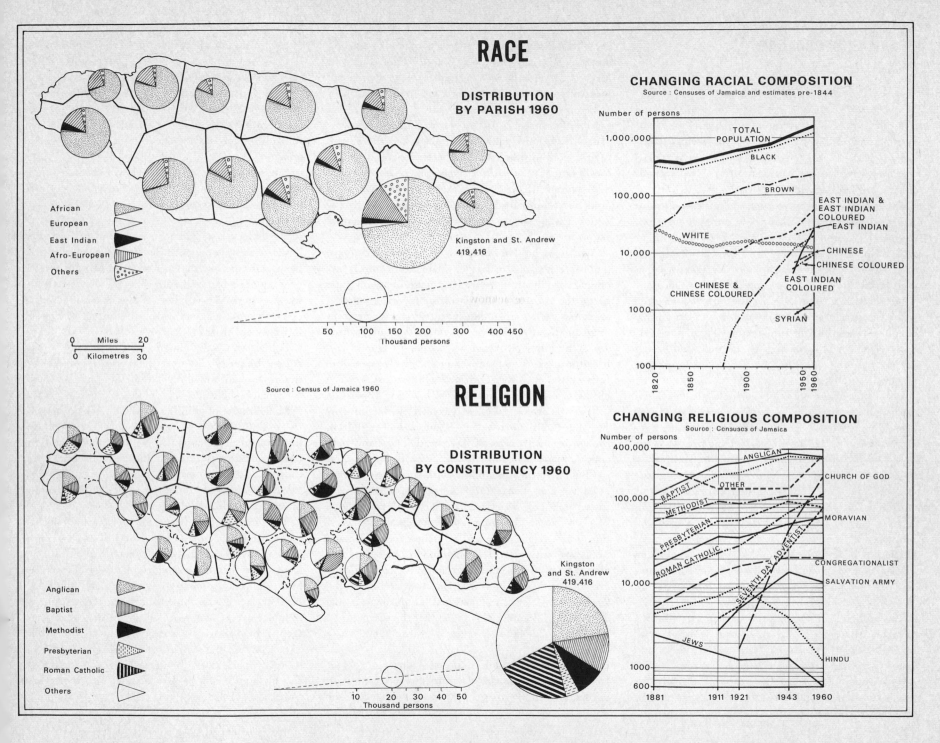

RACE

DISTRIBUTION
BY PARISH 1960

African
European
East Indian
Afro-European
Others

Kingston and St. Andrew
419,416

0   Miles   20
0   Kilometres   30

50   100   150   200   300   400 450
Thousand persons

Source : Census of Jamaica 1960

CHANGING RACIAL COMPOSITION
Source : Censuses of Jamaica and estimates pre-1844

Number of persons

1,000,000

TOTAL POPULATION
BLACK

100,000

BROWN

EAST INDIAN &
EAST INDIAN
COLOURED
EAST INDIAN

WHITE

10,000

CHINESE
CHINESE COLOURED

CHINESE &
CHINESE COLOURED

EAST INDIAN
COLOURED

1000

SYRIAN

100

1820   1850   1900   1950 1960

RELIGION

DISTRIBUTION
BY CONSTITUENCY 1960

Anglican
Baptist
Methodist
Presbyterian
Roman Catholic
Others

Kingston
and St. Andrew
419,416

10   20   30   40   50
Thousand persons

CHANGING RELIGIOUS COMPOSITION
Source : Censuses of Jamaica

Number of persons
400,000

ANGLICAN

BAPTIST   OTHER   CHURCH OF GOD

METHODIST

100,000

PRESBYTERIAN

MORAVIAN

ROMAN CATHOLIC

SEVENTH DAY ADVENTIST

CONGREGATIONALIST

SALVATION ARMY

10,000

JEWS

1000

HINDU

600

1881   1911   1921   1943   1960

12 FAMILY STRUCTURE

Mores prescribe that before a Jamaican marries he must buy or build a house, hold an elaborate wedding, and support a wife who need not go out to work. Confronted with these Victorian ideals, lower class Jamaicans have institutionalized alternative methods of mating and household formation.

Mating is initiated by visiting, and about one-third of all girls have their first baby before they are twenty. After an initial show of annoyance, the girl's mother usually accepts the situation, and the baby's father is given access to the house provided he acknowledges some financial responsibility for the child. Once she has achieved her 'womanship', the girl may proceed to a consensual or common-law union; no formal ceremony is held. By the time they are forty, however, most women have been legally married, and this is regarded as an appropriate status for mature and independent adults.

In addition to the effect of the life-cycle, there is a strong community influence over these mating patterns. Casual liaisons are the rule for part-time migrant labourers in the sugar areas. Among peasant farmers legal and consensual unions are stable, and prevail in proportions that vary with land ownership and productivity. These ecological distinctions are largely filtered out at the parish level, though Kingston is clearly set apart from the rural areas. In the capital common-law unions are rarer, visiting is common, and the incidence of household fragmentation is high both for consensual and marital unions. Furthermore, none of the alternative methods of mating has an exclusive place within a series nor within the individual's life cycle. In Kingston a woman may form a visiting relationship with one man, cohabit with another, revert to visiting with yet another, and finally marry someone different from all three.

Widowhood and separation provide a basis for female household headship; single mothers usually look after their own children in truly matrifocal units.

Female headship occurs in at least a quarter of all rural households, rising to over one-third in Kingston. Matrifocality is expressed in the placement of children. Invariably they reside with their mother's female kin, and women who migrate to the towns frequently send their children back to the country. In many lower-class urban households half-siblings are the norm. One school of thought attributes Jamaican matrifocality to West African polygamy and Ashanti matrilineage. However, this aspect of the lower-class family is essentially a creation of plantation slavery which has been sustained by subsequent structural requirements.

Male household headship is associated with conjugal unions, especially marriage. Male heads rarely accommodate offspring by earlier mates but sometimes house the previous children of their current spouses as well as their mutual descendants. Over 70 per cent of all births in Jamaica are illegitimate, though many are eventually legitimized when their parents marry. Illegitimacy is of no great significance to the Jamaican lower class, but a social distinction does exist between children who are acknowledged by their father and others who are promiscuously conceived. Men usually provide funds to maintain their absent children, though payments cease if their mothers cohabit with another mate. Male household heads will support their spouses' illegitimate children until they leave school.

Upper class behaviour is totally at variance with these practices. Marriage, mating, and parenthood succeed one another in a fashion acceptable to West Europeans. The family and household coincide, and heads are usually male. The middle class includes elements of both cultural traditions, combining a creolized version of Victorian marriage with the keeping of mistresses. Paternal dominance is the norm, and it is among this group that the sharpest distinction is made between a man's legal and illegitimate issue.

The upper and middle strata are endogamous; their liasons with the lower class are rarely legitimized. Irrespective of their own behaviour, members of the upper strata moralize about lower class illegitimacy

and 'promiscuity'. But lower class household structure is different, not deviant. Lack of patterned learning in childhood and problems over the fulfilment of parental roles give rise to tensions. However, they are rarely psychologically crippling or harmful to mental health. Most children are wanted, and are treated with warm affection interspersed with physical chastisement.

Family structure among the lower stratum is often described as 'extended', though this is not expressed in residential units. Rather it consists of a loose network that links distant kindred. Most activities are segregated by sex, and men and women spend little leisure-time together. Among the lower class, women meet at home, in the market, and at church. Men congregate at bars and rum shops, under trees and at street corners. The tie between parents and children, especially mothers and sons, is often closer than the link between marriage partners.

Folk customs still influence child-birth and rearing. A large minority of country deliveries are attended by the nana or untrained local midwife. Until recently it was widely believed that God revealed a woman's ordained quota of children by the number of knots in the umbilical cord of her first-born. Incorrect folk diagnosis of protein-calorie malnutrition – the symptoms are often ascribed to the common cold – still causes high infant mortality in some lower-class areas. Jamaicans are characterized by a fatalistic approach to procreation, life, and death.

The relationship between illegitimacy and the birth rate has been keenly debated. Data suggest that marital unions are more fecund than consensual cohabitation: married women tend to have more than four children, common-law wives less than four. Further factors of importance are the relative infrequency of sexual relations in visiting unions, and the role of separation as an impediment to procreation. Paradoxically, the mass marriage movement launched by the upper classes in the 1940s might have raised the birth rate still higher had it not clashed with lower-class values.

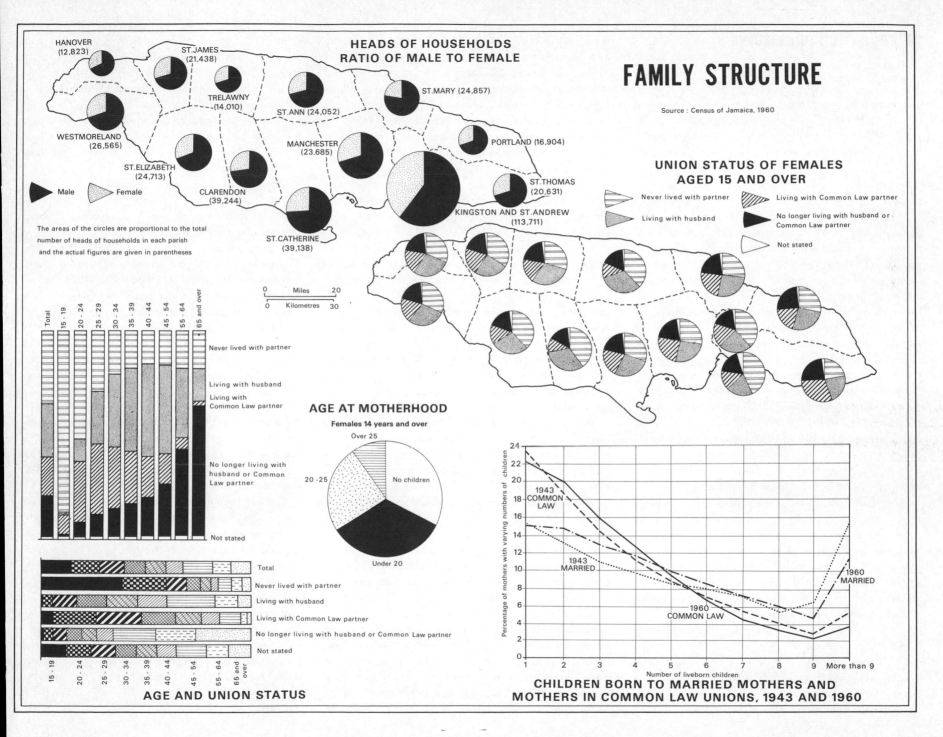

FAMILY STRUCTURE

**HEADS OF HOUSEHOLDS
RATIO OF MALE TO FEMALE**

Source : Census of Jamaica, 1960

HANOVER (12,823)
ST.JAMES (21,438)
TRELAWNY (14,010)
ST.ANN (24,052)
ST.MARY (24,857)
WESTMORELAND (26,565)
ST.ELIZABETH (24,713)
MANCHESTER (23,685)
PORTLAND (16,904)
CLARENDON (39,244)
ST.THOMAS (20,631)
KINGSTON AND ST.ANDREW (113,711)
ST.CATHERINE (39,138)

◀ Male   Female

The areas of the circles are proportional to the total
number of heads of households in each parish
and the actual figures are given in parentheses

Miles 20
Kilometres 30

**UNION STATUS OF FEMALES
AGED 15 AND OVER**

Never lived with partner   Living with Common Law partner

Living with husband   No longer living with husband or Common Law partner

Not stated

AGE AND UNION STATUS

Total
15 - 19
20 - 24
25 - 29
30 - 34
35 - 39
40 - 44
45 - 54
55 - 64
65 and over

Never lived with partner
Living with husband
Living with Common Law partner
No longer living with husband or Common Law partner
Not stated

Total
Never lived with partner
Living with husband
Living with Common Law partner
No longer living with husband or Common Law partner
Not stated

15 - 19
20 - 24
25 - 29
30 - 34
35 - 39
40 - 44
45 - 54
55 - 64
65 and over

AGE AT MOTHERHOOD

Females 14 years and over

Over 25
20 -25
No children
Under 20

CHILDREN BORN TO MARRIED MOTHERS AND MOTHERS IN COMMON LAW UNIONS, 1943 AND 1960

1943 COMMON LAW
1943 MARRIED
1960 MARRIED
1960 COMMON LAW

Percentage of mothers with varying numbers of children
Number of liveborn children
More than 9

33

13 EDUCATION PROVISION

The system of education in Jamaica is complex, and comprises state, private, and religious schools. These are divided into primary and secondary groups. In the early 1960s primary education was provided in infant (5 to 7), junior (7 to 11), senior (11 to 15), and all-age schools, the vast majority being state-run. Secondary schools were originally started by private individuals or religious groups, but most have become the direct responsibility of the government. Despite the importance of education, little more than 3 per cent of the Gross National Product is allocated to it.

The greater proportion of Jamaican children attend all-age schools. In St Thomas and St Elizabeth in the early 1960s no alternative existed for children enrolled in primary education. The most diversified primary system was located in Kingston, St Andrew, St James, Westmoreland and Manchester. In Kingston parish about 40 per cent were in age-graded schools, but there was no provision for infants in St Andrew. The absence of infant facilities in many areas is not surprising: schooling for five- and six-year-olds was not compulsory, and pressures on junior and senior places were intense. In view of current preoccupations with teaching the very young, however, the late starting age of schooling is highly undesirable.

Attendance at school is compulsory for children aged 7 to 15 but rarely enforced. Attendance rates exceed 75 per cent in Kingston and 65 per cent in St Andrew, dropping to about 60 per cent in the rural parishes. There are insufficient class-rooms to accommodate all potential pupils, and the building programme lags behind the birth rate. At the beginning of each academic year children are turned away from schools in the capital: in the rural areas they may not even bother to enroll.

Despite absenteeism, overcrowding persists in most primary schools. Even where verandahs are used as class-rooms the number of desks may be insufficient. Under these conditions it is virtually impossible to form project groups of mobile youngsters, and keeping order becomes a major preoccupation of the teacher. Problems are compounded by the shortage of qualified staff. Most enter the profession as pupil-teachers having passed the Jamaica School Certificate; some may eventually receive in-service training at a college of education. Consequently, children are often taught by adults whose knowledge and intellectual horizons are almost as narrow as their own. In six of the fourteen parishes less than half the staff have been trained as teachers; among the remainder, only in Kingston and St Andrew are more than two-thirds formally prepared for the class-room.

The pupil–teacher ratio is high everywhere. On average there are more than 50 children to each teacher, the ratio being lowest in Kingston and Westmoreland, and highest in St Mary, where it rises to 80:1. If qualified teachers alone are considered, the pupil–teacher ratio is more than doubled. Conditions are most satisfactory in Kingston and St Andrew, but appalling in St Mary, where each qualified member of staff is responsible for more than 160 pupils.

Historically, secondary schools have been the preserve of the well-to-do. This bastion of the middle classes has now been breached by the 11-plus system, though the cultural bias of the examination operates against children from the lower stratum. To compensate for this factor and to discourage private education, the government has established a system whereby 70 per cent of free secondary places are allocated to children from state primary schools. Each parish is served by at least one secondary school, and there are minor concentrations in the urban centres of St Catherine, Clarendon and St James. But almost 50 per cent of the secondary schools are in Kingston, and over half the 20,000 places.

Access to secondary education was once tied to money and status. The system operated in favour of fee-paying whites and browns, and financially mobile immigrants from Syria and China. Since the late 1950s, however, scholarships have placed secondary education within the reach of some black children. Many hope to gain enough General Certificate of Education 'O' and 'A' levels to secure a white collar job or a place at university. To hasten the process of mobility, and to cater for a more comprehensive type of education, a number of junior secondary schools have been set up which cater for 12 to 16 year olds. During the late 1960s all the senior schools were transferred to this sector of the system, and Canada and the World Bank provided funds for 30 junior secondary schools to be built.

Opportunities for higher education are relatively slight. Technical high schools take in about 3,000 children from the primary and junior secondary schools and offer a four-year course leading to the General Certificate of Education. They also operate a day-release scheme and evening classes. Technical institutes are located at Montego Bay and Port Antonio, each being attached to a junior secondary school. They provide pre-apprenticeship training for boys and girls aged 15 to 18 in building, woodwork, metalwork, mechanics, shorthand, typewriting and commercial practice. But there is a paucity of vocational institutes. Carron Hall Vocational School for Girls offers a two-year training in needle-work, embroidery, cooking and household management, while the Knockalva Agricultural Training Centre teaches stock-rearing, poultry-keeping, farm mechanics, and general husbandry. The pinnacle of vocational training is the Jamaica School of Agriculture which prepares farmers, extension workers and civil servants.

Teacher training colleges number only six, and half are in Kingston. In 1968, 826 teachers successfully graduated after a two-year course. The high point of the educational system is the University of the West Indies which was opened in 1948 and has a large campus at Mona. About half the 3,000 students are Jamaican. The university provides undergraduate and post-graduate courses in the humanities, social studies, law, medicine, and sciences. The teaching hospital is world-famous and a major asset to the island. But only about one-third of the Jamaicans who are at university attend locally. Degrees from abroad are highly valued in a community which has traditionally imported its standards.

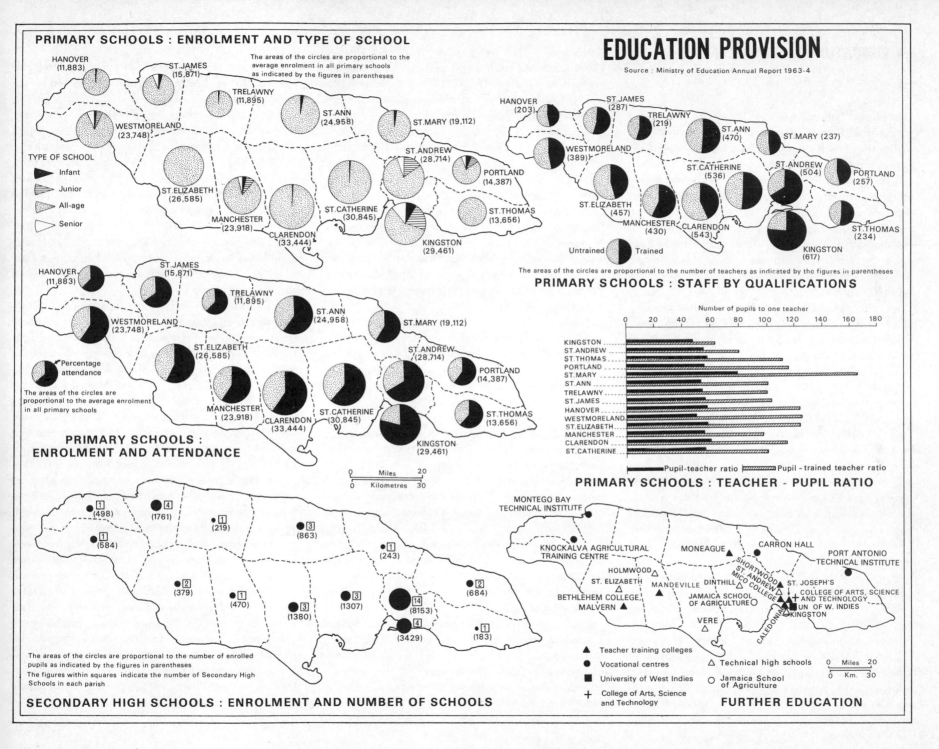

EDUCATION PROVISION

Source : Ministry of Education Annual Report 1963-4

PRIMARY SCHOOLS : ENROLMENT AND TYPE OF SCHOOL

The areas of the circles are proportional to the average enrolment in all primary schools as indicated by the figures in parentheses

HANOVER (11,883)
ST.JAMES (15,871)
TRELAWNY (11,895)
ST.ANN (24,958)
ST.MARY (19,112)
WESTMORELAND (23,748)
ST.ANDREW (28,714)
PORTLAND (14,387)
ST.ELIZABETH (26,585)
MANCHESTER (23,918)
ST.CATHERINE (30,845)
CLARENDON (33,444)
KINGSTON (29,461)
ST.THOMAS (13,656)

TYPE OF SCHOOL
Infant
Junior
All-age
Senior

PRIMARY SCHOOLS : STAFF BY QUALIFICATIONS

HANOVER (203)
ST.JAMES (287)
TRELAWNY (219)
ST.ANN (470)
ST.MARY (237)
WESTMORELAND (389)
ST.CATHERINE (536)
ST.ANDREW (504)
PORTLAND (257)
ST.ELIZABETH (457)
MANCHESTER (430)
CLARENDON (543)
KINGSTON (617)
ST.THOMAS (234)

Untrained   Trained

The areas of the circles are proportional to the number of teachers as indicated by the figures in parentheses

PRIMARY SCHOOLS : ENROLMENT AND ATTENDANCE

HANOVER (11,883)
ST.JAMES (15,871)
TRELAWNY (11,895)
ST.ANN (24,958)
ST.MARY (19,112)
WESTMORELAND (23,748)
ST.ANDREW (28,714)
PORTLAND (14,387)
ST.ELIZABETH (26,585)
MANCHESTER (23,918)
CLARENDON (33,444)
ST.CATHERINE (30,845)
ST.THOMAS (13,656)
KINGSTON (29,461)

Percentage attendance

The areas of the circles are proportional to the average enrolment in all primary schools

PRIMARY SCHOOLS : TEACHER - PUPIL RATIO

Number of pupils to one teacher
0   20   40   60   80   100   120   140   160   180

KINGSTON
ST.ANDREW
ST.THOMAS
PORTLAND
ST.MARY
ST.ANN
TRELAWNY
ST.JAMES
HANOVER
WESTMORELAND
ST.ELIZABETH
MANCHESTER
CLARENDON
ST.CATHERINE

Pupil-teacher ratio   Pupil - trained teacher ratio

Miles 20
Kilometres 30

SECONDARY HIGH SCHOOLS : ENROLMENT AND NUMBER OF SCHOOLS

[1] (498)
[4] (1761)
[1] (219)
[3] (863)
[1] (243)
[1] (584)
[2] (379)
[1] (470)
[3] (1380)
[3] (1307)
[14] (8153)
[2] (684)
[4] (3429)
[1] (183)

The areas of the circles are proportional to the number of enrolled pupils as indicated by the figures in parentheses

The figures within squares indicate the number of Secondary High Schools in each parish

FURTHER EDUCATION

MONTEGO BAY TECHNICAL INSTITUTE
KNOCKALVA AGRICULTURAL TRAINING CENTRE
MONEAGUE
CARRON HALL
PORT ANTONIO TECHNICAL INSTITUTE
HOLMWOOD
ST. ELIZABETH
MANDEVILLE
DINTHILL
SHORTWOOD
ST. ANDREW
MICO COLLEGE
ST. JOSEPH'S
COLLEGE OF ARTS, SCIENCE AND TECHNOLOGY
BETHLEHEM COLLEGE
MALVERN
JAMAICA SCHOOL OF AGRICULTURE
UN OF W. INDIES
CALEDONIA
KINGSTON
VERE

▲ Teacher training colleges
● Vocational centres
△ Technical high schools
■ University of West Indies
○ Jamaica School of Agriculture
+ College of Arts, Science and Technology

Miles 20
Km. 30

35

14 EDUCATIONAL ATTAINMENT

Historically, Jamaica has been an area of educational deprivation. During slavery white children were sent to Britain for schooling and most became absentees. Local grammar schools catered to the free coloureds and Jews, but the slaves were denied a formal training unless it was imparted by the missions. Educational patterns reflected, validated and reinforced the social stratification, and these relationships persisted throughout the post-emancipation period. Between 1835 and 1840 the British Government spent £30,000 per annum on the education of West Indian ex-slaves, but the sum was subsequently decreased, and stopped in 1846. By 1861 the Jamaican legislature was spending no more than one shilling per child per annum. Some whites claimed that blacks were mentally defective; most believed that literacy would teach the lower class to disdain manual labour and dissatisfy them with their station in life.

According to the 1871 census only 16 per cent of the Jamaican population aged over 5 were able to read and write; in Kingston the figure was 40 per cent. In 1892, however, school fees were abolished, and considerable improvements took place. By 1921 over half the population were literate, 80 per cent in Kingston, and 64 per cent in St Andrew. But training in craftsmanship was sadly neglected, and for many years the only source of skilled labour was the reformatory at Stony Hill in St Andrew. It was not until the late 1950s that a major structural change to the system was effected. The People's National Party introduced government-financed scholarships, which were tenable at the secondary schools and awarded on the basis of a competitive examination. The ceiling to lower class aspirations had been breached.

The 1960 census revealed that the majority of Jamaicans had received a primary schooling. Between 1943 and 1960, however, the percentage with secondary education expanded at an unprecedented rate, and this improvement was particularly striking among those aged 15 to 30. The tiny professional group barely increased during this period, but among the younger age-groups the number of those who had never attended school was reduced by over a third.

Jamaican men and women achieve roughly comparable standards. The principal contrasts are between Kingston and the remainder of the island and migration intensifies these discrepancies. Rural areas lack infant training, the majority of children attend primary schools, secondary education is for the few, and only a handful go to university. Most Kingstonians have been to primary school, but university training is not uncommon in the capital; a higher proportion have attended secondary school than in any other area, and infant provision is superior to the rural parishes. In Kingston girls have a noticeably higher level of attainment than boys.

Jamaican education is characterized by low rates of attendance. The proportion not at school fell from 30 per cent to 20 per cent between 1943 and 1960. Irregular schooling is more prevalent in the country districts than in Kingston. Children are expected to help with agricultural tasks and household chores; parents are unaware that learning is a gradual process and that frequent absence is a major handicap.

Illiteracy is virtually uniform throughout rural Jamaica, accounting for about 15 per cent of the population aged ten and over. In Kingston the figure is, of course, lower. Women are everywhere more literate than men, and this is a measure of their more regular schooling. Nevertheless, the rate of literacy has greatly improved during this century, and the category of people who could read but not write has been almost eradicated. Yet functional illiteracy is alarmingly widespread, and lapsed literacy a major problem among the poorest Jamaicans.

Education provides a formal method of socialization, a training-ground for future employment, and a stimulus to individual enquiry. The form and content of any system has a direct impact on the economic efficiency and social cohesion of a society. There are two distinct systems in Jamaica, associated with the secondary schools and what used to be called the primary schools.

Jamaican secondary education is available to about ten per cent of the age-group and is modelled on the British grammar school. Emphasis is given to academic subjects, character-building, morals and team-work. During the colonial period the curriculum was orientated to European tastes and experience; ignorance of local history, geography, agriculture and poverty were the hall-marks of the secondary-school graduate. During the last two decades enrolment has trebled and efforts have been made to make the subject matter more relevant and understandable to Jamaican children. Local history and geography are taught, and many schools use books written by West Indian poets and novelists. These changes have not always received parental sympathy.

While secondary schools remain essentially elitist, affording prestige rather than social utility, primary institutions inculcate respect for superiors. Rote learning is the norm and the discipline often harsh. Creative work is neglected if not actively discouraged. Agricultural training is overlooked and biblical teaching is often a mainstay of the syllabus. Creole is spoken by the children, but standard English is supposed to be the medium of communication in school. Teachers demand from children a form of speech which they themselves do not normally use, even in the classroom. Furthermore, teachers encourage children to aspire to white-collar jobs, though employment opportunities are invariably confined to mechanical, agricultural, and domestic tasks.

The dysfunctional aspects of education rebound on Jamaican society and reinforce other problems and ambiguities associated with family life, race and religion. Information on education alone shows that a cultural gulf of generally unacknowledged proportions separates the upper and lower strata. Furthermore, Jamaicans of low status are continually trying to adjust to goals which are simply not attainable. These frustrations are institutionalized in a self-denigrating folk culture rooted in slavery. The only way to change this situation is through education itself.

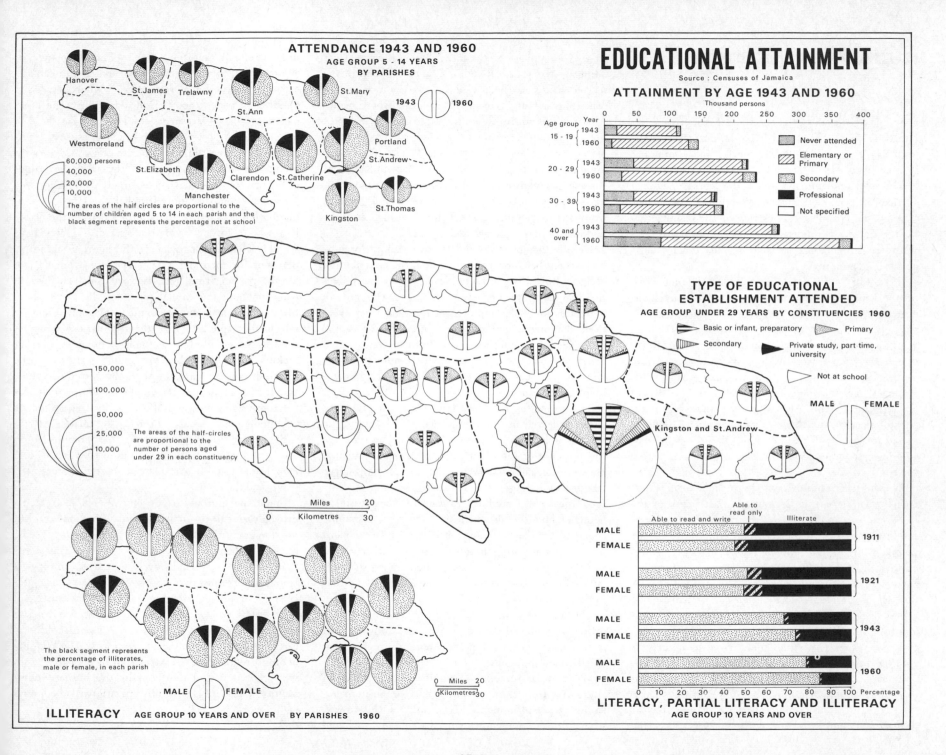

EDUCATIONAL ATTAINMENT

ATTENDANCE 1943 AND 1960
AGE GROUP 5 - 14 YEARS
BY PARISHES

Hanover
St.James
Trelawny
St.Ann
St.Mary
1943   1960
Westmoreland
St.Elizabeth
Clarendon
St.Catherine
Portland
St.Andrew
Manchester
Kingston
St.Thomas

60,000 persons
40,000
20,000
10,000

The areas of the half circles are proportional to the number of children aged 5 to 14 in each parish and the black segment represents the percentage not at school

Source : Censuses of Jamaica

ATTAINMENT BY AGE 1943 AND 1960

Thousand persons

Age group	Year
15 - 19	1943
	1960
20 - 29	1943
	1960
30 - 39	1943
	1960
40 and over	1943
	1960

0 50 100 150 200 250 300 350 400

Never attended
Elementary or Primary
Secondary
Professional
Not specified

TYPE OF EDUCATIONAL ESTABLISHMENT ATTENDED
AGE GROUP UNDER 29 YEARS BY CONSTITUENCIES 1960

Basic or infant, preparatory
Primary
Secondary
Private study, part time, university
Not at school

MALE   FEMALE

150,000
100,000
50,000
25,000
10,000

The areas of the half-circles are proportional to the number of persons aged under 29 in each constituency

Kingston and St.Andrew

0 Miles 20
0 Kilometres 30

ILLITERACY   AGE GROUP 10 YEARS AND OVER   BY PARISHES   1960

The black segment represents the percentage of illiterates, male or female, in each parish

MALE   FEMALE

0 Miles 20
0 Kilometres 30

LITERACY, PARTIAL LITERACY AND ILLITERACY
AGE GROUP 10 YEARS AND OVER

Able to read and write
Able to read only
Illiterate

MALE	1911
FEMALE	
MALE	1921
FEMALE	
MALE	1943
FEMALE	
MALE	1960
FEMALE	

0 10 20 30 40 50 60 70 80 90 100 Percentage

15 EMPLOYMENT AND INDUSTRY

Despite two decades of economic diversification, the Jamaican labour force is still predominantly agricultural (37·8 per cent). Public service and commerce are the next largest employers (24·6 per cent), followed by manufacturing (14·8 per cent), personal service (14·5 per cent) and construction (8·2 per cent). Among men agriculture, construction and manufacturing are the most important groups. Women are concentrated in personal service, manufacturing, agriculture and commerce.

In most of the rural parishes over half the men work on the land, and manufacturing, servicing, and construction are minority pursuits. Manufacturing is strongly associated with sugar processing, construction with the tourist and bauxite industries. The majority of country women work as domestics and concentrate in other services such as commerce and government. Personal service is important in the tourist parishes of St James and St Ann. Agriculture is scarcely more important than manufacturing among women. Regional variations are few for either sex. Only Kingston and, to a lesser degree, Montego Bay deviate greatly from the rural pattern.

In Kingston employment in manufacturing outstrips the numbers in agriculture. Yet many of the factory jobs scarcely deserve the name. According to the 1960 census manufacturing employed 39,000 people in the capital, but the Factory Inspectorate recorded only 17,000 jobs in registered enterprises having more than ten workers. The majority of industrial concerns are small. Many are repair shops, others engage in the petty manufacture of pots, pans and brooms. Women employees are usually no more than seamstresses, while their rural counterparts employ their dexterity in handicrafts.

Even according to the census, tertiary employment exceeds manufacturing in Kingston. Much of this takes the form of domestic service, commerce or government employment; domestic service is the largest employer of women, and other services dominate the male labour force. The inflation of the service sector has been essential for the mopping-up of surplus labour in an urban economy where manufacturing growth has failed to match the expansion of the population. It is highly significant that almost 70 per cent of the increase in the island's classified labour force between 1943 and 1960 took place in Kingston. Among men construction is one of the most outstanding urban pursuits. It received considerable impetus from the expanding market for housing, and the building of new factories and offices.

Despite the growth of the Jamaican labour force by 20 per cent between 1943 and 1960, the contribution of agriculture has contracted. For women the reduction has been greater than for men. The growth industries for male employment have been construction, commerce and other services. Heavy capital investment in mining and manufacturing has created few additional jobs. Expansion of employment for women has been achieved in manufacturing, commerce, and other services.

The processes of expansion and contraction are partly reflected in the average age of workers in the various industries. Traditional primary pursuits are the preserve of the elderly; mining, manufacturing, construction and personal service exemplify a younger labour force. Agricultural labour is eschewed by school-leavers. They flock to the towns and to those rural neighbourhoods which are undergoing economic change. Two major consequences ensue. The modern sector cannot absorb the growth of the labour force, and the depletion of the able-bodied among the agricultural population has been accompanied by a serious decline in output.

The minority of Jamaicans are employers, the majority employed. Self-employment removes a man from surveillance, and peasant agriculture has provided an escape from plantation supervision. Where employment is scarce, self-employment provides an alternative to unemployment. It is common in manufacturing and commerce, especially in the towns, where it is synonymous with handicraft work and market selling. Traditional forms of employment persist in agriculture, and to a lesser extent in manufacturing, construction and commerce, where wives and children provide a body of unpaid labour. The rapid expansion of government employment has been a feature of the post-war period, and is especially important in Kingston. The bureaucracy provides an avenue for advancement where the ascriptive values of the private sector have been largely abandoned.

Women comprise more than half the Jamaican population but account for only 37 per cent of the classified labour force. Overall participation rates have scarcely changed since 1943: the figure is about 84 per cent for men and 43 per cent for women. The female participation rate is very much higher in Kingston, and the capital possesses the best opportunities for female employment. Conversely, the male rate in the capital is lower than the national average, and this is accounted for by the large numbers who are seeking their first job. Outstanding features of the Jamaican economy are the slow absorption of youth, and the rapid decline in employment opportunities for those aged fifty and above. Only the skilled or able-bodied are secure. In Kingston males are absorbed more slowly into, and shed more rapidly from, the work force than they are in the island as a whole. Hopelessness and frustration characterize many of the young and the aged.

Since the end of the Second World War it has proved easier to diversify the Jamaican economy than to alter radically the pattern of employment. The bauxite industry illustrates the problem. It represents a multi-million pound investment, yet employs a labour force of just over 10,000. Moreover, this figure is split almost equally between constructional and agricultural workers on the one hand, and bauxite and alumina operatives on the other. Similar difficulties have been encountered in Kingston. The building of an oil refinery on the waterfront in the early 1960s was greeted with enthusiasm by the business community. The plant is now fully operational and employs eighty workers.

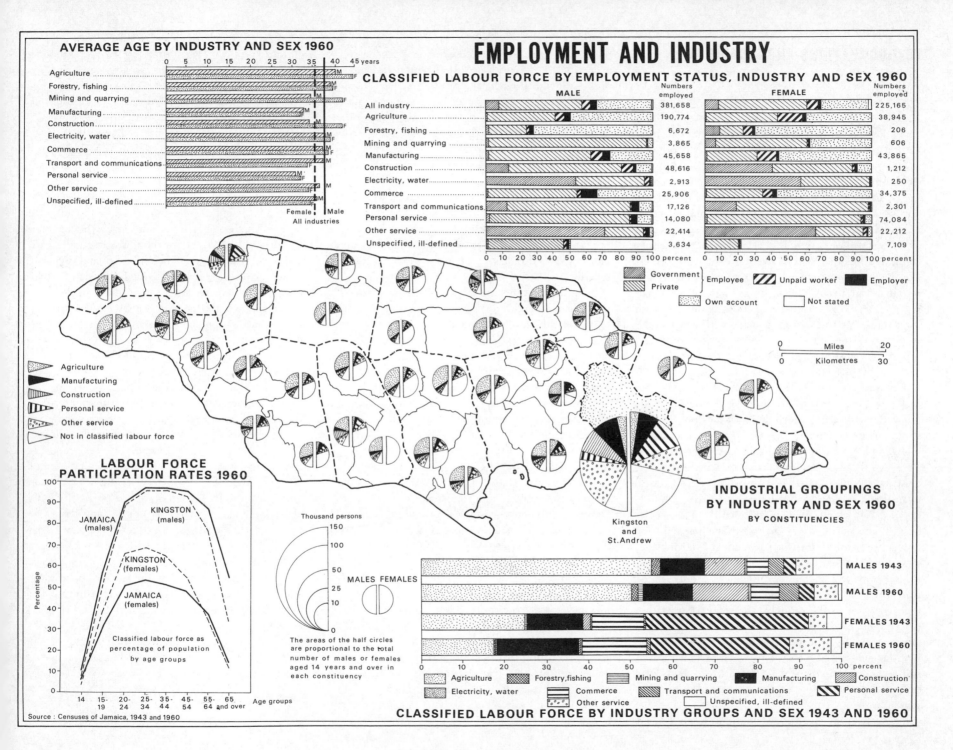

EMPLOYMENT AND INDUSTRY

AVERAGE AGE BY INDUSTRY AND SEX 1960

0 5 10 15 20 25 30 35 40 45 years

Agriculture
Forestry, fishing
Mining and quarrying
Manufacturing
Construction
Electricity, water
Commerce
Transport and communications
Personal service
Other service
Unspecified, ill-defined

Female | Male
All industries

CLASSIFIED LABOUR FORCE BY EMPLOYMENT STATUS, INDUSTRY AND SEX 1960

	MALE	Numbers employed	FEMALE	Numbers employed
All industry		381,658		225,165
Agriculture		190,774		38,945
Forestry, fishing		6,672		206
Mining and quarrying		3,865		606
Manufacturing		45,658		43,865
Construction		48,616		1,212
Electricity, water		2,913		250
Commerce		25,906		34,375
Transport and communications		17,126		2,301
Personal service		14,080		74,084
Other service		22,414		22,212
Unspecified, ill-defined		3,634		7,109

0 10 20 30 40 50 60 70 80 90 100 percent   0 10 20 30 40 50 60 70 80 90 100 percent

Government / Private — Employee   Unpaid worker   Employer
Own account   Not stated

Map legend
Agriculture
Manufacturing
Construction
Personal service
Other service
Not in classified labour force

Kingston and St. Andrew

INDUSTRIAL GROUPINGS BY INDUSTRY AND SEX 1960
BY CONSTITUENCIES

Miles 0 — 20
Kilometres 0 — 30

LABOUR FORCE PARTICIPATION RATES 1960

100
90
80
70
60
50
40
30
20
10
0

JAMAICA (males)
KINGSTON (males)
KINGSTON (females)
JAMAICA (females)

Classified labour force as percentage of population by age groups

Percentage

14   15-19   20-24   25-34   35-44   45-54   55-64   65 and over   Age groups

Thousand persons
150
100
50
25
10
0

MALES FEMALES

The areas of the half circles are proportional to the total number of males or females aged 14 years and over in each constituency

CLASSIFIED LABOUR FORCE BY INDUSTRY GROUPS AND SEX 1943 AND 1960

MALES 1943
MALES 1960
FEMALES 1943
FEMALES 1960

0 10 20 30 40 50 60 70 80 90 100 percent

Agriculture   Forestry, fishing   Mining and quarrying   Manufacturing   Construction
Electricity, water   Commerce   Transport and communications   Personal service
Other service   Unspecified, ill-defined

Source : Censuses of Jamaica, 1943 and 1960

39

16 OCCUPATIONS AND INCOME

Jamaica is a developing country and economically dependent on primary products. Traditionally its population has worked in agriculture or provided goods and services for those employed in this basic industry. According to the 1960 census just over 60 per cent of the island's labour force were engaged in manual and service occupations, 21 per cent were employed in craft and technical jobs, 11 per cent possessed clerical or sales positions, 4 per cent were in supervisory tasks, and less than half of one per cent were professionals. Among women personal service was more important than manual occupations, and professionals were extremely rare. Occupation coincides with social rank. Median status is equated with white-collar work, and the elite monopolize professional and supervisory positions. Beneath these strata are located the mass of the labouring population.

Regional variations in occupational structure are negligible, the only areas to deviate conspicuously from the national pattern being Kingston and the constituency containing Montego Bay. In the capital male employment in the manual and service groups is exceeded by the combined provision of white-collar, craft and technical jobs. The two latter groups vie with manual and service occupations as the major employers of urban labour, though white-collar work is also heavily concentrated in Kingston. The participation rate is lower for women than for men, and in Kingston, where over half are employed, the majority are domestic servants and manual workers. Not only is the concentration of women in the clerical and sales groups higher in the capital than the rural areas, but this proportion is higher than for men. However, most saleswomen are probably market sellers. In Montego Bay the substantial provision of white collar, craft and technical employment, coupled to the high level of female participation, are symptomatic of its urban status.

The pattern of income distribution clearly reflects the spatial variation in occupations. With the single exception of St Catherine, all the rural parishes express an identical financial stratification. In 1960 only a small minority earned over £500 per annum, the majority of males receiving less than £100 and their female counterparts less than £50. These proportions were reversed in the capital and St Catherine. Over one-third of Kingston's male labour force earned over £200 per annum, a sizeable segment in the suburbs receiving over £1,000. Incomes were lower in the agricultural sector (£45 per annum), and highest in construction (£100), utilities (£200) and transport (£92). Wages average £1,000 per annum in the bauxite industry and this has created a regional pattern of inflation.

Inequalities in income distribution are expressed in the Jamaican tax returns. In the early 1960s nine-tenths of the classified labour force earned less than £300 per annum and paid no tax, but almost 20 per cent of the remainder received over £1,000. The possibilities for income redistribution through progressive taxation are quite limited. Skewed incomes are the norm in most countries, but Jamaica experiences extreme conditions. One of the major development problems in Jamaica has been to flatten the curve of income distribution to bring it closer to the line of equality. Whether this process has taken place is a moot point. The island has certainly experienced rapid socio-economic development – if the Gross Domestic Product per capita is any guide. During the 1960s alone per capita incomes at current prices rose from just over £250 to well over £400, and the latter figure would have been much higher with a stable population.

The gap between the rich and the poor is matched by the distinction between aspirations and achievement. Agricultural employment is socially stigmatized, and even country people wish to avoid it. Jamaicans realize that high status is reserved for white collar workers, and that physical toil goes largely unrewarded. A survey of occupational choice among a sample of rural schoolboys showed that the majority hoped to be mechanics, doctors or truck drivers; no-one wanted agricultural work or labouring. Schoolgirls expressed similar preferences, and parents reinforced their children's aspirations. Yet opportunities for well-paid, non-manual jobs are limited in the rural areas.

Kingston's socio-economic characteristics perpetuate the agglomerative forces which have created the modern city. Migrants are drawn by the prospect of higher wages and better jobs, and retailers and manufacturers locate where the market is largest. But in Kingston the gulf between the rich and the poor is not only wider than elsewhere, but more explicit. Manual labour and low wages are the norm in rural Jamaica, and poverty is concealed behind crops and vegetation. However, the ostentatious living of the rich is obvious to the most unperceptive Kingstonian, while the bus journey down the Spanish Town Road is likely to remain in the mind's eye for its expression of human degradation. In this highly polarized urban situation migrants are usually trapped in the slums.

Despite the rapid development of trade unionism since the riots of 1938, the bulk of Jamaican labour remains unorganized. This is due to the high proportion of self-employed farmers and domestic servants and to the nature of the trade union movement itself. The labour scene is dominated by two unions, the Bustamante Industrial Trade Union (BITU) and the National Workers Union (NWU). Neither is a craft union and the leadership of each is essentially middle class. Inter-union rivalry is intense, and they vie to represent the labour force in each factory and estate. The bauxite industry is virtually a NWU stronghold, and the BITU tends to dominate the sugar industry. A gap has been created between privileged, unionized labour, with comparatively good, sophisticated social benefits and pension schemes, and the remainder of employees who enjoy only limited social security. Some of the poor claim that the growth of trade unions has made their chance of obtaining casual employment a good deal less than it was two decades ago.

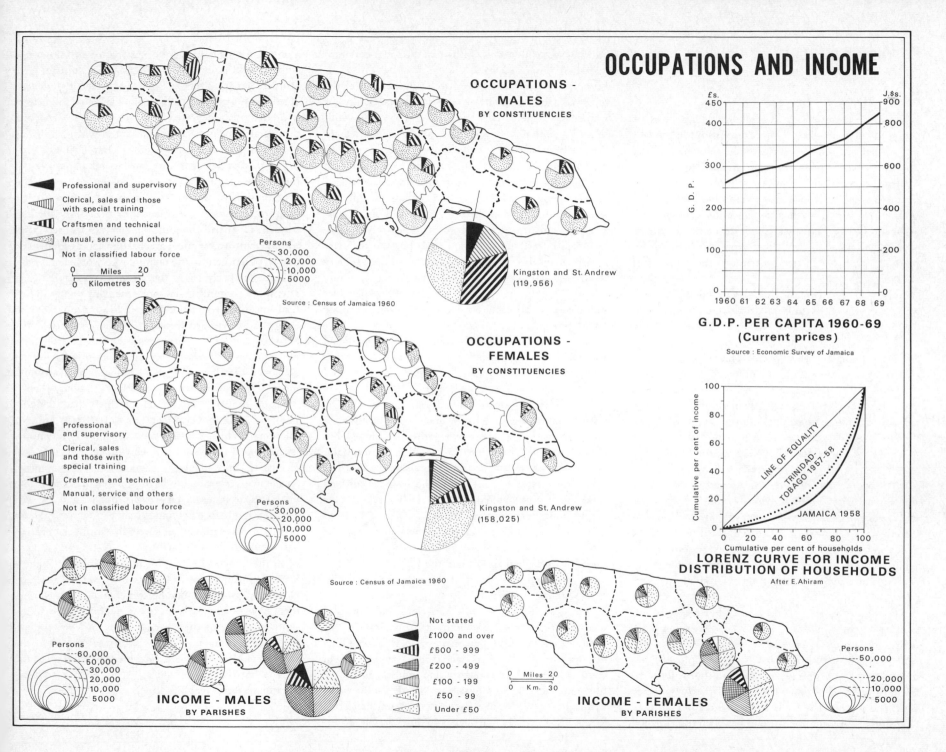

OCCUPATIONS AND INCOME

OCCUPATIONS - MALES
BY CONSTITUENCIES

- ◤ Professional and supervisory
- ◤ Clerical, sales and those with special training
- ◤ Craftsmen and technical
- ◤ Manual, service and others
- ◁ Not in classified labour force

0 Miles 20
0 Kilometres 30

Persons
30,000
20,000
10,000
5000

Kingston and St. Andrew (119,956)

Source : Census of Jamaica 1960

OCCUPATIONS - FEMALES
BY CONSTITUENCIES

- ◤ Professional and supervisory
- ◤ Clerical, sales and those with special training
- ◤ Craftsmen and technical
- ◁ Manual, service and others
- ◁ Not in classified labour force

Persons
30,000
20,000
10,000
5000

Kingston and St. Andrew (158,025)

Source : Census of Jamaica 1960

G.D.P. PER CAPITA 1960-69
(Current prices)

Source : Economic Survey of Jamaica

LORENZ CURVE FOR INCOME DISTRIBUTION OF HOUSEHOLDS
After E. Ahiram

LINE OF EQUALITY
TRINIDAD-TOBAGO 1957-58
JAMAICA 1958

Cumulative per cent of income
Cumulative per cent of households

INCOME - MALES
BY PARISHES

Persons
60,000
50,000
30,000
20,000
10,000
5000

- ◁ Not stated
- ◤ £1000 and over
- ◤ £500 - 999
- ◤ £200 - 499
- ◤ £100 - 199
- ◤ £50 - 99
- ◁ Under £50

0 Miles 20
0 Km. 30

INCOME - FEMALES
BY PARISHES

Persons
50,000
20,000
10,000
5000

17 UNEMPLOYMENT

Jamaica has experienced continuously high rates of unemployment since the Great Depression. In the late 1930s a British official described unemployment as the island's principal problem, and emphasized the seriousness of the situation among school-leavers. Rapid population growth since that period has perpetuated labour surplus. According to the 1960 census, 12·6 per cent of the classified labour force were unemployed, and subsequent estimates put the figure at 20 per cent, rising to 30 per cent among the group aged 16 to 25.

Almost 60 per cent of the island's unemployment was concentrated in the capital in 1960. High rates of unemployment were located in St James and the south-coast parishes, and the remainder was distributed among the rural areas. The relationship between urbanization and unemployment provides a geographical expression of the gap between perceived and realized opportunity. Urban-rural differences affect the character of the unemployed. In rural districts the majority are school-leavers looking for their first job. But in Kingston this group accounts for only one-third of the unemployed. Kingston's out-of-work women are frequently engaged in the home, and the majority of men previously obtained work but lost it. Rural school-leavers soon migrate to Kingston if they cannot find work. Over one-third of the city's males and a half of the females who were looking for their first job in 1960 had been born in the rural parishes, and most of this group was under 21 years of age.

The population of Jamaica has been slowly accumulating in Kingston, and so too has unemployment. As long ago as 1936 it was estimated that 11 per cent of the city's labour force was unemployed, and that 40 per cent of this group was rural-born. By 1946 the level of unemployment had risen to nearly 16 per cent, and in 1960 the figure reached 18.4 per cent. In Kingston cyclical unemployment has been transformed into a permanent, secular feature of the socio-economic scene. Two levels of adaptation have emerged. Service activity – le tertiaire refuge – has been inflated to provide employment for domestic servants, washer women, gardeners, yard-boys and odd-job men – but at wages which barely exceed subsistence rates. In West Kingston many of the older people have abandoned the search for employment, and rely on 'scuffling' or scraping a living from a variety of illegal or quasi-legal activities such as begging, stealing and selling scrap culled from the city's rubbish dumps. The men and women involved in these activities are technically speaking self-employed, but the majority regard themselves as unemployed and so does society at large. Unemployment does not necessarily imply idleness, but the very existence of scuffling provides a socio-economic index of poverty and extreme population pressure.

In Jamaica it is essential to think of employment and unemployment as occupying a continuum. As well as those who are unemployed for periods of several months, there are many who work for only a few weeks in each year or for a few days in each week. The distinction between those who are employed on a part-time basis and those who are unemployed but obtain a variety of occasional tasks is difficult to sustain. About one-quarter of the labour force worked for less than five days in the week before the 1960 census, and rural under-employment is particularly marked. One of the most persistent problems has been associated with the seasonal character of the sugar industry. The crop is cut between January and June and followed by a dead season when almost half the labour force is laid off. Furthermore, the end of the sugar harvest coincides with the slump in tourism.

Setting aside these seasonal variations, the industrial sectors recording the highest rates of unemployment are construction and personal service, followed by manufacturing, electricity and water, transport and communications. The construction industry is susceptible to short-term fluctuations in demand, while domestic servants have no security of tenure and rely for employment on personal recommendation. Commerce, mining and public service record low unemployment rates and so too does agriculture. The low rate in agriculture is explicable by the high degree of self-employment and the coincidence of the census with the sugar harvest. However, evidence suggests that rural Jamaicans are disenchanted with conditions in agriculture. In the 1950s, for example, it was estimated that 62 per cent of the males and 36 per cent of the females in rural areas were looking for work. The contribution of the various industrial sectors to the total rate of unemployment produces an expected pattern. Over half the jobless men are in construction and agriculture, while personal service accounts for nearly 50 per cent of the unemployed women.

Since the early 1950s the Jamaican government has attempted to combat unemployment by giving industrial incentives to foreign and local capitalists. In Kingston, however, these efforts have created only between ten and twenty per cent of the factory employment which was required. It is now generally conceded that it is difficult to generate mass employment using orthodox capitalistic techniques; most modern industry is capital- rather than labour-intensive. The government has had to face another dilemma. While wanting to modernize the economy it has been reluctant to encourage technological changes if they involve a reduction in employment. Successive governments have opposed mechanization in the sugar industry on social grounds, and permits are required before equipment can be imported. However, a certain amount of surreptitious mechanization has occurred. In some areas the reduction in employment has been effected by refusing jobs to school-leavers in preference to laying-off registered workers. Nevertheless, rural unemployment and impoverishment have been greatly increased by this process in the southern sections of the sugar belt. In Vere for example, the number of cane-cutters employed in the vicinity of Mitchell Town decreased from nearly 1,000 to 200 between 1965 and 1968, an 80 per cent reduction in three years.

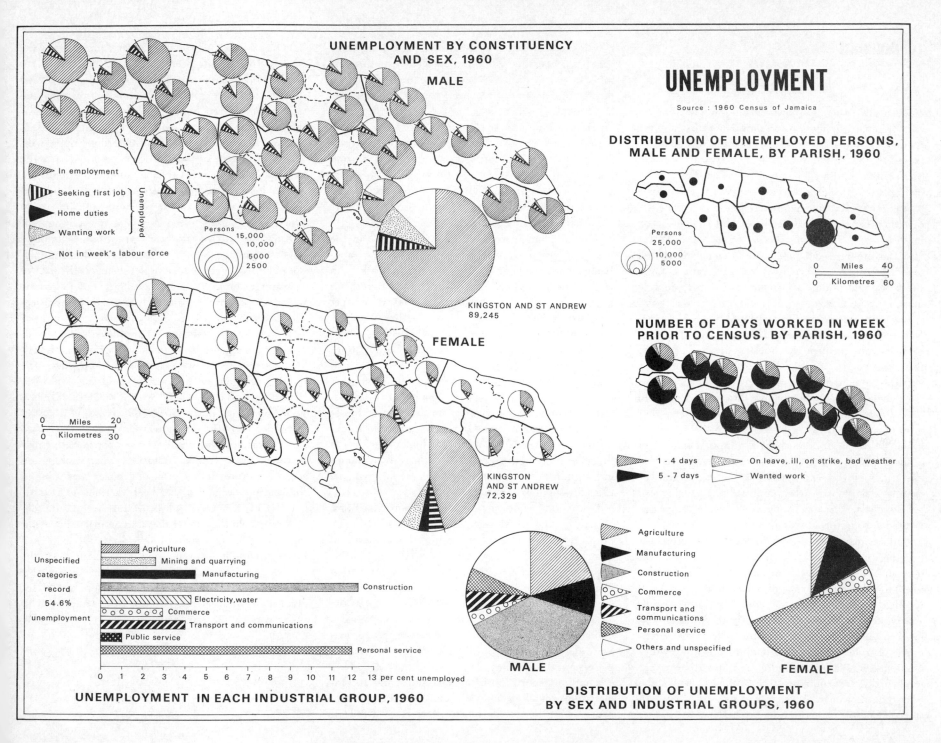

UNEMPLOYMENT BY CONSTITUENCY AND SEX, 1960

MALE

In employment

Seeking first job ⎫
Home duties ⎬ Unemployed
Wanting work ⎭

Not in week's labour force

Persons
15,000
10,000
5000
2500

KINGSTON AND ST ANDREW
89,245

FEMALE

0 Miles 20
0 Kilometres 30

KINGSTON AND ST ANDREW
72,329

UNEMPLOYMENT

Source : 1960 Census of Jamaica

DISTRIBUTION OF UNEMPLOYED PERSONS, MALE AND FEMALE, BY PARISH, 1960

Persons
25,000
10,000
5000

0 Miles 40
0 Kilometres 60

NUMBER OF DAYS WORKED IN WEEK PRIOR TO CENSUS, BY PARISH, 1960

1 - 4 days   On leave, ill, on strike, bad weather

5 - 7 days   Wanted work

Unspecified categories record 54.6% unemployment

Agriculture
Mining and quarrying
Manufacturing
Construction
Electricity,water
Commerce
Transport and communications
Public service
Personal service

0 1 2 3 4 5 6 7 8 9 10 11 12 13 per cent unemployed

UNEMPLOYMENT IN EACH INDUSTRIAL GROUP, 1960

Agriculture
Manufacturing
Construction
Commerce
Transport and communications
Personal service
Others and unspecified

MALE   FEMALE

DISTRIBUTION OF UNEMPLOYMENT BY SEX AND INDUSTRIAL GROUPS, 1960

18 HOUSING

Since emancipation housing conditions in Jamaica have been deplored by numerous commissions of enquiry. A source as impartial as the 1943 census described almost half the buildings as bad. The typical Jamaican house comprised a single-room, wooden hut run up from planks of timber or scraps of debris. Frequently it was infested with termites. Three-quarters of the dwellings had no bathing facilities, and kitchens were located outside the main structure of the house. Water closets were rare and pit-latrines the norm. Shared tenements were essentially urban in location. Only the upper and middle strata possessed large, durable houses, inside kitchens, toilets and baths. There was a strong correlation between social rank and house-type.

The dichotomy between Kingston and the rural parishes runs through the housing data collected by the 1960 census. Owner-occupation is essentially a rural phenomenon, most parishes recording over half their dwellings in this category. Small farmers build on their own property, while land-less labourers rent a ground-let on which to construct a movable chattel house. In the sugar areas there is a limited amount of accommodation in estate barracks. Renting is the norm in Kingston, and tenancy is common wherever there is a substantial urban population. Squatting still occurs on the backlands, but the largest camps are located in Kingston and Montego Bay.

Building materials vary with locale. Concrete has become more common in the last two decades, but only in Kingston does it account for over half the dwellings. The majority of rural homes are still wooden, particularly in the lowlands at the eastern and western extremities of the island. Brick is confined to the towns and in Kingston reflects the persistence of a few eighteenth- and nineteenth-century buildings. St Mary, Clarendon and St Catherine are noteworthy for their wattle dwellings, while the limestone parishes – St Ann, Trelawny, St Elizabeth and Manchester – record a high percentage of houses constructed of other materials. In some of these parishes timber-frame houses with a stone-and-mortar infill, known as Spanish Wall, are common. The spread of concrete buildings has been hastened by government housing schemes carried out after the 1951 hurricane. Between 1946 and 1957 26,000 people were housed in government projects, the majority being in Kingston. Additional improvements in rural housing have been sponsored through the Farm Development Programme. Galvanized-iron roofs threaten to become ubiquitous, making redundant the picturesque palm thatch of the south-eastern lowlands.

Substantial improvements have been made in the public provision of water. In 1943 over half the population had to collect their own requirements from rivers, ponds, streams and wells. By 1960 two-thirds of all dwellings had access to tap- or tank-water. Yet only the townspeople can expect to have supplies piped into their dwelling or yard. Elsewhere, public standpipes are the norm. Important regional variations are recorded. Natural supplies are the principal source in Hanover, Westmoreland, St Catherine, Portland, and St Mary, where the rainfall is heaviest and the stream density greatest. In the dry parishes of Manchester, St Elizabeth, and St Ann, private catchments are essential. Public standpipes perform a valuable, if inadequate, function in the squatter camps in Kingston. Some squatters open up the fire-hydrants to secure supplies of drinking water.

Urban-rural contrasts are brought out even more clearly by the distribution of toilet facilities. The proportion of dwellings with water closets increased from 10 to 20 per cent between 1943 and 1960, but more than four-fifths are still concentrated in Kingston. Elsewhere in Jamaica pit-latrines account for over three-quarters of the facilities, except at the western end of the island where virtually no modern sanitation is available. Even in Kingston pit-latrines are widespread – though illegal – and serve almost 40 per cent of the dwellings.

Kingston records both the best and worst accommodation, and long hours of sunshine are the sole palliative for the capital's tenement- and yard-dwellers.

The Department of Housing was responsible for the construction of just over 7,000 units in Jamaica between 1963 and 1969, 1,000 of which were provided in slum-clearance schemes in Kingston. During the same period private housing guaranteed by the government produced 4,400 units in the capital, and accounted for the greater part of the suburban growth. The government has found it easier to underwrite the loans of other agencies than to supply the funds required for low-income housing. The poor are quite unable to make reliable repayments for long-term loans; squatters are often expelled, never rehoused. In Kingston 1965 was the best year for house-building, but less than 2,500 units were completed in the various public and private schemes. Yet such is the pace of the capital's growth that an annual target of 3,250 new units was required to maintain the highly unsatisfactory situation which existed in 1960.

Judged by the standards of the developing world, housing and amenities in Jamaica are by no means bad. To British eyes, however, they are appalling. The housing problem is an aspect of the island's poverty syndrome, and is associated with low levels of living, poor wages and rapid population increase. In Kingston city-ward migration and unemployment have created a massive slum. The ramifications of poor housing may be traced in the family, education, urban ecology and social structure. It is typical of Jamaica that some of the best public housing has been carried out as a by-product of, if not as a substitute for, agricultural development. In the capital the housing market is manipulated by the upper and middle strata for their own ends. Middle-income housing is facilitated by the government; public housing is inadequate and costly; tenanted slums are tolerated; squatter camps are eradicated; and priority is given to the expansion of the sewered area into the suburbs.

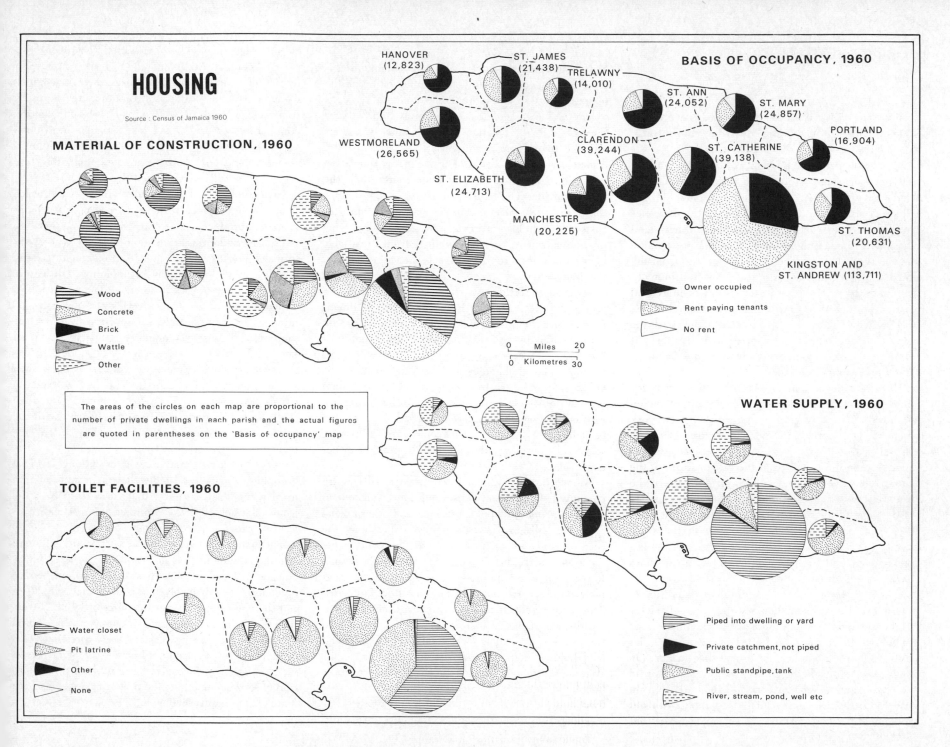

HOUSING

Source : Census of Jamaica 1960

MATERIAL OF CONSTRUCTION, 1960

Wood
Concrete
Brick
Wattle
Other

BASIS OF OCCUPANCY, 1960

HANOVER
(12,823)

ST. JAMES
(21,438)

TRELAWNY
(14,010)

ST. ANN
(24,052)

ST. MARY
(24,857)

PORTLAND
(16,904)

WESTMORELAND
(26,565)

CLARENDON
(39,244)

ST. CATHERINE
(39,138)

ST. ELIZABETH
(24,713)

MANCHESTER
(20,225)

ST. THOMAS
(20,631)

KINGSTON AND
ST. ANDREW (113,711)

Owner occupied

Rent paying tenants

No rent

0 Miles 20
0 Kilometres 30

The areas of the circles on each map are proportional to the number of private dwellings in each parish and the actual figures are quoted in parentheses on the 'Basis of occupancy' map

WATER SUPPLY, 1960

Piped into dwelling or yard

Private catchment, not piped

Public standpipe, tank

River, stream, pond, well etc

TOILET FACILITIES, 1960

Water closet
Pit latrine
Other
None

45

19 RURAL SETTLEMENT

Two distinct types of rural settlement have evolved in Jamaica; they are associated with the sugar plantation and the peasantry.

Sugar settlements are a product of the resurgence of cane-growing since 1900, not a direct continuation from the eighteenth century. At Hampden in the Queen of Spain's Valley near Falmouth, the flat canelands are dominated by two buildings which stand adjacent to one another – the plantation great house and the sugar factory. The great house dates from the end of the eighteenth century, its fabric a testimony to the durability of the plantocracy, if not of individual planter families. The factory is the economic life-line of those who live in the sugar area. Together with the garage, power station, workshops and distillery, it stands in a yard or compound which can be sealed off from the remainder of the estate.

The great house acts as the organizing focus for social patterns and relationships. Senior staff are housed in bungalows located close to the mansion, and work as engineers, electricians, and accountants. Many are expatriates, especially Scots. A few barracks are provided near to the factory, but the vast majority of the labour force live in street villages on the edge of the cane. The post office, school and church congregate on the edge of the old plantation, but in recent years have been engulfed by the expansion in the sugar acreage. The social stratification of the plantation is a finely-graded hierarchy, and social status declines sharply with distance from the great house.

On some estates the nucleation of workers' homes is stronger than at Hampden, and the urban character of the settlement more obtrusive. The main road leading to the sugar factory often possesses groceries and rum shops, a butcher, baker and shoe-maker. On the pavement outside the grocery shops vendors spread their fruit and vegetables for sale. Behind the main road footpaths lead into family yards filled with old wooden huts. The entire locality might have been lifted from an urban slum.

The outstanding feature of the sugar communities is their dependence on a single economic staple and the seasonality of the work. At the beginning of the crop season the local unemployed are rapidly absorbed into the labour force, together with migrants who flock into the town from neighbouring villages and more distant parts of the island. The incoming population creates a recurrent social revolution transforming the rhythm of life. The housing situation becomes more acute, the newcomers create changes in the constitutions of households, setting up new unions and altering previous alliances. Earnings fluctuate from a relatively high level in the crop to bare subsistence, or less, in the dead season.

Some sugar settlements, such as Lionel Town, are recognized urban areas; others possess only rudimentary service functions. The sugar communities are characterized by paternalism, social distance, racial hostility, and sectional organizations. Trade unions are the most influential bodies, and the National Workers' Union and the Bustamante Industrial Trade Union maintain offices in most nucleations. The whites are isolated among the sugar proletariat. Despite the revitalizing influence of newcomers from Britain, social relationships within the white group soon become jaded.

Among the peasantry in rural Jamaica, villages are composed of clusters of houses and shops, and contain the local primary school, post office and other official agencies. Villages are usually strung out along the road or roads which promoted their growth; some successful villages have become towns, like Christiana. In most rural communities, however, the settlement pattern is dispersed and linked by circuitous footpaths. This pattern reflects the spontaneous, haphazard process by which the emancipated slaves burrowed into the interior, as well as local conditions of relief and land holding. Where there are motor-roads, a discontinuous ribbon of development is characteristic, household clusters forming foci for the more dispersed dwellings.

Topography is critical for community formation, ridges attenuating the frequency and intensity of interpersonal contact. Rural folk tend to mate within their local group, and communities possess their own mores. Community and kinship structures are mutually reinforcing: co-operative farm work is based upon the community, so too are cricket teams. Individuals know their own community well and possess numerous details about their neighbours; but they are vague about adjacent communities.

Each community has its own stratification, but race is of less importance than in the sugar areas. Shopkeepers, produce-dealers, teachers, civil servants, politicians and priests are important. However, informal leadership, as distinct from economic power, usually resides with men of middling age whose economic status rouses little envy. Their position in informal associations such as cricket clubs, unregistered thrift or co-operative groups is strong by popular support. Likewise, community solidarity in rural Jamaica depends upon the network of social relationships: it cannot be gauged by material symbols such as the presence of a church. The real community rituals take place at the wake or nine-night, when death leads to a demonstration of solidarity with the bereaved. Formal associations imposed by the government frequently discount these factors, neglect community boundaries, and remain essentially artificial groupings. Agricultural and welfare associations fail to involve the small farmers; their leadership is in the hands of strangers to the community – teachers, welfare workers, and other newcomers.

The dichotomy between sugar settlements and small farming communities is not rigid. In Christiana polyculture is the norm, but many rural settlements are much more deeply involved in commercial agriculture and their settlement pattern is more ordered. Nevertheless, an interesting paradox emerges. The spatial regularities of the sugar estate are expressions of a rigid hierarchy; they do not connote a high degree of social coherence. In contrast the haphazard distribution of settlement among the peasantry belies a strong sense of community feeling.

RURAL SETTLEMENT

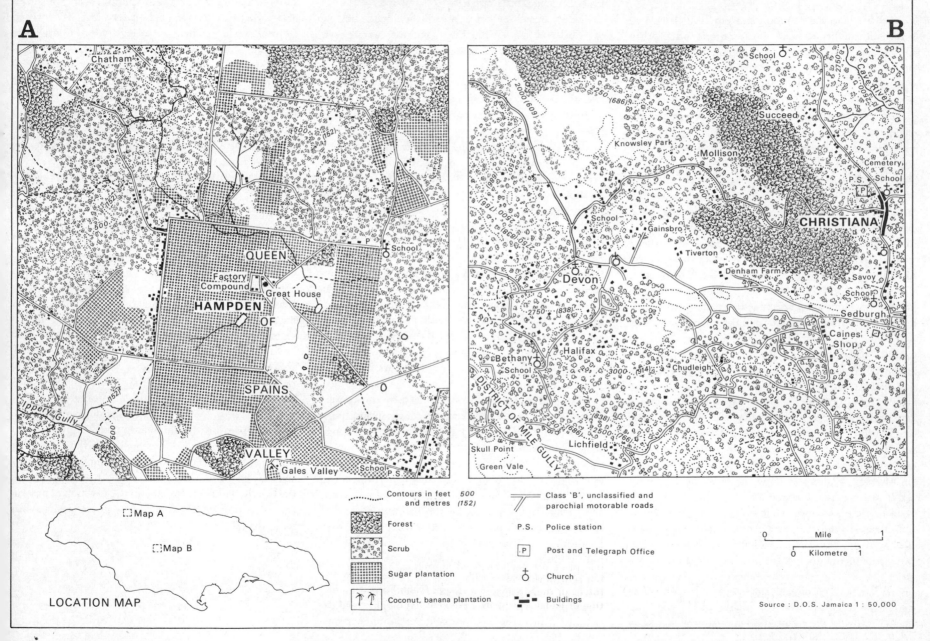

A

Chatham
500 (152)
500
QUEEN
Factory Compound
Great House
HAMPDEN
OF
SPAINS
VALLEY
School
Gales Valley
School
P.S.
Ippery Gully

B

School
2750 2600
Cave River
2000 (609)
2250 (686)
2500 (766)
Succeed
Knowsley Park
Mollison
Cemetery
P.S. School
CHRISTIANA
School
Gainsbro
Tiverton
Denham Farm
Savoy
School
Sedburgh
Devon
2750 (838)
Caines Shop
Bethany
School
Halifax
Chudleigh
3000 (914)
DISTRICT OF MILE GULLY
Skull Point
Lichfield
Green Vale

LOCATION MAP

☐ Map A

☐ Map B

····	Contours in feet *500* and metres *(152)*
(Forest)	Forest
(Scrub)	Scrub
(Sugar)	Sugar plantation
↑↑↑	Coconut, banana plantation

Class 'B', unclassified and parochial motorable roads

P.S.   Police station

P   Post and Telegraph Office

☥   Church

▪▪▪   Buildings

0   Mile   1

0   Kilometre   1

Source : D.O.S. Jamaica 1 : 50,000

20 SETTLEMENT HIERARCHY

Cities articulate the economic system, and changes in economic conditions result in alterations to the urban hierarchy. The historical development of Jamaica's dual economy is reflected in the pattern of urbanization. The earliest towns were ports which handled the export of sugar, rum and molasses, and the import of slaves and manufactured goods. Inland centres remained of minimal importance and depended upon the exchange of slave-produced commodities which were sold or bartered in the Negro or Sunday Markets. After emancipation the sugar ports declined, internal marketing expanded, and an additional set of central places emerged to serve the peasant-farming communities which were established in the interior.

The generic distinction between ports and market centres lacks functional validity. Produce markets are, and always have been, located in all the urban nodes, and in many smaller nuclei which lack the status of towns. Markets are consumer-orientated, and their distribution closely follows population patterns. The Blue Mountains and Cockpit Country are devoid of central places, but Kingston has eight markets, the majority located close to the city centre. In rural Jamaica the populated districts are served by a regularly-spaced network of markets, situated between five and eight miles apart. But Jamaican roads and tracks are notoriously winding, and country traders, who transport produce to the towns, often cover considerable distances. Many take a truck into Kingston on Thursday nights to supply the city's hucksters for the Friday and Saturday markets.

Fruit and vegetables are low-order goods. They are comparatively inexpensive and are bought on a regular, if not a daily, basis. The smaller rural nucleations can be expected to support the retailing of these necessities. But as a commodity becomes more expensive and less frequently purchased, its range or market area increases. It is essential for higher order goods to locate in towns where the market is largest. Kingston contains one-quarter of the island's entire population, and provides the complete range of goods for its own citizens as well as high order goods for the other towns and rural districts.

The urban system is largely explained by the nesting of retail and service functions. But the hierarchy is most clearly expressed in demographic terms. In Jamaica towns are defined as settlements having more than 1,000 inhabitants, and comparative data are available for 1943, 1960 and 1970. Census material for 1970 is incomplete: the tabulations published so far refer only to the ten largest towns plus four ports of smaller size. Although shifts in urban boundaries between 1960 and 1970 are explicitly indicated in the census report, there is no means of knowing what alterations were effected between 1943 and 1960. The urban hierarchy is dominated by Kingston, which had 506,000 inhabitants in 1970. The capital was more than twelve times the size of its closest rivals, Montego Bay (42,800) and Spanish Town (41,600). Some systems of cities are regularly graded, the second settlement recording half the population of the largest, the third one-third the population of the largest, and so on. In Jamaica this rank-size rule breaks down, especially at the top of the hierarchy, and the urban network is characterized instead by primacy. Kingston's historical role as colonial capital and principal port is a causal factor in this situation.

In 1943 19 towns were recognized by the census, rising to 35 in 1960. The majority of these additional settlements had less than 2,500 inhabitants. Although there were some important changes in rank between 1943 and 1960 – Montego Bay replacing Spanish Town as the second city, Mandeville rising from fifteenth to sixth, Port Maria dropping from eighth to fourteenth, and Ocho Rios appearing in the listing for the first time to take tenth place – subsequent alterations have been minor. In the period 1960 to 1970 Mandeville moved up to fifth and Morant Bay to eighth. But only one place has been changed in each case, and the top ten remain the same. All except Ocho Rios are chief towns of their respective parishes. While the population of Jamaica grew by 2 per cent per annum between 1960 and 1970, Spanish Town recorded increases of 11 per cent, and May Pen (6·4 per cent), Montego Bay (6·1 per cent), Mandeville (4·6 per cent) and Morant Bay (4·4 per cent) expanded at rates well above the national average. Furthermore, all benefited from boundary changes. Kingston's growth was relatively slow (3·0 per cent per annum), but even if the underenumeration is disregarded its absolute increase (130,000) was greater than the total population of the next four largest settlements put together. Although the second- and third-largest towns are beginning to whittle down Kingston's lead, most settlements remain small. Ocho Rios, the tenth town in 1970, had less than 7,000 inhabitants.

Two patterns of urbanization emerge. In 1960 16 out of the 35 towns were coastal, as were 7 of the top 10. According to the limited data for 1970 the same situation exists, but the third, fourth and fifth towns (Spanish Town, May Pen and Mandeville) are located inland, and are among the most rapidly growing centres. These three towns form the core of a second zone of urbanization extending westwards from Kingston via Spanish Town, Old Harbour, May Pen, Porus, Mandeville, and Santa Cruz to Black River, with a secondary network running inland from May Pen linking Chapelton, Frankfield, Spaldings and Christiana. Heavy in-migration must be occurring in the most rapidly expanding towns; some of this is undoubtedly step-wise, and directed up the urban hierarchy. The five largest settlements are all economic growth points. Kingston provides capital functions and engrosses most of the new industry; Montego Bay is the centre for tourism; Spanish Town has new housing and industry; and May Pen and Mandeville are both associated with the bauxite industry. But not all the towns have grown. Falmouth and Black River have been stagnant for more than three decades.

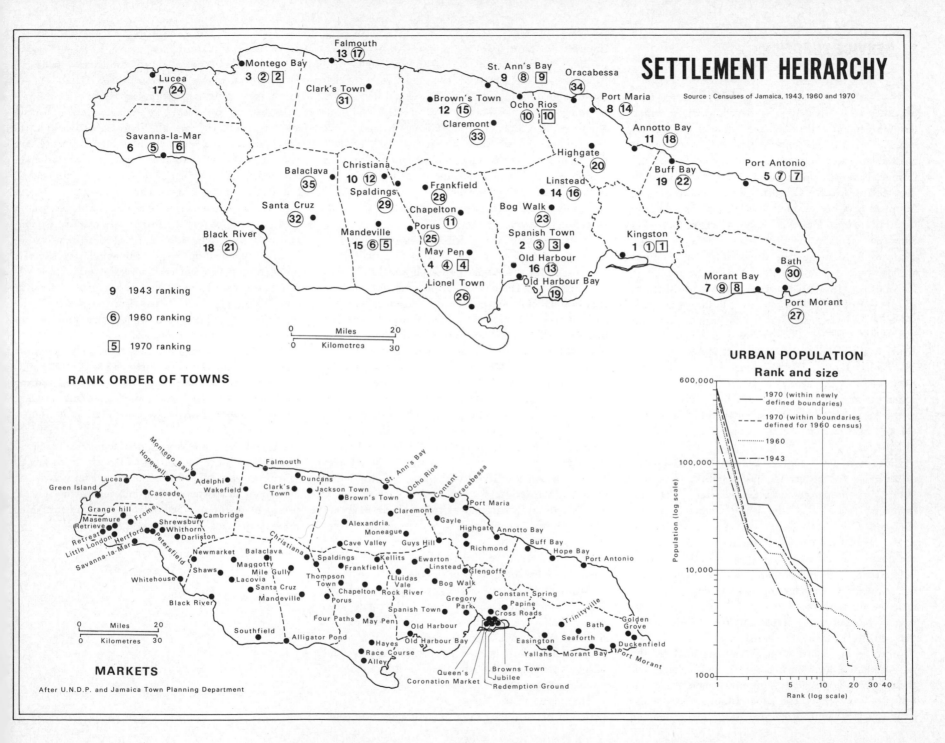

SETTLEMENT HEIRARCHY

Source : Censuses of Jamaica, 1943, 1960 and 1970

9 1943 ranking

⑥ 1960 ranking

⑤ 1970 ranking

Falmouth 13 ⑰

Montego Bay 3 ② ②

Lucea 17 ㉔

Clark's Town ㉛

St. Ann's Bay 9 ⑧ ⑨

Oracabessa ㉞

Port Maria 8 ⑭

Brown's Town 12 ⑮

Ocho Rios 10 ⑩

Claremont ㉝

Annotto Bay 11 ⑱

Savanna-la-Mar 6 ⑤ ⑥

Highgate ⑳

Buff Bay 19 ㉒

Port Antonio 5 ⑦ ⑦

Balaclava ㉟

Christiana 10 ⑫

Spaldings ㉙

Santa Cruz ㉜

Frankfield ㉘

Linstead 14 ⑯

Chapelton ⑪

Porus ㉕

Bog Walk ㉓

Spanish Town 2 ③ ③

Kingston 1 ① ①

Mandeville 15 ⑥ ⑤

May Pen 4 ④ ④

Old Harbour 16 ⑬

Old Harbour Bay ⑲

Bath ㉚

Morant Bay 7 ⑨ ⑧

Port Morant ㉗

Black River 18 ㉑

Lionel Town ㉖

Miles 0 — 20
Kilometres 0 — 30

RANK ORDER OF TOWNS

MARKETS

After U.N.D.P. and Jamaica Town Planning Department

Montego Bay
Hopewell
Lucea
Green Island
Grange hill
Masemure
Retrieve
Little London
Frome
Shrewsbury
Whithorn
Darliston
Hertford
Petersfield
Savanna-la-Mar
Adelphi
Wakefield
Cascade
Cambridge
Newmarket
Shaws
Whitehouse
Balaclava
Maggotty
Mile Gully
Lacovia
Santa Cruz
Mandeville
Black River
Southfield
Alligator Pond
Falmouth
Duncans
Jackson Town
Clark's Town
Brown's Town
Christiana
Spaldings
Frankfield
Thompson Town
Chapelton
Porus
Four Paths
Hayes
Race Course
Alley
St. Ann's Bay
Ocho Rios
Content
Oracabessa
Port Maria
Claremont
Gayle
Alexandria
Moneague
Cave Valley
Guys Hill
Kellits
Ewarton
Lluidas Vale
Rock River
Linstead
Bog Walk
Spanish Town
May Pen
Old Harbour
Old Harbour Bay
Gregory Park
Highgate
Richmond
Glengoffe
Constant Spring
Papine
Cross Roads
Queen's
Coronation Market
Browns Town
Jubilee
Redemption Ground
Annotto Bay
Buff Bay
Hope Bay
Port Antonio
Trinityville
Bath
Golden Grove
Easington
Seaforth
Duckenfield
Yallahs
Morant Bay
Port Morant

Miles 0 — 20
Kilometres 0 — 30

URBAN POPULATION
Rank and size

— 1970 (within newly defined boundaries)

--- 1970 (within boundaries defined for 1960 census)

···· 1960

-·-· 1943

Population (log scale)

600,000
100,000
10,000
1000

Rank (log scale)

1   5   10   20 30 40

49

21 SERVICE FUNCTIONS

Services may be divided into two groups: those which have an economic base and are essentially geared to financial transactions, and those that are socially orientated and cater to people's well-being. Among the former, banks are an outstanding example. Banks in Jamaica are British-, Canadian-, or American-owned, but plans have been made to place a majority share in the hands of local investors. About a half are located in Kingston, which contains seven times as many branches as Montego Bay. Important concentrations are also recorded in May Pen, Mandeville and Ocho Rios. Banks are often situated in centres which are too small to be classified as towns. Instances are provided by the branches at Grange Hill, Frome, Hampden and Monymusk, all of which are foci for the sugar areas. Conversely, many recognized towns are without banks, though all these cases ranked beneath twenty-first in the urban hierarchy and had less than 3,000 inhabitants in 1960. Kingston clearly emerges as the financial hub of the island. In addition to the cluster of commercial banks, it also possesses the Bank of Jamaica.

Cinemas are much more heavily concentrated in the urban areas. The pattern is adjusted both to the distribution of potential clients and the residence of local investors. Almost half the island's cinemas are in Kingston. Other settlements with cinemas are located to the west of the capital, in the ports and resorts of the north coast, and in three sugar 'towns', Duckenfield, Grange Hill and Frome. Kingston's cinemas fall into three classes: older, open-air buildings situated near the city centre or in the slum area; air-conditioned theatres concentrated at Cross Roads; and a drive-in cinema on the St Thomas road.

Most of the social services are provided by the government. Education is considered elsewhere, but the supply of books gives some impression of the diffusion of knowledge. The Jamaica Library Service has established a hierarchy of provision. Major lending libraries are located in the principal town of each parish, with branches in the larger settlements. The rural districts are served by 150 book centres which usually open for a few hours each week and are manned by volunteer staff. A bookmobile service is run from Kingston, St Elizabeth, and St Ann. A free postal service links branch libraries, and a stock of over half-a-million books is available throughout the island. Registered readers number more than a quarter of a million. Some of the libraries have special collections, and individual libraries arrange educational and cultural programmes.

Public hospitals are distributed according to administrative convenience as well as to social need. Each parish has at least one general hospital located in the chief town. The coastal periphery is better served than the interior, since ten of the fourteen parishes have their main centre on the coast. Specialized medical facilities are confined to Kingston, where there is a children's hospital, a sanitorium, and a maternity hospital (Jubilee). Moreover, Kingston possesses the island's only mental institution; in the late 1960s it had 2,500 inmates. The teaching hospital of the University of the West Indies is also located in Kingston, and supplies Jamaicans with a wide range of medical services. The only specialist facility located outside Kingston is the leprosarium (the Hansen Home), which is situated near Spanish Town and is staffed by Marist Sisters.

Hospitals rarely have more than 150 beds. Many are old, overcrowded and gravely under-staffed. To reduce the pressure on these institutions and to supply medical services more directly to the rural areas, the government has set up a lower tier of about 150 health centres and dispensaries. They treat lesser ailments, and refer the complicated cases to the hospitals. Free medical services are available to the poor, and the remainder of the population pay for treatment at a rate proportional to their income. Private facilities and hospitals are also available for those wealthy enough to be able to afford them.

The impact of these medical services is clearly revealed in the declining rates of adult and infant mortality, and this is a major tribute to the island's 1,000 doctors and 3,000 qualified midwives. Jamaica's health problem has been transformed into one of morbidity rather than mortality. Heart diseases, vascular lesions, neoplasms, pneumonia, infant diseases and gastro-enteritis are all common, and to control these complaints considerable improvements are needed both in curative and preventive medicine. There are still only about 3,000 beds in the public hospitals, one to 600 persons. The doctor–patient ratio has been halved since 1943 but even so stands at 1:2,000. Moreover, the majority of medical personnel practise in Kingston, and the rural districts are heavily dependent on the government clinics. Dentists number only 150 and each serves about 10,000 patients; the majority of the population, of course, never enter a surgery. There are less than 40 opticians in the entire island, and it is little wonder that Woolworths is a major supplier of spectacles.

In general, there is a close relationship between the size of a settlement and the range and importance of its functions. But at the bottom of the hierarchy many small settlements lack the more important services, while a number of tiny sugar 'towns' are quite significant. Montego Bay is clearly the 'capital' of the north coast, and the Prime Minister has announced plans to establish an office in the town. But by no means all Jamaicans use official institutions. Banks have an equivalent in 'partners' – an informal saving scheme prevalent among the lower classes – and the untrained midwife or 'nana' is important in rural areas.

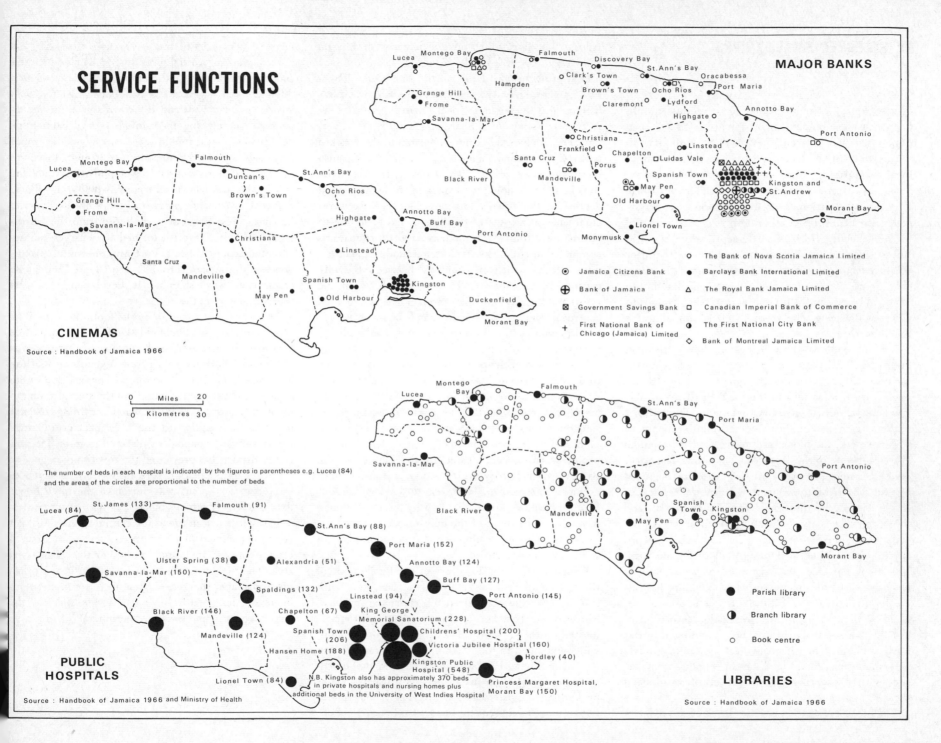

SERVICE FUNCTIONS

MAJOR BANKS

CINEMAS

Source : Handbook of Jamaica 1966

○ The Bank of Nova Scotia Jamaica Limited

⊙ Jamaica Citizens Bank
● Barclays Bank International Limited

⊕ Bank of Jamaica
△ The Royal Bank Jamaica Limited

⊠ Government Savings Bank
□ Canadian Imperial Bank of Commerce

＋ First National Bank of Chicago (Jamaica) Limited
◐ The First National City Bank

◇ Bank of Montreal Jamaica Limited

Scale:
0 — Miles — 20
0 — Kilometres — 30

The number of beds in each hospital is indicated by the figures in parentheses e.g. Lucea (84) and the areas of the circles are proportional to the number of beds

PUBLIC HOSPITALS

Lucea (84)
St. James (133)
Falmouth (91)
St. Ann's Bay (88)
Port Maria (152)
Ulster Spring (38)
Alexandria (51)
Savanna-la-Mar (150)
Annotto Bay (124)
Spaldings (132)
Buff Bay (127)
Black River (146)
Linstead (94)
Port Antonio (145)
Chapelton (67)
King George V Memorial Sanatorium (228)
Mandeville (124)
Childrens' Hospital (200)
Spanish Town (206)
Victoria Jubilee Hospital (160)
Hansen Home (188)
Hordley (40)
Kingston Public Hospital (548)
Lionel Town (84)
N.B. Kingston also has approximately 370 beds in private hospitals and nursing homes plus additional beds in the University of West Indies Hospital
Princess Margaret Hospital, Morant Bay (150)

Source : Handbook of Jamaica 1966 and Ministry of Health

LIBRARIES

● Parish library
◐ Branch library
○ Book centre

Source : Handbook of Jamaica 1966

51

22 SELECTED SMALL TOWNS

Spanish Town was founded in 1534 to rehouse the inhabitants of the colony's first capital, which had been established at Sevilla La Nueva near St Ann's Bay on the north coast. Its location fitted exactly the Spanish ideal formulated in the Law of the Indies. Spanish Town was situated about six miles inland from Passage Fort, and its position ensured protection from privateers. The Plain of St Catherine provided a level site for a planned, grid-iron settlement, while the Rio Cobre supplied drinking water and transport. After the British conquest Spanish Town became the planters' centre. Reduced to penury by the decline in the sugar industry and the removal of the capital to Kingston in 1872, the town stagnated for almost a hundred years.

Most travellers from Kingston hurry through Spanish Town by car or train. Motorists making for the north coast must wind through the narrow streets; those with destinations in the western towns of May Pen and Mandeville have an easier route. The outlines of the Spanish plan can be detected from the alignment of the streets; the blocks are square, and quite unlike those laid out by the British in Kingston. The park, which occupies the site of the original plaza, is graced by the facade of the ruined Governor's residence, King's House, by the ornate Rodney Memorial, and the former legislative chamber which serves as the parish office for St Catherine. The town also contains the Anglican cathedral. During the past decade Spanish Town has been reinvigorated as a satellite of Kingston, and the enumerated population has increased from 14,700 in 1960 to 41,600 in 1970. Much of the housing in the core of the town remains squalid, but new suburbs have been completed to the north and east. Twickenham Park has emerged as a major industrial estate, and vies in economic importance with the surrounding plantations of bananas and sugar.

The origins of *Montego Bay* may be traced to Mantica Bahia, a hog port which revictualled Spanish ships on the voyage to and from the mainland. Protected by a minor promontory to the north, and watered by a small stream, known as The Creek, the settlement was hampered at the beginning of the British period by the restrictive policy of the Board of Trade. By the 1770s, however, it emerged as the emporium of the western part of the island, and traded with the Spanish territories as a free port. The repeal of the Free Port Acts in 1822, coupled to emancipation, led to a rapid decline in the town's fortunes. Montego Bay's re-emergence as a town of significance has been due to international tourism. A modern airport terminal was completed in 1959. Hotels cluster around the Doctor's Cave beach, which lies midway between the city centre and the airport. The contrast between the resort and the city centre is extreme. The commercial centre is subject to flooding and physical decay: tourists who venture into the shopping area are liable to abuse.

The growth of the population from 23,600 in 1960 to 42,800 in 1970 has created socio-economic tensions. Suburbs have expanded to the north of the old town, but much of the periphery is occupied by squatter camps. Dwellings in the shanty towns have increased by 75 per cent in the last decade. Further problems have been created by the closure of the Barnett sugar factory which stood at the southern entrance to the town. However, these economic difficulties have been partially offset by the creation of a free port to the south of the built-up area. In the near future the Urban Development Corporation plans to redevelop the waterfront.

When sugar was planted across the fertile floor of the Queen of Spain's Valley in the late eighteenth century a port was required to export the produce. This was established at *Falmouth*, a planned settlement located on the seaward side of the mangrove swamps which extended to the north of Martha Brae. Within less than thirty years Falmouth became the fourth most important town in Jamaica. Its prosperity is expressed in Georgian facades and its superb courthouse. But Falmouth's subsequent history has been one of unrelieved decay. Until the early 1970s the wharf exported wet sugar, lightered to ocean-going vessels anchored in the bay, and it imported a few consumer durables. But sugar has been switched to the bulk loader at Ocho Rios and the town's economy is dependent on retailing and administration. Falmouth's population was 3,700 in 1960 and 3,900 in 1970. Although the older houses are maintained, there are no residential or tourist developments within the town. The majority inhabit poor, wooden dwellings.

Port Antonio stands on two of the finest harbours in Jamaica. West Harbour is sheltered from the North-East Trades by Navy Island, and its wharves can accommodate large vessels. Port Antonio rose to prominence with the banana trade in the 1870s. Through its connection with shipping it developed a modest tourist industry in the 1920s.

The town is hemmed in by the foothills of the Blue Mountains. Upper Titchfield stands on the peninsula between the harbours and contains the prosperous old houses. Port Antonio proper extends around the head of East Harbour. Dwellings of poorer quality lie adjacent to the court house and the stores. Employment depends on administration, retailing, banana handling, and selling to the occasional cruise ship. Heavy rainfall, coupled to distance from an international airport, has prevented the town's emergence as a resort. Its population rose from 7,800 in 1960 to 10,400 in 1970, but redefinition of the town boundary was largely responsible.

In small Jamaican towns the central business district (CBD) is confined to a few streets, and social status is often expressed by house-type rather than residential area. The higher a settlement's position in the urban hierarchy and the more open it is to modern influences, the greater the social differentiation, the larger the CBD, and the more peripheral the elite.

SELECTED SMALL TOWNS

Source : D.O.S. Jamaica 1 : 50,000

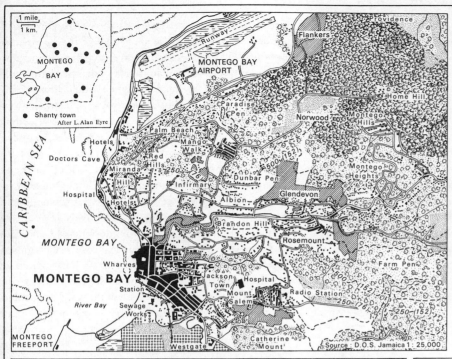

Montego Bay map:

1 mile / 1 km.

MONTEGO BAY

• Shanty town
After L. Alan Eyre

Runway
MONTEGO BAY AIRPORT
Flankers
Providence
Home Hill
Paradise Pen
Norwood
Montego Hills
Palm Beach
Mango Walk
Montego Heights
Hotels
Doctors Cave
Red Hills
Miranda Hill
Infirmary
Dunbar Pen
Hospital
Hotels
Albion
Glendevon
Brandon Hill
CARIBBEAN SEA
Rosemount
MONTEGO BAY
Farm Pen
Wharves
Jackson Town
Hospital
Station
Mount Salem
Radio Station
River Bay
Sewage Works
MONTEGO FREEPORT
Catherine Mount
Westgate

Source : D.O.S. Jamaica 1 : 25,000

Port Antonio map:

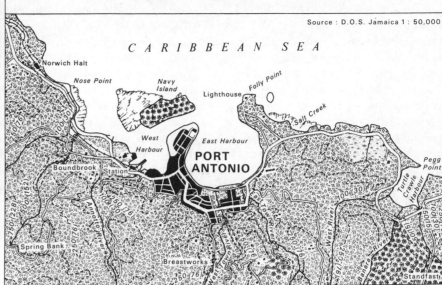

CARIBBEAN SEA

Norwich Halt
Nose Point
Navy Island
Lighthouse
Folly Point
Salt Creek
West Harbour
East Harbour
PORT ANTONIO
Boundbrook Station
Pegg Point
Turtle Crawle Harbour
Spring Bank
Breastworks
Standfast

Spanish Town map:

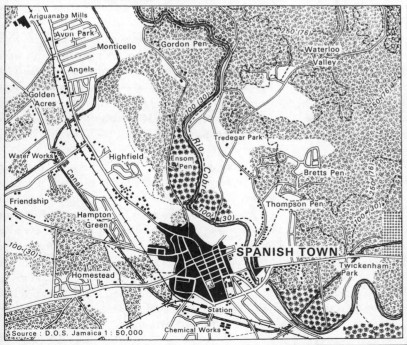

Ariguanaba Mills
Avon Park
Monticello
Gordon Pen
Waterloo Valley
Angels
Golden Acres
Water Works
Tredegar Park
Highfield
Ensom Pen
Rio Cobre
Bretts Pen
Friendship
Thompson Pen
Hampton Green
SPANISH TOWN
Homestead
Twickenham Park
Station
Chemical Works

Source : D.O.S. Jamaica 1 : 50,000

Falmouth map:

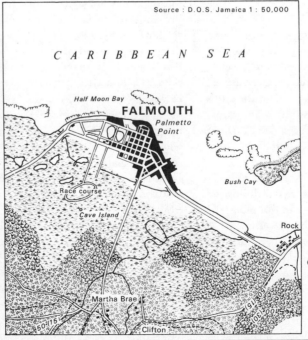

Source : D.O.S. Jamaica 1 : 50,000

CARIBBEAN SEA

Half Moon Bay
FALMOUTH
Palmetto Point
Race course
Bush Cay
Cave Island
Rock
Martha Brae
Clifton

Legend:

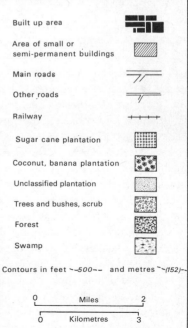

- Built up area
- Area of small or semi-permanent buildings
- Main roads
- Other roads
- Railway
- Sugar cane plantation
- Coconut, banana plantation
- Unclassified plantation
- Trees and bushes, scrub
- Forest
- Swamp

Contours in feet ~–500–~ and metres ~–(152)–~

0   Miles   2
0   Kilometres   3

Kingston is the capital, principal port, chief retailing centre and primate city of Jamaica. The settlement was founded to provide a refuge for victims of the earthquake which destroyed Port Royal in 1692. Incorporated in 1802, the city became the capital of Jamaica seventy years later. Kingston's growth has been especially rapid since 1920, and in 1970 its population exceeded half a million. The built-up area has spread across the Liguanea Plain, and the newest suburbs reach the foothills of the Blue Mountains. Through a process of sifting and sorting certain social groups and functions have been concentrated in different localities. The city's socio-economic patterns do not consist of randomly distributed elements, but reflect the orderly arrangement of land values. Land values in Kingston decline with distance from the city centre and market forces determine the location of land uses.

Land use in Kingston during the early 1960s may be examined under two major headings: concentrated zones and dispersed elements. Most of the grid which had been laid out during the seventeenth and eighteenth centuries was occupied by the central business district (CBD). It provided a central place for the city's transactions, and contained the most important shops, banks and private offices. On the edge of the CBD, and especially to the north-west, concentric zones of poor, medium and good quality housing succeeded one another in a northerly direction. In West Kingston, however, the slums were confined to a wedge following the alignment of the Spanish Town Road. An industrial estate had been established by the government at Three Miles in West Kingston, but some light industry was scattered throughout the commercial area. Warehousing and wholesaling lay between the business district and the port, and visiting ships moored against the finger piers.

Subsidiary commercial centres were located at Cross Roads and Half Way Tree, while smaller sub-centres composed of grocers, barbers' shops and pharmacies were situated at Matilda's Corner, Mary Brown's Corner, and Papine. Retail premises were also distributed along main lines of communication, while food shops and bars occupied street corner sites throughout the densely populated tenements. Food was sold on the pavements of the down-town area, though vending was legally restricted to a number of emporia, the largest being the Coronation Market on the Spanish Town Road.

The earliest public offices were built on King Street after the earthquake and fire of 1907. With the expansion of the functions of government after the Second World War, offices were established in the large Victorian houses which lay to the north-east of the commercial area. Government departments moved inland away from expensive and congested sites near the city centre. By 1960 East and South Race Course were lined with ministries – all within easy access of the House of Representatives.

Public utilities clustered like beads along the thoroughfares linking the city centre with the suburbs. Proximity to main lines of communication was also an important factor in the location of churches, theatres, cinemas, and sports and social clubs; Cross Roads and Half Way Tree were major centres for recreational activity. Parks were confined to the Parade (Victoria Park), Race Course (George VI Memorial Park) and Hope Botanical Gardens. West Kingston suffered from serious under-provision of public open space and sports grounds. In this respect it compared unfavourably with East Kingston, which eventually received the National Stadium. The penitentiary, mental hospital, Up Park Camp, King's House, and the campus of the University were all located in the eastern sector of the city.

Within the central business district land values declined from the centre towards the periphery. The peak land value intersection was situated at the junction of King Street and Barry Street, and was occupied by a bank and multiple store. High class comparison shopping was confined to King Street, and the western portion of the CBD was divided between Syrian dry goods shops and a China Town. Developed around the grocery trade at the end of the nineteenth century, the latter contained supermarkets, laundries, restaurants and bars. The eastern portion of the CBD included a professional quarter which housed insurance brokers, real estate agents, solicitors, doctors and dentists. It enjoyed proximity to the law courts and public transport facilities on King Street, yet bore lower property values than the retail area.

Land values also affected the distribution of social groups. The upper class could afford a long journey to work and a location at the edge of the town. In the outskirts land values were comparatively low, properties large, the houses well-constructed, and the population sparse. Conversely the poor were crammed into dilapidated tenements close to the city centre or confined to yards and government housing schemes in West Kingston. Housing of medium quality occupied an intermediate position – socially, economically and geographically between these extremes. There was a tendency for the quality of buildings to be related to their age, and for residential land use to reflect patterns of urban growth.

During the last decade significant changes have taken place in Kingston. An office complex has been created at New Kingston, to the north of the Half Way Tree Road, and a number of shopping plazas have been established to provide services for the rapidly expanding suburbs. These two processes have led to the relative decline of the CBD. Land speculation and property development have proved highly lucrative. The Foreshore Development Corporation has constructed Newport West in the marshes near the industrial estate. Another private company has built a causeway across Hunt's Bay to give direct access from the city to the new town which it has constructed at Portmore. Under the watchful eye of the government's Urban Development Corporation the finger piers in the old port have been dismantled, and the waterfront adjacent to the city centre is under-going re-development. However, the comprehensive renewal of West Kingston still awaits attention.

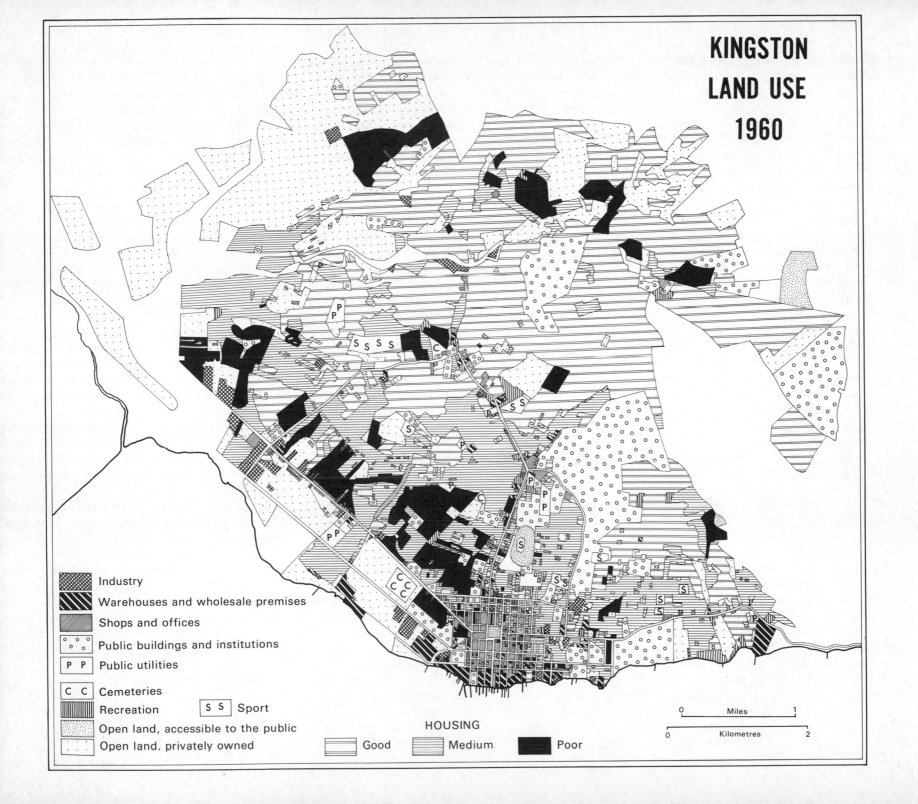

KINGSTON LAND USE 1960

Industry

Warehouses and wholesale premises

Shops and offices

Public buildings and institutions

P P Public utilities

C C Cemeteries

Recreation   **S S Sport**

Open land, accessible to the public

Open land, privately owned

HOUSING

Good   **Medium**   **Poor**

0   Miles   1

0   Kilometres   2

24 KINGSTON: POPULATION AND HOUSING

Kingston is the fourth-ranking city in the West Indies after Havana, Santo Domingo and San Juan. Between 1943 and 1960 the city's population increased by 86 per cent to 379,600. In 1960 alone, the annual increment approached 20,000 – a figure almost equivalent to the entire population of Montego Bay, the second largest town in Jamaica. Preliminary results from the 1970 census show that the city's rapid growth has been maintained during the last decade, though the rate of increase has dropped. However, substantial under-enumeration is suspected. Kingston parish together with St Andrew, which includes the mountains on the edge of the built-up area, recorded 550,000 inhabitants in 1970, and the increase during the preceding ten years was just over 3 per cent per annum.

The distribution of population in 1960 coincided closely with the pattern of land use: densities increased from north to south and from east to west. The central business district and port recorded less than 100 persons per hectare (40 per acre), but the ratio rose to between 250 and 1000 per hectare (100 and 400 per acre) on the periphery of these areas. The largest concentration and highest densities were associated with the tract running north-westwards from the city centre along the Spanish Town Road to Cockburn Gardens. Accommodation in this zone comprised wooden or concrete tenements, shack yards and various types of government housing. The buildings were predominantly single-storey; households rarely possessed more than one room; and, except for government housing, virtually all the accommodation was rented. In the tenements dwellings had been built one behind the other and entire plots were engulfed. A similar situation existed in the yards where ground lots were usually rented, and huts constructed on them by the tenants. Moderate densities were recorded to the north and east of the previous zone, and the property comprised better quality bungalows. A high proportion was rented,

and some had been sub-divided for use by several families. Although isolated concentrations of population occurred in shanties on the banks of the storm-water gullies, densities of less than 25 persons per hectare (10 per acre) prevailed throughout the northern suburbs. The majority of the housing was in good repair, ownership was common, and the accommodation comprised spacious modern dwellings set within large, carefully-tended gardens.

Overcrowding of dwellings was one of the clearest indices of population pressure. A density of more than two persons per habitable room and a ratio of more than eight persons to each hygienic water closet have been used as measures of overcrowding by the Jamaica Town Planning Department. The most severely overcrowded areas were the tenements and yards in the south of the city, and especially those in West Kingston. The northern suburbs enjoyed far better conditions. Overcrowding was associated with poor quality housing; but its incidence was more logically explained by the distribution and density of population. Some overcrowding occurred where densities exceeded 25 persons per hectare (10 per acre) and severe conditions where it surpassed 250 persons per hectare (100 per acre). In 1960 the Central Planning Unit estimated that 80,000, or one-fifth of the city's population, were living in overcrowded accommodation.

Population pressure cannot be measured solely in quantitative terms: many qualitative factors have to be taken into account. Migration is a major component of population growth in the capital. Over the years, newcomers from the rural areas and small towns have concentrated in West Kingston and some of the older tenements to the east of the central business district. These overcrowded sections of the city were inadequately provided with sewerage facilities. Cases of tuberculosis of the respiratory system and of typhoid were unique to them, and supplied additional evidence for overcrowding. Some townspeople adapted to conditions of enduring poverty by squatting. In 1961 the police estimated their number at 20,000. Located primarily on government-owned land, they were concentrated either on the fringe of the tene-

ments or in the outskirts of the city. Squatters' dwellings consisted of one-room huts constructed from packing cases and fish-barrels, cardboard and polythene. Few public amenities were available, and pit latrines, though illegal, had to be dug, and water collected from stand-pipes or stolen from fire-hydrants. By establishing these camps the squatters made two gains. They secured accommodation for which they paid no rent, and occupied areas with densities of population lower than those recorded in the tenements and yards. It is a grave error to associate population pressure solely with high densities.

Between 1960 and 1967 Kingston had to absorb about 130,000 additional inhabitants, and this greatly intensified the housing problem. In most years the output of all types of government-supported accommodation has barely exceeded 1,000 units, and the greater proportion has been provided by mortgage-insurance schemes, which have drawn their residents from the more densely populated, middle status areas. The Sanitary Survey of Kingston and St Andrew shows that the concentration of population in the slum areas has substantially increased. Between 1960 and 1967 almost 50 per cent of the city's total population growth was absorbed by the overcrowded areas which lie adjacent to the Spanish Town Road. The situation was aggravated by the obliteration of squatter camps at Boy's Town, Back o' Wall and Moonlight City. Many of the occupants of these camps settled in the tenements and yards or established new shanties in West Kingston. Government housing for the poor has been negligible, and accommodation in the schemes for urban renewal in West Kingston has been distributed in a partisan fashion. Paradoxically, the struggle in West Kingston has not been for structural change, but to secure power for one's political party, and access via the party to resources, such as housing, which are in chronically short supply.

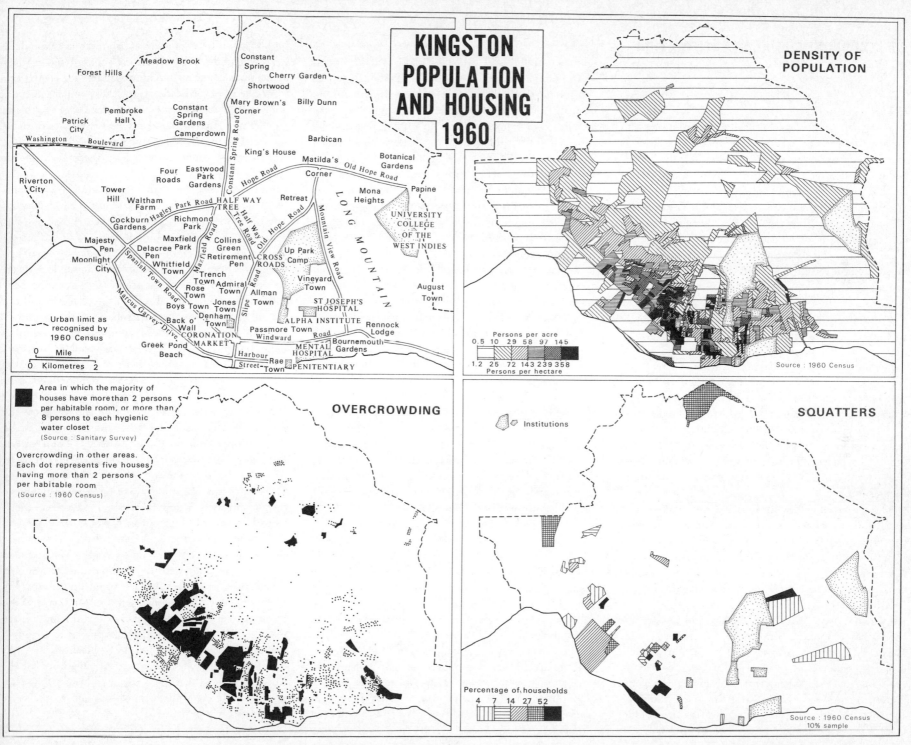

KINGSTON POPULATION AND HOUSING 1960

Forest Hills
Meadow Brook
Constant Spring
Cherry Garden
Shortwood
Pembroke Hall
Constant Spring Gardens
Mary Brown's Corner
Billy Dunn
Patrick City
Camperdown
Washington
Boulevard
Barbican
King's House
Riverton City
Four Roads
Eastwood Park Gardens
Hope Road
Matilda's Corner
Old Hope Road
Botanical Gardens
Papine
Tower Hill
Waltham Farm
Hagley Park Road
HALF WAY TREE
Retreat
Mona Heights
Cockburn Gardens
Richmond Park
Half Way Tree Road
Old Hope Road
Mountain View Road
LONG MOUNTAIN
UNIVERSITY COLLEGE OF THE WEST INDIES
Majesty Pen
Maxfield Park
Collins Green
Retirement Pen
CROSS ROADS
Up Park Camp
Moonlight City
Delacree Pen
Whitfield Town
Maxfield Road
Trench Town
Admiral Town
Slipe Road
Vineyard Town
August Town
Rose Town
Allman Town
Spanish Town Road
Boys Town
Jones Town
Denham Town
St JOSEPH'S HOSPITAL
Marcus Garvey Drive
Back o' Wall
CORONATION MARKET
Passmore Town
Windward Road
ALPHA INSTITUTE
Rennock Lodge
Greek Pond Beach
Harbour Street
Rae Town
MENTAL HOSPITAL
Bournemouth Gardens
PENITENTIARY

Urban limit as recognised by 1960 Census

0 Mile
0 Kilometres 2

DENSITY OF POPULATION

Persons per acre
0.5 10 29 58 97 145
1.2 25 72 143 239 358
Persons per hectare

Source : 1960 Census

OVERCROWDING

Area in which the majority of houses have more than 2 persons per habitable room, or more than 8 persons to each hygienic water closet
(Source : Sanitary Survey)

Overcrowding in other areas. Each dot represents five houses having more than 2 persons per habitable room
(Source : 1960 Census)

SQUATTERS

Institutions

Percentage of households
4 7 14 27 52

Source : 1960 Census
10% sample

57

25 KINGSTON: SOCIAL STRATIFICATION

Kingston is composed of three hierarchically arranged strata which have been culturally, economically and racially determined. The city's social structure is clearly expressed in its spatial organization; the 'haves' occupy the expansive suburbs in the north and east of the city, while the 'have nots' concentrate in central Kingston and the slums of the Spanish Town Road. The gulf between these groups was created by historical factors and is perpetuated by contemporary problems. Almost 20 per cent of the city's work force were unemployed in 1960, and labour surplus is most problematic in the overcrowded districts of West Kingston.

Cultural distinctions reinforce the socio-economic patterns. Each stratum practises different institutions. Male household headship, marriage, denominational Christianity and secondary education characterize the upper echelon: consensual cohabitation, extra-residential mating, female household headship, Afro-Christian cults, sects, and low levels of education typify the lower stratum. The middle stratum maintains a syncretic culture derived from the other elements. The closer the pattern conforms to the West European norm, the higher the status of the group in question.

The polarization of whites and blacks is expressed in social and spatial dimensions. Whites are confined to the elite suburbs, blacks are concentrated in West Kingston. But segregation is by no means extreme. Some blacks enter the suburbs as householders, others as servants. People of mixed descent are located socially and geographically between the blacks and whites, and merge with each. Syrians and Jews repeat the distribution of the whites. The Chinese are closely associated with the brown group but also maintain a separate commercial enclave in the city centre. In contrast, the East Indians share the low status of the blacks; they, too, reside in West Kingston. The city's social stratification has often been ascribed to colour.

But the presence of the Oriental immigrants and the upward mobility of blacks have complicated the model.

The upper stratum is composed of whites, Syrians and Jews with small accretions of browns, Chinese and blacks. This group dominates the commercial, professional, and industrial life of the capital. Its members are isolated from the mass of the black population and insulated from the syndrome of poverty which typifies West Kingston. The upper stratum is internally stratified by colour and class. All members mix freely on public occasions and subscribe to multiracialism; but private functions are racially exclusive. Blacks are rarely invited to white homes, and whites, Syrians and Jews remain endogamous.

Median status is associated with the racially mixed groups, the Chinese, and a growing number of blacks. Shade snobbery is most important in this section of the population. Members of the stratum are firmly established in East Kingston and to the south of the Half Way Tree Road. They occupy a wide range of positions, but are commonly employed as teachers and civil servants or in white collar posts in industry and commerce. The civil service has provided a major avenue for the advancement of blacks; in 1960 they accounted for almost three-quarters of government employees in Kingston. Politicians and trade-unionists are also drawn from this segment of the population. The black-white mixtures are the core of the middle stratum and regard themselves as the heirs of the British governing class. They adopt a superior attitude to the blacks, and indulge in a love-hate relationship with the whites. The Chinese are the city's grocers, endogamy is the norm, and the group is only partially assimilated to the creole middle stratum. But the younger generation has rapidly secured higher education, adopted creole values, broken away from the paternalistic grocery system, and penetrated the white collar and professional enclaves.

The lower stratum is composed of blacks together with relatively small numbers of East Indians and persons of mixed descent. Lower class men work as labourers or artisans, and women are engaged as seamstresses and domestic servants. Three ranks can be distinguished: unionized labour, non-unionized workers and the unemployed. The more impoverished elements are concentrated in the slums and segregated from the superordinate strata. East Indians form a semi-endogamous minority disdained by the black population. Hinduism and the caste system are in an advanced state of decay, and only the Bombay merchants retain more than a few vestiges of Indian culture.

Mobility between strata depends upon acculturation, though money is also essential for advancement. The three social strata form relatively closed systems and only the status-gap minorities – the Chinese, Syrians and Jews – have achieved a high degree of upward mobility. Distinctions of status are underwritten by occupation: members of the trade unions constitute a working-class elite; white collar posts in the private sector depend on patronage. Cultural pluralism militates against social cohesion, and colour is important both psychologically and symbolically. But if the white bias has provided a social cement, black racism has emerged to challenge the myth of consensus.

More than a decade ago Kingston was the centre of activity for the Ras Tafari cult, which rejected white domination, deified Haile Selassie, Emperor of Ethiopia, and advocated migration or 'repatriation to Africa'. The Ras Tafari were concentrated in the squatter camps but rapidly extended their influence throughout West Kingston. Since 1968 a more intellectual version of black power has been developed by social scientists at the University of the West Indies, and is current among the city's youth. Their philosophy is anti-imperialistic and hostile to foreign capital; they assert that 'black is beautiful' and that the society needs to be reconstructed in the image of the black majority. Most political leaders in Kingston are negroid and contend that black power is already a reality. They accept the notion of black dignity, but dismiss black power leaders as 'misguided socialists'. The latter retort that the brown and black ruling class are culturally and politically 'white', and as oppressive as the British imperialists.

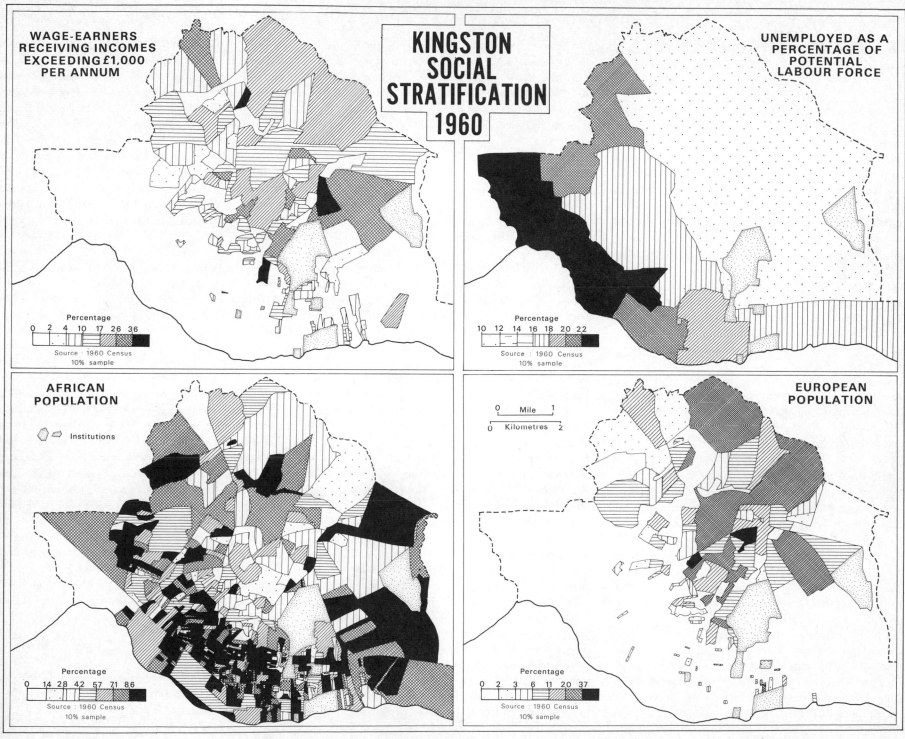

KINGSTON SOCIAL STRATIFICATION 1960

WAGE-EARNERS RECEIVING INCOMES EXCEEDING £1,000 PER ANNUM

Percentage

0 2 4 10 17 26 36

Source : 1960 Census
10% sample

UNEMPLOYED AS A PERCENTAGE OF POTENTIAL LABOUR FORCE

Percentage

10 12 14 16 18 20 22

Source : 1960 Census
10% sample

AFRICAN POPULATION

Institutions

Percentage

0 14 28 42 57 71 86

Source : 1960 Census
10% sample

EUROPEAN POPULATION

0 Mile 1
0 Kilometres 2

Percentage

0 2 3 6 11 20 37

Source : 1960 Census
10% sample

26 ELECTORAL PATTERNS, 1938-62

The post-emancipation period in Jamaica was brought to an end by the riots of 1938. Two national figures emerged: Alexander Bustamante, the founder of the Bustamante Industrial Trade Union (BITU), and his cousin, Norman Manley, a distinguished, Oxford-educated barrister, who in 1938 launched the People's National Party (PNP). The PNP's object was to create social justice in a colony steeped in inequality. It demanded independence in the firm belief that only local leaders would put Jamaican interests above those of the imperial power.

In 1944 Britain allowed the first general election to be held in Jamaica on the basis of universal adult suffrage, and it seemed likely that union and party would be linked. But on the eve of the election the Jamaica Labour Party (JLP) was created as the political wing of the BITU. Barely half the electorate voted, but the charismatic Bustamante swept to victory, taking 22 out of the 32 seats with 41 per cent of the votes. Independents won 5 constituencies, while the PNP obtained the same number of seats. Manley himself was defeated in St Andrew.

Adult suffrage destroyed the white ruling class as a political force, though they retained considerable influence as nominated members of the legislative council and as senior civil servants. Yet there was no mass support for the PNP. Social equality seemed a chimera, and nationalization of sugar and public utilities smacked of expropriation. The PNP compounded its problems by adopting a sophisticated political language unintelligible to the peasantry; and this further emphasized the gulf between Manley's middle class colleagues and the rural population. The JLP produced no policy, but relied upon Bustamante's captivating oratory and paternalistic touch. He skilfully manipulated the nationalization issue, warning small farmers that a PNP government would confiscate their land. A conservative at heart, he led a static revolution which simply perpetuated the colonial system.

Almost two-thirds of the electorate turned out at the 1949 election, and the PNP improved its performance. Party organization had been improved, and the Trades Union Congress (TUC) affiliated to the party. Moreover, Bustamante's charisma had been cramped by office. The JLP polled 42·7 per cent of the votes, the PNP 43·5 per cent; and Manley was returned for a constituency in St Andrew. The JLP secured 17 seats, the PNP 13 and independents 2. A two-party system was created, each backed by a trade union movement.

The long period of constitutional decolonization was punctuated by a number of electoral campaigns. In 1952 the PNP expelled its Marxist element, which took the TUC into the political wilderness, and created the National Workers Union (NWU), led by Manley's younger son, Michael. Previously the PNP had depended upon the urban middle class, though many were suspicious of the Marxist cell. After the 1952 purge, however, their wholehearted support was forthcoming. The basis of the party was gradually extended. Its espousal of West Indian Federation, retreat from socialism, and adoption of capitalistic development strategy, won substantial upper class backing. Furthermore, the party improved Manley's image with the lower stratum, casting him as 'the man of destiny'. These changes, coupled to proven charges of corruption against JLP politicians, ensured a PNP victory at the 1955 election. The party took 50 per cent of the vote and 18 seats.

By the mid 1950s two very similar parties dominated the political scene. Both were controlled by members of the middle stratum, but each possessed a different style of leadership, historical development, and trade-union base. All three social strata were divided in their political loyalties. Jamaica's membership of the West Indies Federation provided the major issue during the late 1950s. When federal elections were held in 1958 the JLP and PNP formed the cores of rival inter-territorial parties. The JLP mobilized the rural electorate to great effect, warning that Manley would sell them out to the small islands. Fifty-three per cent of the electorate voted – a smaller proportion than in national campaigns – the JLP securing 53 per cent of the poll. It came as something of a surprise to the JLP, therefore, when they were beaten in the snap election in 1959. The PNP were much more formidable when fighting on the record of their domestic achievements. The original 32 seats had been expanded to 45, the PNP obtaining 29, with 54 per cent of the poll. JLP bailiwicks were confined to the sugar-growing areas, and reflected the strength of the BITU. Safe PNP seats were located in an economically developing tract running north-eastwards across the island from Westmoreland to St Mary. In Kingston all but two seats – St Andrew West Rural and St Andrew South Western – returned PNP candidates.

The JLP, enlivened by the inclusion of young intellectuals among its leadership, vigorously pursued the federal issue. A referendum was held in September 1961, the PNP campaigning for continued membership, the JLP against. Just over 60 per cent voted, 54 per cent favouring withdrawal. The rural electorate was decisively against federation. In Kingston, the middle- and upper-class suburbs voted overwhelmingly for the security of federation, but the slums returned a resounding rejection. Interpreting the referendum as a vote of no confidence in the government, the JLP demanded an election before independence. In April 1962 they polled 50 per cent of the vote and secured 26 of the 45 seats. Safe PNP constituencies were situated in Westmoreland, St Elizabeth, St Ann, and the suburbs of the capital, and the party gained St Andrew West Rural. However, the marginal constituency of Kingston Western fell to the JLP, despite the intervention of the People's Political Party, a racist organization headed by Millard Johnson with some support from the Ras Tafari. The PNP regime had favoured the urban middle classes and lost the election. Jamaica was led into independence by Alexander Bustamante.

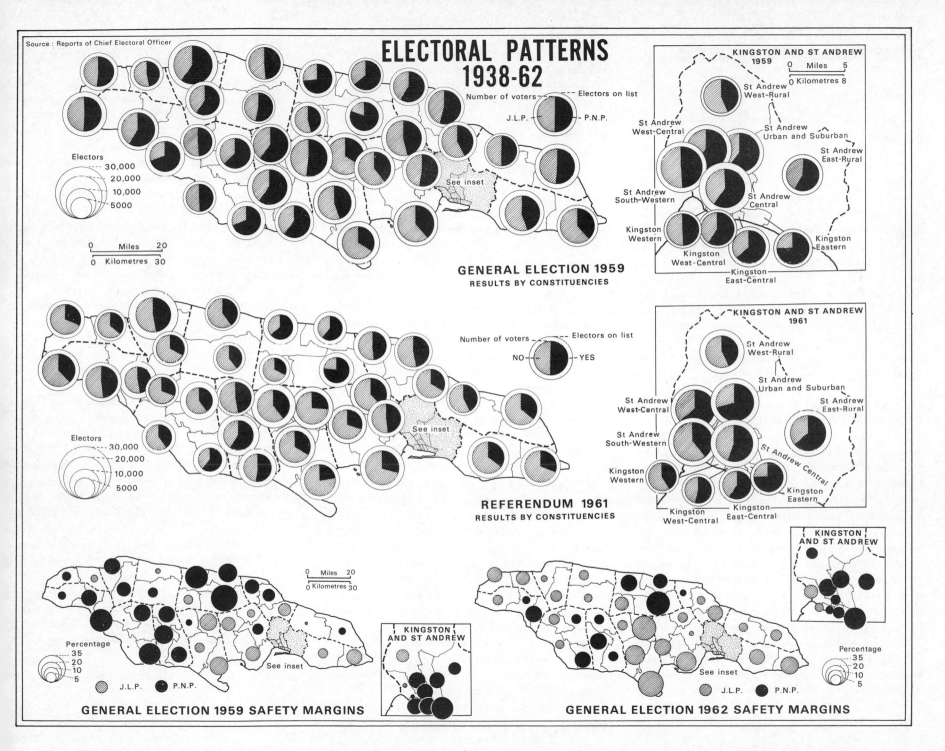

ELECTORAL PATTERNS 1938-62

Source : Reports of Chief Electoral Officer

KINGSTON AND ST ANDREW 1959

0   Miles   5
0   Kilometres   8

St Andrew West-Rural

St Andrew West-Central

St Andrew Urban and Suburban

St Andrew East-Rural

St Andrew South-Western

St Andrew Central

St Andrew East-Rural

Kingston Western

Kingston Eastern

Kingston West-Central

Kingston East-Central

Number of voters — — — Electors on list

J.L.P. ⬤ P.N.P.

Electors
30,000
20,000
10,000
5000

0   Miles   20
0   Kilometres   30

See inset

GENERAL ELECTION 1959
RESULTS BY CONSTITUENCIES

KINGSTON AND ST ANDREW 1961

St Andrew West-Rural

St Andrew West-Central

St Andrew Urban and Suburban

St Andrew East-Rural

St Andrew South-Western

St Andrew Central

Kingston Western

Kingston Eastern

Kingston West-Central

Kingston East-Central

Number of voters — — — Electors on list

NO ⬤ YES

Electors
30,000
20,000
10,000
5000

See inset

REFERENDUM 1961
RESULTS BY CONSTITUENCIES

Percentage
35
20
10
5

J.L.P.   P.N.P.

See inset

KINGSTON AND ST ANDREW

GENERAL ELECTION 1959 SAFETY MARGINS

KINGSTON AND ST ANDREW

Percentage
35
20
10
5

J.L.P.   P.N.P.

See inset

GENERAL ELECTION 1962 SAFETY MARGINS

61

27 ELECTORAL PATTERNS, 1963-72

An improvement in social relations took place in Jamaica after independence. The sense of 'being free', the election of a new government formed by the Jamaica Labour Party (JLP), the skilful use of political patronage, the initiation of schemes for urban renewal, and the promise of economic development, produced a relatively calm period which contrasted with the last years of the colonial period.

The first general election after independence was held in 1967. The Peoples' National Party (PNP) was led once more by Norman Manley, but the JLP was headed by Donald Sangster, who had acted as Prime Minister for the ailing Sir Alexander Bustamante during the last stages of the previous government. Both parties still drew their support from all levels of the society; and each favoured economic growth, foreign investment, and gradual social change.

Fifty-three seats were contested, 8 more than in 1962. The JLP polled 50·7 per cent of the vote, and the PNP just over 49 per cent. The PNP's share was 0·5 per cent higher than in 1962, and the party secured 20 seats, compared with 19 five years earlier. However, the JLP obtained 33 seats, 7 more than in 1962, though its share of the poll increased by only 0.7 per cent. Political strongholds remained basically similar to those at the 1962 election. The JLP dominated the parishes adjacent to the capital and the western constituencies within and bordering upon Hanover. PNP support remained strong in parts of Kingston, St Mary, St Ann, Manchester and St Elizabeth, and seats were captured in St James, Trelawny and Westmoreland. But while the PNP expanded its geographical base, the JLP coasted to easy victories in the new seats which had been created in the southern sugar belt. Moreover, the JLP reduced the PNP's stranglehold on Kingston, narrowly winning two more constituencies; in the capital the PNP led the JLP by 6 seats to 5.

In 1968 Walter Rodney, a Guyanese lecturer at the University of the West Indies at Mona was barred from re-entering Jamaica after attending a congress of black writers in Montreal. University students objected to his exclusion, rioting took place in Kingston, and a black power movement was born. Public opinion became increasingly sceptical of the benefits of foreign capital, alarmed at the rising tide of unemployment, and critical of the JLP government. When a general election was held in 1972 a large swing to the PNP was recorded.

The PNP was headed by Michael Manley, Norman Manley's younger son, and the JLP by Hugh Shearer, who had succeeded to the leadership on the death of Sir Donald Sangster. Manley promised 'better must come', and the electorate responded by giving him 56·1 per cent of the poll, the largest proportion of the national vote ever secured by either party in a Jamaican election. Thirty-seven of the 53 constituencies went to the PNP. JLP victories were confined to areas peripheral to the capital, and many of these seats became marginal. The island's largest settlements have all become PNP strongholds, and only one town of any note – Morant Bay – is in JLP territory. In Kingston the dominance of the PNP has been restored, and 9 of its 11 candidates were returned. Yet the two seats in the Kingston slums remained faithful to the JLP, and their safety margins were increased.

Although about 80 per cent of the electorate voted in 1967 and 1972, some political scientists have rejected the idea that the PNP and JLP are 'mass parties'. Indeed, one commentator has described the struggle at the hustings as 'cuckoo politics'; in his opinion the parties go into hiding during the period between elections but rush out noisily declaring their presence whenever it is necessary to secure a popular mandate. The lack of a clear ideological difference between the parties, the personal character of the Jamaican leadership, the absence of keen public debate, and the impotence of the parties in the face of Jamaica's agricultural and unemployment problems, have left the mass of voters politically apathetic.

One explanation of the high turn-out at the elections is the steady decline in voter registration since 1959. Despite the rapid growth of the population, the total number of voters in 1972 was less than in 1944. Barely one-third of the population was placed on the electoral roll, and low registration was strongly associated with the towns. But the larger settlements are known to attract adult migrants; from the demographic point of view urban voter registration should have been higher than in rural districts. It is likely that eligible persons in PNP-dominated constituencies encountered more difficulties in registering their names than persons in areas controlled by their rivals.

Additional reasons for the high electoral turn-out are attributable to the party system. Both the PNP and JLP are multiple-class coalitions and each has a strong trade union wing; shop-floor rivalry is carried over into the electoral process. Furthermore, the PNP and JLP operate extensive networks of patronage and these bind the non-unionized lower class into the political system. Political largesse runs to homes and jobs. If the spontaneous benefits of economic growth are minimal, the swing of the political pendulum rewards different segments of the lower class.

Regularities in Jamaican electoral behaviour can be detected. Successful parties have always taken two successive elections and no more; the JLP in 1944 and 1949, the PNP in 1955 and 1959, and the JLP in 1962 and 1967. The PNP victory in 1972 has perpetuated this sequential pattern and ensured the first change of government since independence. Each time a new party has come to power the island has experienced a wave of optimism which has carried it through the next election. Disillusion and outright discontent have welled up in its second term, and it has then been defeated by the opposition. Nevertheless, this electoral cycle has been contained within the two-party system: neither the white conservatives of the colonial period nor the black power advocates since independence have disrupted the electoral balance.

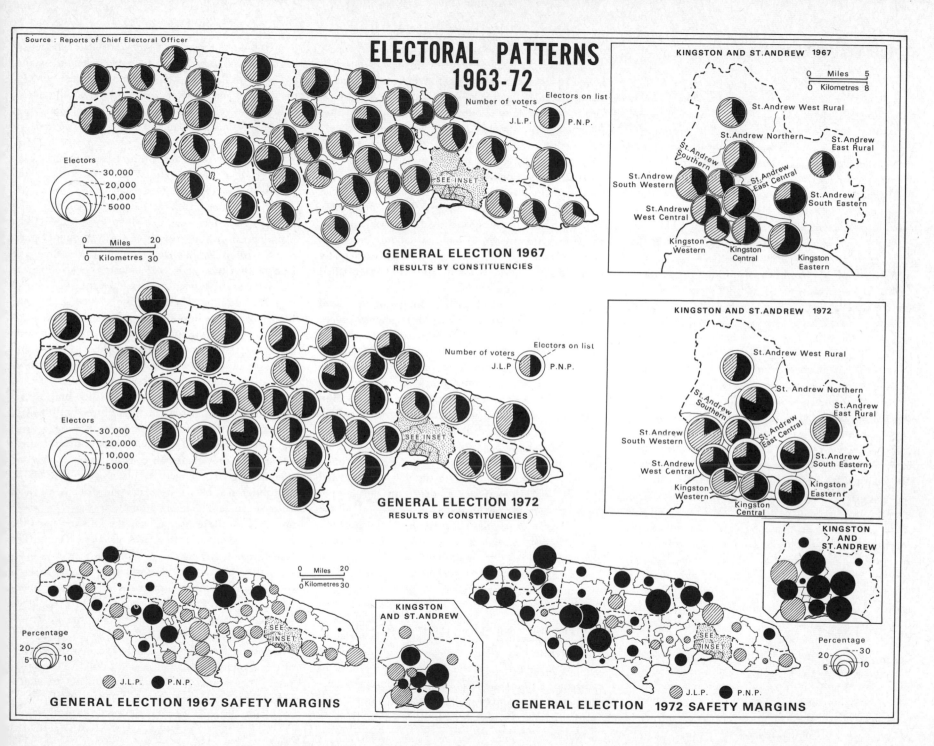

ECONOMIC DEVELOPMENT

Since the end of the Second World War successive Jamaican governments have attempted to develop and diversify the economy. Social change has been predicated on economic growth. While offering hope to the impoverished, this policy has guaranteed the upper and middle classes against expropriation of their possessions. The People's National Party once advocated state socialism but no government has been elected with a brief to redistribute resources in this manner. Government activity has been confined to infrastructural improvements, subsidies to farmers, incentives to manufacturers and hoteliers. Orthodox capitalistic lines of development have been followed, based on local savings, overseas loans and foreign investment. The economic returns have been excellent, the social benefits slight.

Jamaica has a dual economy. Almost half the population is dependent on agriculture, in which small farming is a major element. Production for subsistence lies at the heart of the small farming system, though most peasants market ground provisions, bananas and fruit. Sugar planting and manufacturing is the most export-orientated activity in this traditional sector. The contrast between peasant and planter remains an important facet of the plural framework of Jamaican society. Peasants cultivate their own land, subsist, make low capital investments, rely on hand labour, and have their own tenurial system; sugar plantations are highly capitalized, employ labour, are mechanized, and hold title to their land in an orthodox manner. Nevertheless, sugar also contrasts with the manufacturing, tourist and bauxite-alumina industries which have developed since the Second World War. This modern sector, like the sugar industry, is based on foreign as well as local capital, but its technology belongs to the twentieth century. The bauxite industry represents a multi-million dollar investment by North American companies.

Jamaica's gross domestic product at current prices more than doubled during the 1960s. The fastest growing sectors were mining and manufacturing, followed by construction. The latter industry expanded rapidly in 1967, and reflected a boom in tourist provision and a variety of infrastructural improvements. Manufacturing output, which includes sugar processing, improved steadily, but the contribution of mining surged upwards as new prices for bauxite were negotiated, and more and more ore was converted locally to alumina. The most depressing aspect of the 1960s was the levelling off of agricultural output after 1967. This was due to drought, labour problems, and the contraction of the agricultural labour force. Exports of staple crops such as sugar and bananas actually declined, and subsidies for peasant production failed to stimulate output.

These economic shifts have had important social and spatial implications. The growth industries are capital- rather than labour-intensive. Direct employment in the factories established under the tax incentive programme accounts for about 13,000 jobs. Bauxite mining and alumina processing requires only 6,000 workers, and direct employment in tourism barely exceeds another 6,000. Yet agriculture, which is the least capitalized and slowest growing sector employs about 35 per cent of the labour force. Furthermore, economic enclavism has been expressed spatially. Tourism and bauxite mining have created 'islands' of development on the coast and in the interior, engendered local inflation, and raised the reserve price of labour. Forward and backward linkages between sectors are often conspicuous by their absence, and the diffusion of innovations from growth points to the agricultural periphery has been a slow or non-existent process.

Most new manufacturing industry has been concentrated in Kingston, and the process of agglomeration has proceeded apace. Dispersal of factories to rural sites has been confined to parishes adjacent to the capital. In addition to the benefit of proximity to Kingston, both St Catherine and St Thomas returned politicians who were prominent in governments formed by the Jamaica Labour Party. Despite these improvements, a massive concentration of job seekers has developed in Kingston; unemployment and underemployment have become endemic. Kingston contains the richest and poorest Jamaicans; the oil refinery stands within a few hundred metres of squatter camps where shoe making and pot making are carried out by hand.

Three major national plans have been prepared for Jamaica since the Second World War, but spatial aspects of development have been ignored or played down. Even the Five Year Independence Plan, 1962 to 1967, failed to mention either regional or town planning. More recently, the Town Planning Department, United Nations Development Programme, the land authorities and the Industrial Development Corporation have been involved in various aspects of regional planning, including the choice of optimal locations for new developments. Yet no regional planning agency exists to integrate the social and economic aspects of development within a spatial context, and no single organization has been set up to administer the most complex settlement, Kingston.

The relationship between inequality and spatial factors is most apparent in agriculture. Only half of Jamaica is suitable for cropping or pasture, but one thousand owners control about half the cultivable area. Almost certainly their half contains the best soils and is concentrated on the coastal plains and inland valleys. The difference between upland and plain is pregnant with social and economic implications. The plains nurtured the slave plantations; the hills provided the emancipated slaves with a taste of independence. The plains are not only coastal, but their produce goes overseas; the uplands provide for subsistence and supply the network of internal markets. The uplands cannot sustain population increase, but the plains might do so if cultivation were intensified and the system of land holding were reformed.

Unplanned population growth has undermined many of the economic advances made during the last thirty years. Aspirations of the rural population to white-collar jobs and higher education compound Jamaica's problems. But lack of government or even local control affects many spheres. Jamaica's economy is mixed and open. It is dependent on foreign markets and requires preferential prices for its agricultural exports. An economic recession in the United States results in fewer tourists; strikes at British ports cause loss of banana shipments; United States' stockpiling policy limits or expands bauxite exports. Decision-making is often out of Jamaican hands. The head offices of the bauxite and sugar companies are in Canada, the United States and the United Kingdom. Jamaicans may have a majority share in most of the banks, but orders still come from London, New York, Chicago or Montreal.

Criticism of this pattern of dependence has been the keynote of the writings of the New World Group at the University of the West Indies in Kingston. Since the mid-1960s they have expressed and published opinions highly critical of Jamaica's 'neo-colonialist' government, of the organization of the bauxite, sugar and banana industries, and of the role played by foreign-owned banks and insurance companies. More specifically, they have argued for the nationalization and regional integration of the bauxite industry; the regional re-organization of banana production; the use of cane land to produce food, thus relieving population pressure and cutting imports; and the redeployment of bank investments away from the most lucrative sectors toward areas of national priority, especially agriculture. The cornerstone of this programme is the creation of a Caribbean economic community which will treat Jamaica as one element in a regional development programme. While some of these prescriptions are divorced from the realities of the situation, others suggest approaches to Jamaica's problems which are slowly winning favour in political circles.

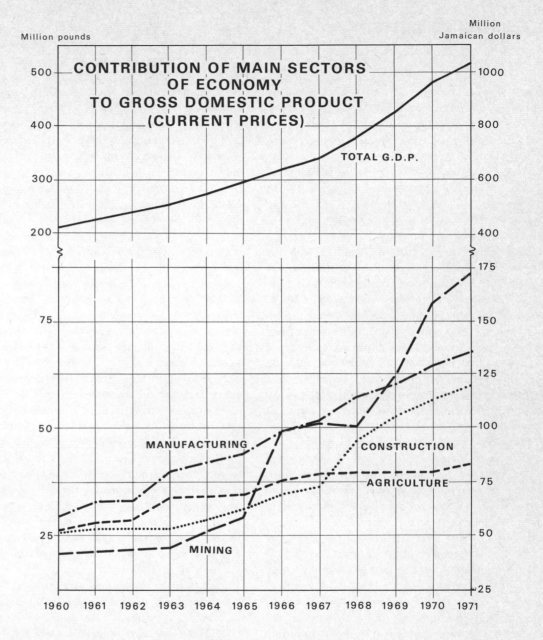

Million pounds

Million Jamaican dollars

CONTRIBUTION OF MAIN SECTORS
OF ECONOMY
TO GROSS DOMESTIC PRODUCT
(CURRENT PRICES)

TOTAL G.D.P.

MANUFACTURING

CONSTRUCTION

AGRICULTURE

MINING

1960 1961 1962 1963 1964 1965 1966 1967 1968 1969 1970 1971

28 AGRARIAN STRUCTURES

Despite the diversification of the Jamaican economy in the period since the Second World War, agriculture remains of vital importance. It employs about 35 per cent of the labour force and accounts for a similar proportion of visible exports. Nevertheless, the performance of this sector has given cause for concern. Exports of staple products declined in the late 1960s; food imports have rapidly increased; and the gap between average earnings in agriculture and the rest of the economy has tended to widen.

About 1,000 proprietors monopolize half the cultivated area. Yet three-quarters of the farmers possess under 2 hectares and control less than 15 per cent of this land. Only in the mountainous parishes of St Andrew and Manchester do medium-sized farms account for more property than the large estates. Declining farm numbers and sizes were recorded between 1954 and 1968: farms dropped from 199,000 to 185,000, their area from 724,000 to 610,000 hectares (1,788,000 to 1,507,000 acres). One-third of the reduction in farm land was concentrated in the 2 to 10 hectare (5 to 25 acre) category. Speculation in the north-coast tourist areas, urban expansion, purchases by the bauxite companies, and consolidation of holdings hastened the process. However, farms of less than 2 hectares (5 acres) increased in number, and fragmentation reduced the average size of unit from 0·7 to 0·6 hectares (1·8 to 1·5 acres).

Although 75 per cent of the smallest farms are owned, tenural problems remain. Many farmers still do not possess legal proof of land ownership, despite the Facilities for Titles Law enacted in 1955. Leases are usually held on an annual basis and give no recompense for improvements made by tenants. An unquantifiable proportion of small freeholds constitute family land, which is in joint ownership. Many farmers still lack bankable securities, and renters mine the land with multiple croppings. Family land is rapidly reduced to house plots – as relatives may claim a share of the produce, residents usually ignore its agricultural capabilities. Moreover, parcellation of holdings is the norm among small farmers, and this considerably reduces the productivity of labour.

Withdrawal of land from agriculture, coupled to population growth, cut the farm area per capita from 0·52 to ·032 hectares (1·3 to 0·8 acres) between 1954 and 1968. Concern has been expressed about the amount of potentially productive land which is uncultivated or inefficiently employed. In 1959 the basis for land taxation was changed from improved to unimproved valuation, the object being to intensify use, especially on 'ruinate'. About half the parishes have been re-valued on this basis, but the assessments have proved too low to effect change. In 1962 estimates placed idle or under-utilized land at 80,000 to 200,000 hectares (200,000 to 500,000 acres), or 8 to 20 per cent of Jamaica's cultivable area. A Land Utilization Act was passed in 1966, and most holdings of more than 40 hectares (100 acres) have subsequently been inspected. By early 1968 some 340,000 hectares (840,000 acres) had been appraised and just over 10 per cent judged idle. Under-utilized property was concentrated in the southern, moisture-deficient parishes stretching from St Elizabeth to St Catherine. A more exhaustive examination of 700 holdings subsequently revealed even higher percentages of idle land, especially on farms of 80 to 200 hectares (200 to 500 acres). Farmers receiving Idle Land Notices are required to submit plans for developing their land, and the majority have done so. Those unwilling or unable to carry out the changes forfeit their land, and the government implements the improvements. This scheme is intended as a stimulus to intensification, not as a means to appropriation.

Land shortage among small farmers has traditionally been resolved by land settlements. The earliest were founded by the Baptists immediately after emancipation. The colonial government became involved after 1865, but since the First World War no frontier has existed, and the process has continued in a context of rising population pressure. Most of the schemes established since 1929 are located in marginal areas – in the periphery of the Blue Mountains, on the edge of the Cockpit Country, and at the extremities of the island. Some of the land has been purchased from absentees; much of it is in poor condition; rarely has it been dispensed in economic units; and invariably the beneficiaries have been non-farmers, chosen for political reasons. During the 1960s the average size of units was raised to 3·6 hectares (9 acres), almost double the size of the pre-1962 distribution, but there are signs that the process is running down. Over the decades the PNP has been less enthusiastic about land settlements than the JLP. Land settlement has been carried out in a piecemeal fashion, and has accelerated the fragmentation of property.

Since 1945 a series of schemes has been devised to foster agricultural development. The Farm Improvement Scheme of 1949 prepared the way for the Farm Development Scheme, the Agricultural Development Programme, and the Farmers' Production Programme. Between 1955 and 1968 subsidies totalling £3,500,000 and loans worth £4,250,000 were paid out. But they had virtually no impact on production, and little of the money was put to the purposes for which it was intended. Output on small farms actually declined between 1955 and 1960. Jamaica's closest approximation to regional agricultural development has been the creation in 1969 of 13 land authorities, many of them almost coincidental with parish boundaries. These agencies have been modelled on the pioneer work of the Yallahs Valley Land Authority (a smaller entity than the Yallahs Land Authority) and the Christiana Land Authority, which were established in the early 1950s. Wide powers are vested in these regional organizations to prevent soil erosion and rehabilitate land and people. Previous experience at Christiana and Yallahs suggests that extension services need to take greater cognizance of the social characteristics of the peasantry. Roads may be built, houses improved, and conservation introduced, but substantial improvements in the farming system have not taken place. Without access to more, better quality land, small farmers will remain impoverished.

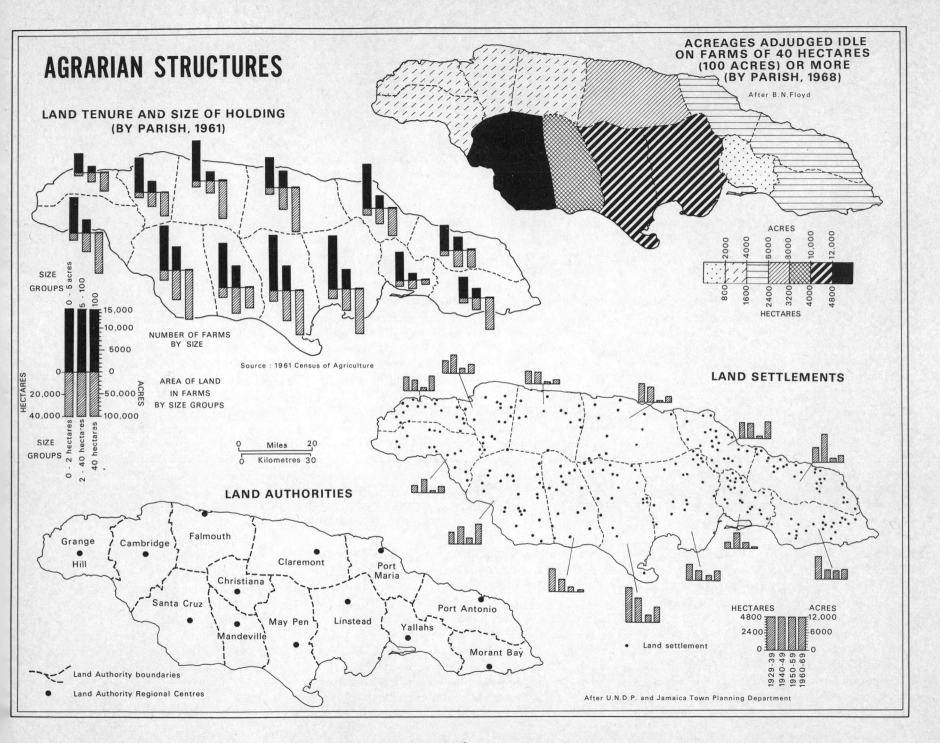

AGRARIAN STRUCTURES

ACREAGES ADJUDGED IDLE ON FARMS OF 40 HECTARES (100 ACRES) OR MORE (BY PARISH, 1968)

After B.N.Floyd

ACRES

2000   4000   6000   8000   10,000   12,000

800   1600   2400   3200   4000   4800

HECTARES

LAND TENURE AND SIZE OF HOLDING (BY PARISH, 1961)

SIZE GROUPS

0 - 5 acres
5 - 100
100

15,000
10,000
5000
0

HECTARES

20,000
40,000

ACRES

50,000
100,000

SIZE GROUPS

0 - 2 hectares
2 - 40 hectares
40 hectares

NUMBER OF FARMS BY SIZE

AREA OF LAND IN FARMS BY SIZE GROUPS

Source : 1961 Census of Agriculture

0   Miles   20
0   Kilometres   30

LAND SETTLEMENTS

HECTARES   ACRES
4800   12,000
2400   6000
0   0

1929-39   1940-49   1950-59   1960-69

• Land settlement

LAND AUTHORITIES

Grange Hill
Cambridge
Falmouth
Claremont
Christiana
Port Maria
Santa Cruz
May Pen
Linstead
Port Antonio
Mandeville
Yallahs
Morant Bay

- - - Land Authority boundaries
• Land Authority Regional Centres

After U.N.D.P. and Jamaica Town Planning Department

67

29 SMALL FARMING

The plural framework of Jamaican society was established during the eighteenth century; its dual economy during the nineteenth. Within the agricultural sector the dichotomy between peasant and planter is expressed in terms of size of holding, tenure, capital, labour, marketing, technology and system of cropping. Planters had first choice of the land, small farmers came off second best. There is a clear geographical distinction in Jamaica between the good terrain, where the emphasis is on the crop, and the poor where it is on the people.

Over half the population live in farming communities scattered throughout the densely populated, mountainous interior. Holdings are usually less than 2 hectares (5 acres) and only half the farmers work full-time on their own land. Most peasants rely upon family labour, augmenting it at seed-time and harvest by combining in 'day for day' and 'morning sport' or by hiring extra hands. Agricultural machinery is confined to the larger units, and small farmers depend on animal traction, the hoe, spade and cutlass. About half their produce is consumed at home or carried weekly to the local market by the country trader – often the farmer's wife. The remainder is sent overseas. Since the middle of the nineteenth century the peasantry has made a substantial contribution to the export economy of the island. Pimento, ginger, cocoa and coffee are exclusively peasant crops: sugar and bananas are grown almost equally on small and large holdings. The farming system employed by the peasantry is more flexible than the plantation – if only in the choice of crops to be grown. Small farmers may eat, sell or export their produce.

Polyculture is an outstanding feature of the small-farming system. Peasants grow as many as 20 different crops, and mixed planting is the norm. Spices, fruit, beverages and medicinal plants are grown outside the farmer's kitchen. The best land is devoted to cash-crops. Bananas and coffee are favoured in the Christiana area, the former providing shade cover. Corn, Irish potatoes, citrus, gungo peas, sugar, cassava and taro are inter-cropped. The roadside is lined with a variety of yams, and napier grass is cut for fodder. Plant mixing was probably practised on the Negro grounds during slavery. Nowadays extension officers advise against the method, arguing that single-crop fields produce better results. But the farmer believes that irrespective of disease, bad weather or depressed prices, all his crops will not fail him.

Bananas and coffee bushes are carefully treated with kitchen garbage and tree mulch. Ideally other areas should be cropped for about two years and then either fallowed or put to pasture. However, this type of shifting cultivation is not feasible where farms are very small or rapid population increase is taking place. Despite their awareness of the loss of nutrients, peasants apply very little fertilizer, government subsidies notwithstanding. Peasants possess virtually no capital, and climatic hazards often cancel out the effects of fertilization; higher yields would be eaten by the family, and no additional funds would be available to purchase new supplies of fertilizer.

On the edge of the Cockpit Country where fields are often confined to steep-sided depressions or dolines, crops are stratified, bananas and coffee being located on the richer down-wash, subsistence crops on the higher slopes. Boulders and stones have to be collected into piles to enable a tilth to be maintained. Some of the poorest land consists of rocky limestone outcrops, and each pocket of red earth supports one plant of corn or cassava. In the Blue Mountains the high relief, heavy rainfall, and steep slopes have resulted in extensive sheet erosion and gullying. In the Yallahs Valley 75 per cent or more of the topsoil has been removed from about half the area, and subsoil and parent material revealed. Almost three-quarters of the cultivated land is on slopes of at least 30°, the principal use being for ground provisions and food forest. A soil scientist working in the valley in the early 1950s recommended that most of the area should be stripped of its population and turned into a forest reserve. But in view of the high population densities occurring throughout Jamaica, it was hardly feasible to resettle 12,000 people from the valley. An alternative strategy was adopted, and a land authority established in Yallahs to conserve and develop the region. Erosion has been checked and a variety of soil conservation techniques applied. Terracing and contour-planting have been more successful than most other innovations, partly because of the inducements offered, and partly because they have required inputs of labour rather than capital.

Peasants are by definition ill-educated and conservative. Land confers status and provides security; small farmers will not raise loans against their property. Approaches to life and agriculture are fatalistic, and the belief dies hard that only large farmers are good cultivators. Reluctance to form formal organizations is coupled to a willingness to settle intra-community disputes out of court. Superstition is rife and influences cultivation practices. The majority of small farmers take their cue to plant from horoscopes published in *Macdonald's Farmers Almanac*. Poverty breeds jealousy, and successful country folk frequently encounter obeah, or black magic.

Small farming is technically bad, yet economically it represents a reasonable response to the conditions under which it is practised. Attitudes to small farming are essentially ambivalent. Commissions of enquiry since 1897 have paid lip-service to the importance of the peasantry, land settlements have been created, roads have been built into isolated areas, extension services are available, and an Agricultural Marketing Corporation has been in existence since 1963. Yet these improvements are not reflected in productivity, and most small farmers want their children to leave agriculture. Rising population in rural Jamaica has been alleviated by migration to the towns, and emigration to Britain. Many streets in the Lambeth area of London are occupied by neighbours from the Yallahs Valley, and remittances provide an important source of finance in numerous farming communities.

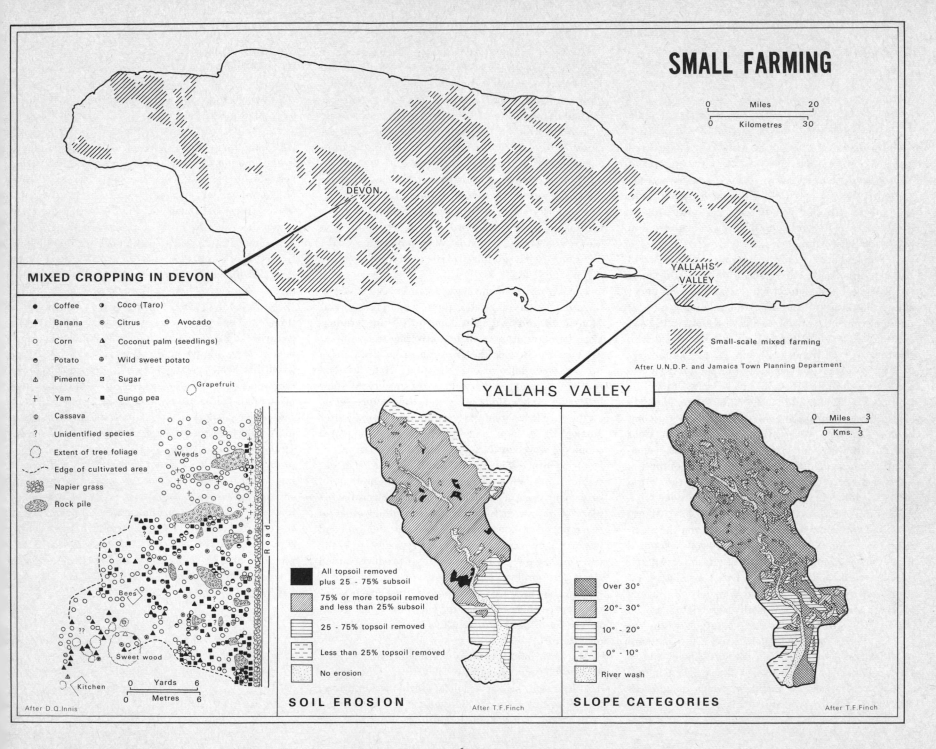

SMALL FARMING

0 — Miles — 20
0 — Kilometres — 30

DEVON

YALLAHS VALLEY

⬚ Small-scale mixed farming

After U.N.D.P. and Jamaica Town Planning Department

MIXED CROPPING IN DEVON

●	Coffee	◑	Coco (Taro)
▲	Banana	◉	Citrus	⊖ Avocado
○	Corn	△	Coconut palm (seedlings)
◓	Potato	⊕	Wild sweet potato
△	Pimento	⊘	Sugar
+	Yam	■	Gungo pea
⊕	Cassava		

? Unidentified species

◯ Extent of tree foliage

〰 Edge of cultivated area

🝆 Napier grass

🝆 Rock pile

Grapefruit

Weeds

Road

Bees

Rock

Sweet wood

Kitchen

0 — Yards — 6
0 — Metres — 6

After D.Q.Innis

YALLAHS VALLEY

SOIL EROSION

■ All topsoil removed plus 25 - 75% subsoil

▨ 75% or more topsoil removed and less than 25% subsoil

▤ 25 - 75% topsoil removed

▦ Less than 25% topsoil removed

░ No erosion

After T.F.Finch

SLOPE CATEGORIES

▨ Over 30°

▨ 20°- 30°

▤ 10° - 20°

▦ 0° - 10°

░ River wash

0 — Miles — 3
0 — Kms. — 3

After T.F.Finch

30 EXPORT CROPS: SUGAR

At the end of the seventeenth century Jamaica rapidly became dependent on the production of sugar; planters of British stock divided the island into estates; and their labour requirements were met by imports of Negro slaves shipped from West Africa. Sugar cane expanded along the fertile, well-drained coastal plains and embayments, and penetrated the interior valleys. By the late eighteenth century a monoculture had been established with sugar as king.

The nineteenth century, in contrast, was a period of contraction. Cane was retained only on the most fertile soils, and marginal land was sold and put under alternative crops. Planters attributed the demise of the industry to the emancipation of the slaves in 1834 and to their gradual loss of protection in the British sugar market between 1846 and 1854. The fact remains, however, that Jamaica's output of sugar fell continually after 1805, while indebtedness among the planters was discernible by the end of the eighteenth century, and rampant after 1800. Furthermore, competition from cheaper, slave-produced sugar in Cuba and Puerto Rico, followed at the end of the nineteenth century by the rapidly growing output of European beet, depressed the price on the world market and compounded Jamaica's problems. A modest recovery was made during the First World War, but the boom soon collapsed. During the economic depression of the 1930s sugar and rum accounted for only one-seventh of the value of Jamaica's exports.

The development of the modern sugar industry was stimulated by the Second World War and consolidated by the system of internationally agreed quotas and prices. More than half the island's output is now exported to the United Kingdom under the Commonwealth Sugar Agreement, and the remainder sold to Canada, which buys at world market prices but pays a small rebate, and to the USA, which operates its own quota system. During the late 1960s, Jamaica exported between 386,000 and 427,000 tonnes (380,000 and 420,000 tons) of sugar per annum, or more than twenty times the figure recorded in 1900. The sugar area has expanded again, and canes are grown in many of the districts which were cropped at the end of the eighteenth century. Economies of scale have been achieved by amalgamating estates and establishing central factories. Whereas each of the small eighteenth century estates possessed its own sugar mill, often producing a few hundred tonnes, by 1970 the entire island was served by only fifteen factories. The majority are owned by public companies rather than families, and the two largest, at Frome and Monymusk, are part of the West Indies Sugar Corporation, itself a subsidiary of the British refining firm of Tate and Lyle.

The expansion of the sugar area has been achieved by the growth of estates through purchase, as at Monymusk, and by the development of cane farming. Cane farmers, many of them cultivating steep slopes, produce almost half the Jamaican crop. They make pre-arranged deliveries to the sugar factories, and receive payments which reflect the quality of their cane: the estates alone grow and manufacture sugar. As the sucrose content of cane diminishes rapidly after cutting, it is important that each producing area should be served by a 'factory in the field'. The manufacturing process involves the crushing of cane, extraction and boiling of the juice, and the production of brown sugar. This is usually refined abroad at its place of import, though one concern produces white sugar for local consumption. Molasses and rum are important by-products of the factory industry. In the late 1960s, exports of sugar and sugar products earned about £20 million (J$40 million), or more than one-quarter the value of all domestic exports. Furthermore, sugar processing accounted for one-fifth of the contribution made to the Gross Domestic Product by the manufacturing sector.

The sugar industry still faces many problems. It is a high-cost producer, and probably would not survive if all its output had to be sold at world market prices. Labour costs are a major item and are constantly rising as the two labour unions compete to represent the work-force. During the past decade the estates have attempted to mechanize the industry, but in view of the high rate of unemployment, the government has retarded the process. Although cutting is still done by hand, cane loading is largely mechanized on most estates, and so too are ploughing, planting and weeding. Some estates have retrenched their labour force by refusing to take on school leavers, and this is having unfortunate repercussions. As many as 60,000 people find employment in the industry during the crop season from December to June. During the dead season, however, when the rattoons are mulched, the new canes planted, and repairs made to the farm and factory, work exists for only about half that number. Another difficulty stems from the small size of many of the factories. Those with an output of less than 20,600 tonnes (20,000 tons) of sugar per annum are threatened unless they can increase their capacity. The factories at Barnett, Caymanas, and Richmond Llandovery were closed in the late 1960s, while Serge Island has been kept open by the government at the request of the cane farmers. Decreases in output have been recorded each year due to droughts, disputes, cane fires and, so it is alleged, labour shortages. Furthermore, the industry has been under sharp attack from Jamaican radicals who argue that sugar is no longer profitable, and that exports simply offset the cost of importing food which could be grown on cane land and would absorb a larger percentage of the labour force. In view of its contribution to employment and the export economy, the government has decided to support the sugar industry, and has negotiated the purchase of land belonging to the West Indies Sugar Corporation and Barnett Estate for re-sale to cane farmers.

EXPORT CROPS
SUGAR

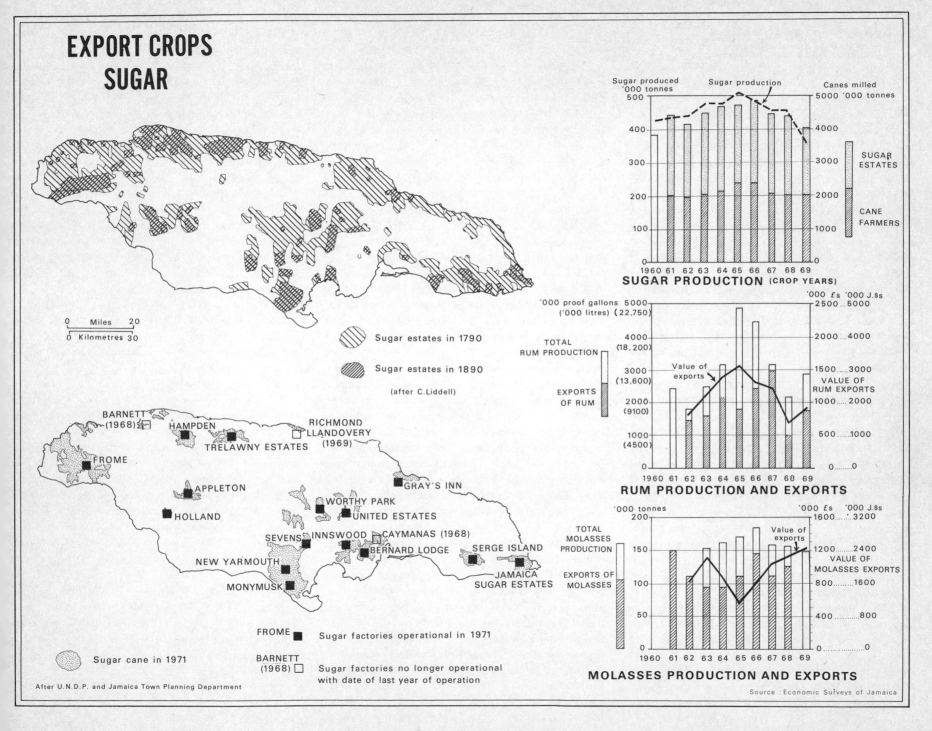

Miles 0 — 20
Kilometres 0 — 30

Sugar estates in 1790

Sugar estates in 1890

(after C. Liddell)

BARNETT (1968)
HAMPDEN
TRELAWNY ESTATES
RICHMOND
LLANDOVERY (1969)
FROME
APPLETON
HOLLAND
GRAY'S INN
WORTHY PARK
UNITED ESTATES
SEVENS
INNSWOOD
CAYMANAS (1968)
BERNARD LODGE
SERGE ISLAND
NEW YARMOUTH
MONYMUSK
JAMAICA SUGAR ESTATES

Sugar cane in 1971

FROME ■ Sugar factories operational in 1971

BARNETT (1968) □ Sugar factories no longer operational with date of last year of operation

After U.N.D.P. and Jamaica Town Planning Department

SUGAR PRODUCTION (CROP YEARS)

Sugar produced '000 tonnes
Sugar production
Canes milled '000 tonnes
SUGAR ESTATES
CANE FARMERS

RUM PRODUCTION AND EXPORTS

'000 proof gallons ('000 litres)
'000 £s '000 J.$s
TOTAL RUM PRODUCTION
EXPORTS OF RUM
Value of exports
VALUE OF RUM EXPORTS

MOLASSES PRODUCTION AND EXPORTS

'000 tonnes
'000 £s '000 J.$s
TOTAL MOLASSES PRODUCTION
EXPORTS OF MOLASSES
Value of exports
VALUE OF MOLASSES EXPORTS

Source: Economic Surveys of Jamaica

31 EXPORT CROPS: BANANAS, CITRUS FRUIT, COCONUTS

The *banana* industry developed during the 1870s through the efforts of an American, Captain Baker. The area adjacent to Port Antonio was rapidly drawn into the commercial venture, and both peasant and planter benefited in the process. Bananas accounted for more than half the island's exports from the end of the nineteenth century until 1938, the rise of the industry coinciding with the nadir of sugar. But the more recent history of the banana has been fraught with problems. Panama and Leaf-Spot diseases reduced exports from 24 million stems in 1938 to 6 million stems in 1946, and the contribution of the industry to total exports fell from 19 to 8 per cent between 1953 and 1968. Depressed prices were a major factor in the 1950s, but its subsequent decline has been relative to the development of bauxite. In 1962, banana output was twice the 1946 figure.

Most small farmers grow bananas, but the main producing areas are located in the coastlands of St Thomas, Portland and St Mary, and the shale inliers around Christiana and Cambridge. Well-drained soils and rainfall in excess of 150 cm (60 in.) are ideal; the plantations in St Catherine, together with the neighbouring sugar estates, require irrigation. The banana is a tuber, and the old plant is cut down to be replaced by new suckers. It is extremely fragile and hurricanes may destroy the entire crop. However, the banana fits well into the small-farming system. It requires only low capital inputs, yields quickly and continually, and combines well with other crops. During the last 30 years the Lacatan variety has almost completely replaced the disease-prone Gros Michel. But yields are barely half those achieved in Martinique and Ecuador. Reduced output results from the pattern of planting which is employed. Until the early 1960s fruit was bought by the bunch rather than by weight, and bananas were widely spaced to encourage bunch yields. Furthermore, producing areas in Jamaica are confined to poorer soils, and small farms use little or no fertilizer.

Bananas are still the island's second most important agricultural export after sugar. During the 1960s the curve of production has closely conformed to a normal distribution: slight increases were recorded until 1966, followed by a decline each year until 1969, the steep drop in the last section of the graph being due to drought. The value of exports has tended to follow a similar pattern, though prices have raced ahead of production, reaching their peak as late as 1968. The boom since 1962 has largely been due to West Cameroon's loss of Commonwealth preference in the British market. By the mid 1960s over 90 per cent of United Kingdom requirements were met by Jamaica and the Windward Islands. A price-war ensued between Fyffes, a subsidiary of the United Fruit Company, which handles the bulk of Jamaica's exports, and Geest, which markets Windward Island bananas. In 1967 the suppliers agreed to share the UK market, Jamaica supplying 52 per cent of British needs. But in 1970 Fyffes unilaterally broke the pact, claiming that Jamaica was not able to supply its quota and that the quality of bananas had declined. A request was made to the British Government for permission to import bananas from the Ivory Coast. Early in 1971 the original agreement was confirmed after arbitration.

The Banana Board has launched a replanting programme to increase production and improve quality. More than half a million pounds are being invested, and a new, high yielding variety, Valery, is being introduced. However, some Jamaican economists also believe that the industry should be rationalized to make it more competitive. As trucking costs from the interior to the ports are high, they suggest that only those areas with locational advantages should remain in production. Even with adjustments along these lines it is unlikely that the industry could continue without sheltered access to the UK market. However, that market is characterized by inelastic demand.

The principal *citrus* groves are located in the middle Rio Minho valley between May Pen and Frankfield, though trees flourish on most well-drained soils where the rainfall exceeds 150 cm (60 in.). Four-fifths of the registered growers possess no more than 15 trees, and citrus production is an important element in the polycultural practice of most small farmers. Grapefruit are grown, together with numerous varieties of orange, and a local orange-tangerine hybrid known as the ortanique. Fruit packing and processing have developed at May Pen, Bog Walk and Kingston. Canneries produce fruit segments and juice; citrus oils and marmalade are also marketed.

Despite optimistic post-war forecasts about the future of the citrus industry, exports to the UK have been cut back, and most of the output is sold in Jamaica. Increases in the value of exports between 1960 and 1965 were due to the demand for canned segments and juices and the fresh-fruit trade in ortaniques. But prices in Britain have been static for a long period as a result of intense competition between Spain, Israel and South Africa. The hotel industry in Jamaica may eventually provide a major outlet, and the Citrus Growers Association has launched an expansion programme designed to establish 5,000 hectares (12,500 acres) of new seedlings.

Coconuts are grown on coastal estates, especially at the east end of the island. Many of the groves are also used as cattle pastures and some are planted with sugar or bananas. Trees are slow-maturing, and insurance schemes protect producers from wind damage. A number of coconut products are exported, especially coconut shell, frozen coconut and coconut shell charcoal. Copra is most important for local consumption, and a number of extractive works are located in Portland and St Thomas. The island was self-sufficient in edible oils, fats and soap, but production decreased in the late 1960s due to labour disputes and the dramatic spread of lethal yellow disease. The Coconut Industry Board is encouraging growers to replace Jamaica Talls with the Malayan Dwarf, a more disease-resistant variety.

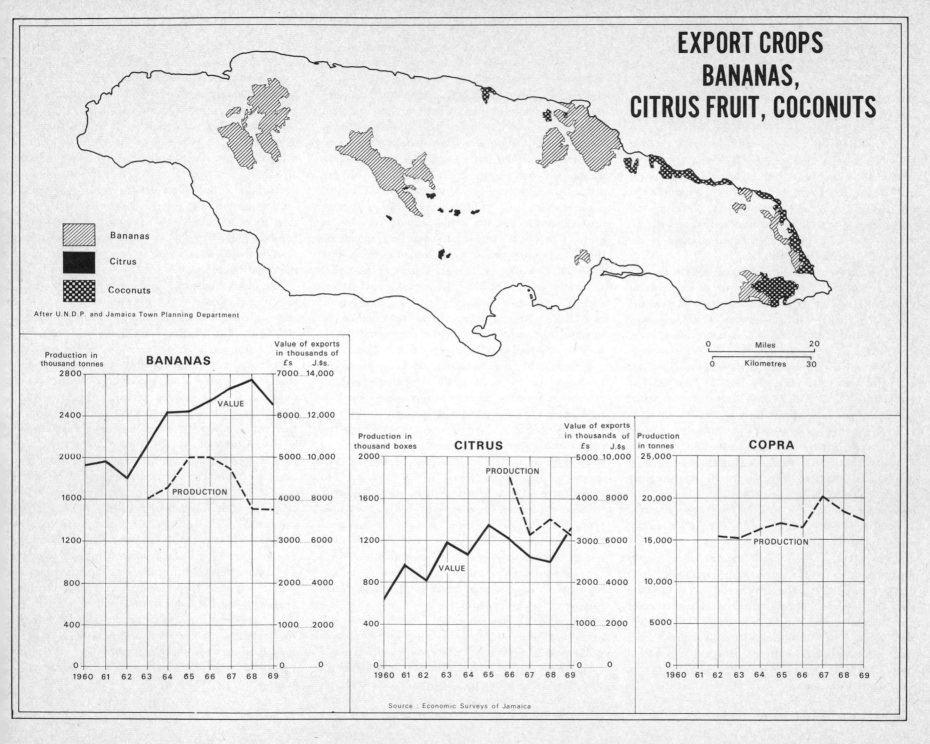

EXPORT CROPS
BANANAS,
CITRUS FRUIT, COCONUTS

Bananas
Citrus
Coconuts

After U.N.D.P. and Jamaica Town Planning Department

0 Miles 20
0 Kilometres 30

BANANAS

Production in thousand tonnes

Value of exports in thousands of £s   J.$s.

VALUE
PRODUCTION

1960 61 62 63 64 65 66 67 68 69

CITRUS

Production in thousand boxes

Value of exports in thousands of £s   J.$s

PRODUCTION
VALUE

1960 61 62 63 64 65 66 67 68 69

COPRA

Production in tonnes

PRODUCTION

1960 61 62 63 64 65 66 67 68 69

Source : Economic Surveys of Jamaica

32 EXPORT CROPS: COFFEE, COCOA, PIMENTO, GINGER

During the eighteenth and nineteenth centuries properties growing *coffee* were established in the Blue Mountains and in the uplands of Manchester and St Elizabeth. As late as 1830 the crop ranked second in importance to sugar. Coffee production diminished in the middle of the nineteenth century, however, and output was gradually concentrated in the hands of small settlers. By 1900 the robusta variety was replacing the less resistant arabica.

Coffee is now a small farmer's crop and grown on a variety of soils at elevations between 150 and 2,000 m (500 and 6,000 ft). Bushes do best where the rainfall exceeds 150 cm (60 in.). The main producing areas are located in the uplands of Clarendon, Manchester and St Ann. The Blue Mountains have given their name to coffee of internationally recognized quality, but cultivation is largely confined to the upper part of the Yallahs Valley. At high altitude bushes grow without shade; nearer sea-level they are usually cultivated beneath a canopy of bananas. Ripe coffee berries are taken to processing factories located in the main growing areas; wet coffee is dried, sorted and graded at a finishing plant in Kingston. Three factories roast and grind coffee for domestic use.

Government involvement in the coffee industry began shortly after the Second World War, at a time when soil erosion and general neglect were causing concern. The Coffee Rehabilitation Scheme concentrated on extension services, the establishment of coffee nurseries, and the erection of coffee cleaning and curing works, and was the first of a number of developments which sought to revitalize the industry. But despite government subsidy, small farmers have lacked the land to expand production, and growth in output has been due to large land owners, especially the bauxite companies.

In the last decade the quantity and value of exports has fluctuated widely, and the proportion of output exported has fallen from about 70 per cent in 1955 to less than one-third in 1968. Yet supplies have failed to meet the demand of local manufacturers of instant coffee. The Coffee Industry Board has found it profitable to export high quality produce and import cheaper beans for blending from Haiti and Trinidad. A Coffee Rehabilitation and Resuscitation Programme was started in 1969. By 1974 it was hoped to have planted 2,000 hectares (5,000 acres), and to have revived 3,200 hectares (8,000 acres) of existing coffee.

Cocoa, also, is a small-farmer's crop and grown throughout the interior of the island. The 800 m (2,500 ft) contour provides an upper limit to cultivation, and the best producing soils have developed on shales. Main producing areas are located in the higher and wetter parts of St Mary, Clarendon and Hanover. Each is served by a fermentary. Cocoa was an important crop in Jamaica before the introduction of the banana; its re-emergence on the commercial scene has been achieved since the Second World War.

Although the government embarked upon a Cocoa Expansion Scheme in 1957, the subsequent performance of the industry has been disappointing. Subsidies have been provided for small farmers, millions of seedlings distributed, and various infrastructural improvements carried out. The value and volume of exports has fluctuated, but the overall trend has been downward since 1960. Small holders have failed to provide the high standard of cultivation required; Black Pod disease, Cherelle Wilt and rodents have taken their toll of the crop. Jamaica has produced barely one-third of the cocoa it could have sold. But not all the industry's problems are domestic. World cocoa prices have fluctuated since the mid 1950s, and negotiations have only recently produced an international price agreement.

Pimento, or allspice, is grown in the wet limestone uplands of Jamaica. Its aroma combines the qualities of cinnamon, nutmeg and clove. Originally it was a spontaneous crop sown by birds. Research has shown that the pulp surrounding the berry has to be removed before planting, and the government now grows and distributes seedlings. Pimento trees grow in cattle pastures and in the food forest maintained by small farmers. Berries are picked between July and September and dried on barbecues before being sent to the government clearing house in Kingston. Since 1969 strict government control of quality has been maintained. Exports comprise the dried spice, pimento siftings, which are used in the production of cattle food, and pimento oil, which is derived from the crushed leaves and is employed in perfumes, food flavouring and medicines. Jamaica is one of the world's leading producers of pimento, and exports are more than twice as valuable as those of coffee and cocoa combined. Exports fluctuated during the 1960s, but have improved since 1965; 1969 was the best year in the whole decade.

The cultivation of *ginger* dates from the period of slavery and it is now grown by small farmers. The crop is ideally planted at heights of about 650 m (2,000 ft). During the last hundred years continuous cultivation has resulted in disastrous soil erosion. In 1964 its contribution to foreign exchange earnings was greater than either coffee or cocoa. But exports have subsequently fallen away very quickly, and rises in world market prices in 1969 and 1970 have failed to arrest the decline. Ginger is notorious among small farmers as an exhauster of soil nutrients. Moreover, growers have encountered difficulties in obtaining labour for peeling. About half the island's exports go to the USA, almost one-third to the United Kingdom.

The agricultural sector has failed miserably during the last decade. All the major export crops have recorded declining output; only pimento has shown improvements. Agricultural exports have failed to create development capital for investment in services or other sectors of the economy. Rural incomes have remained low and highly skewed. Migration has drained some of the best qualified country folk to the towns or to jobs overseas. Thirty-two per cent of local food needs have to be imported, or double the proportion recorded in 1950. Consequently the visible trade deficit has widened.

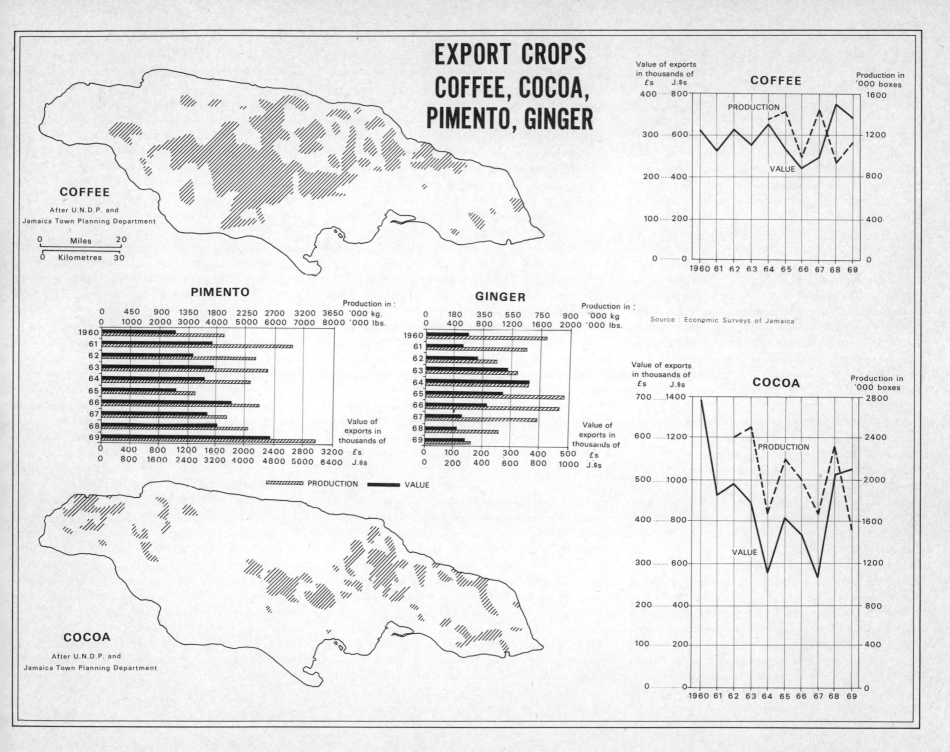

EXPORT CROPS
COFFEE, COCOA, PIMENTO, GINGER

COFFEE

After U.N.D.P. and
Jamaica Town Planning Department

Miles 0 — 20
Kilometres 0 — 30

PIMENTO

Production in : '000 kg.
0   450   900   1350   1800   2250   2700   3200   3650   '000 kg.
0   1000   2000   3000   4000   5000   6000   7000   8000   '000 lbs.

1960
61
62
63
64
65
66
67
68
69

Value of exports in thousands of
0   400   800   1200   1600   2000   2400   2800   3200   £s
0   800   1600   2400   3200   4000   4800   5600   6400   J.$s

GINGER

Production in : '000 kg :
0   180   350   550   750   900   '000 kg :
0   400   800   1200   1600   2000   '000 lbs.

1960
61
62
63
64
65
66
67
68
69

Value of exports in thousands of
0   100   200   300   400   500   £s
0   200   400   600   800   1000   J.$s

▨▨▨ PRODUCTION   ▬▬ VALUE

COFFEE

Value of exports in thousands of
£s   J.$s
400 — 800
300 — 600
200 — 400
100 — 200
0 — 0

Production in '000 boxes
1600
1200
800
400
0

PRODUCTION
VALUE

1960 61 62 63 64 65 66 67 68 69

Source : Economic Surveys of Jamaica

COCOA

Value of exports in thousands of
£s   J.$s
700 — 1400
600 — 1200
500 — 1000
400 — 800
300 — 600
200 — 400
100 — 200
0 — 0

Production in '000 boxes
2800
2400
2000
1600
1200
800
400
0

PRODUCTION
VALUE

1960 61 62 63 64 65 66 67 68 69

COCOA

After U.N.D.P. and
Jamaica Town Planning Department

33 LIVESTOCK AND POULTRY

The Jamaican diet is notoriously deficient in protein. Beef, milk and eggs are undersupplied and expensive. Despite the high elasticity of demand for livestock products, they account for barely one-quarter of the value of Jamaica's agricultural output. Imports of cream, butter and cheese amount to more than £3 million each year.

Cattle rearing is predominantly in the hands of large landowners. Penkeepers and sugar planters maintain big herds, and Reynolds Bauxite is the principal beef-producer in the island. In 1961 the major cattle parishes were St Ann, Westmoreland, St Elizabeth and St Catherine. Lack of specialization characterized most localities with the exception of St Ann and St Catherine, where dairying was well-developed, and Clarendon and St Elizabeth where dairying was in its infancy. Small farms tended to produce dual purpose cattle for milk and for beef; draft beef was associated with the estates.

Cattle production coincides with the most extensive grasslands and the largest areas of improved pasture. Subsidies for the seeding of pasture have hastened the spread of guinea grass and pangola, but substantial numbers of cattle still graze the ruinate. Generally, the grasslands occupy areas which experience rainfall deficiency and drought. But in southern St Elizabeth flypenning is used to intensify the farming system. Savanna grass is cut to mulch the ground; donkeys' dung and urine fertilize the soil. Vegetable crops are obtained with these dry farming techniques.

Pigs and goats are kept by a host of small farmers. Pigs are bought young and allowed to root in the yard adjacent to the peasant's house. They act as garbage disposers, and provide a valuable source of cash when sold for meat. Goats are reared for milk and for the butcher. Curried goat is a Jamaican delicacy. The parishes with the largest head of small stock are St Elizabeth, St Catherine, Manchester and St Ann. The distribution of pigs and goats tends to be associated with areas of cattle production. Goats usually outnumber pigs, though the converse occurs in the vicinity of Kingston.

Chickens are ubiquitous; even the rent-yards in the capital have poultry cages. But the major chicken-producing areas lie adjacent to the Kingston market. In St Mary and St Catherine much of the commercial output of eggs and poultry is in the hands of large operators.

The dairying industry has developed fairly rapidly during this century. Selective breeding to produce a heat- and disease-resistant strain of cattle began at the end of the First World War. European dairy stock were crossed with imported Zebu cattle. The Jamaica Hope was recognized as a dairy herd in 1952. These cattle inherit about 80 per cent of their genes from the Jersey, 15 per cent from the Zebu, and 5 per cent from the Holstein. The Jamaica Hope is an early maturing animal, calves well, and has a lactation period which is much longer than that found in many other tropical dairy breeds.

A significant landmark in the development of dairying in Jamaica was the opening of a milk condensery in 1940. The condensery was built by Jamaica Milk Products at Bybrook in northern St Catherine. Its capacity far exceeded the total milk output at that time, and it was established largely to stimulate expansion. Many of the collecting routes operated by the condensery served areas where very little milk was produced, the object being to encourage cattle keeping. Field officers employed by the condensery gave technical advice to farmers, and co-operated with the Department of Agriculture to promote improved breeding. But the condensery unwittingly encouraged the proliferation of very small producers.

Annual milk output stood at 28 million litres (6 million gallons) in 1943, and rose to 38·6 million litres (8·5 million gallons) in 1954. By the early 1950s about one-quarter of all the milk produced in Jamaica was consumed fresh in Kingston. Since 1954 Bybrook has increased its operations and opened cooling stations at Montpelier and Mandeville. Yet the volume of milk supplied to the condensery has dropped from 14 million litres (3 million gallons) in 1954 to under 9 million litres (2 million gallons) in 1969. To enable the condensery to expand its output, increasing imports of dry skimmed milk have been required. It seems almost certain that the volume of milk going fresh to the market has risen at the expense of supplies to the condensery – not as a result of increased output.

During the Farmers Production Programme which ran between 1963 and 1968, plans were made to raise annual milk production from 45 million litres (10 million gallons) to 135 million litres (30 million gallons) in 1973. Loans were provided to enable farmers to purchase equipment and buildings, and a heifer acquisition programme was organized. Moreover, the Livestock Development Division introduced an artificial insemination service. Careful vigilance was maintained to detect and exclude imported cattle bearing rinderpest and foot and mouth disease.

A significant development in the fresh milk market has been the emergence of a milk-processing and wholesale distributing company called Royal Cremo. In 1968 this firm took over the North Shore Dairies of Montego Bay; the joint enterprise handled more than 5 million litres (1 million gallons) a year. The company collects from contracted farmers and markets pasteurized and homogenized milk. Consequent upon these developments, important changes have taken place in the location of milk production. Output has declined in the north coast parishes and increased in St Thomas, St Catherine, Clarendon and St Elizabeth, all of which either contain or lie adjacent to major urban markets for fresh milk.

The overall distribution of livestock reflects climatic and vegetational aspects of the physical environment. But dairying, pig keeping and poultry raising have concentrated near Kingston and within the rapidly urbanizing parishes to the west of the capital. Here market forces outweigh the physical factors of location.

LIVESTOCK AND POULTRY

Source : Agricultural Census of Jamaica 1961-62

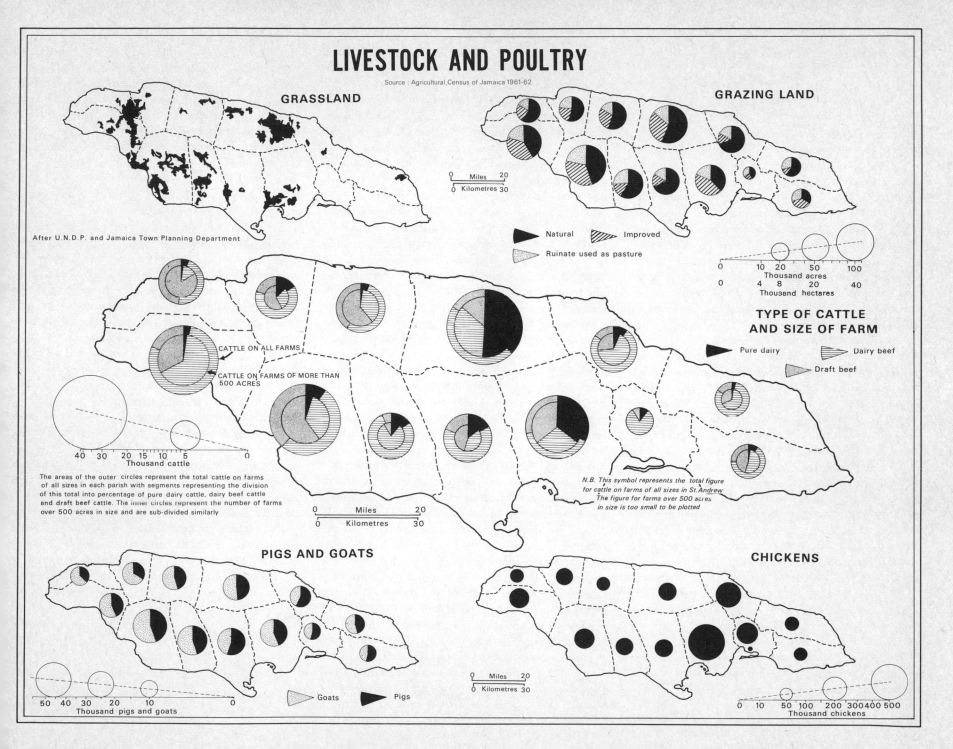

GRASSLAND

After U.N.D.P. and Jamaica Town Planning Department

0 Miles 20
0 Kilometres 30

GRAZING LAND

Natural   Improved

Ruinate used as pasture

0   10   20   50   100
Thousand acres
0   4   8   20   40
Thousand hectares

TYPE OF CATTLE AND SIZE OF FARM

Pure dairy   Dairy beef

Draft beef

CATTLE ON ALL FARMS

CATTLE ON FARMS OF MORE THAN 500 ACRES

40   30   20   15   10   5   0
Thousand cattle

The areas of the outer circles represent the total cattle on farms of all sizes in each parish with segments representing the division of this total into percentage of pure dairy cattle, dairy beef cattle and draft beef cattle. The inner circles represent the number of farms over 500 acres in size and are sub-divided similarly

N.B. This symbol represents the total figure for cattle on farms of all sizes in St. Andrew. The figure for farms over 500 acres in size is too small to be plotted

0 Miles 20
0 Kilometres 30

PIGS AND GOATS

50   40   30   20   10   0
Thousand pigs and goats

Goats   Pigs

CHICKENS

0 Miles 20
0 Kilometres 30

0   10   50   100   200   300 400 500
Thousand chickens

Despite many centuries of timber felling, forests still cover 266,600 hectares (660,000 acres) of upland, or 24 per cent of Jamaica's area. Gazetted forest reserves and crown lands account for about 110,700 hectares (274,000 acres), and are divided between the two main mountain areas. Montane mist forest typifies the Blue Mountains; wet limestone forest envelopes the high limestone plateaux. The Portland Ridge and Hellshire Hills support only a stunted vegetation, and the main reserve of commercial timber lies in the Cockpit Country. Privately-owned forests adjoin the national reserves, but are difficult to exploit because of the thinness of the usable stands, and problems of accessibility.

A policy of afforestation has been actively pursued since the Second World War, first as a means of conserving soil and water, and since 1962 to secure timber production and watershed protection. Afforestation targets were steadily raised during the 1960s. By the beginning of 1970 about 6,500 hectares (16,000 acres) had been planted by the Forestry Department, mostly in the reserves. The aim is to double the afforested area by 1975, and a substantial programme of plant distribution is maintained to supply government agencies, private individuals, bauxite companies, land authorities, and organizations engaged in community development. The most important species of tree produced in Forestry Department nurseries are the Caribbean Pine, Mahoe, Honduras Mahogany and Eucalyptus.

Private landowners receive a £25 per hectare (£10 per acre) subsidy and free distribution of seedlings. But few acceptors have been found. In view of the lack of interest in afforestation and the absence of cleared sites for future development within the national reserve, the Forestry Department has wanted to extend the area under its control. However, a pilot survey of the Buff Bay River Valley has revealed that 60 per cent of the area is in parcels of less than 20 hectares (50 acres); a complicated programme of land consolidation will be necessary to create viable wood-lots.

The Watershed Protection Commission has devoted its attention to selected regions within the major drainage basins. During the last decade the commission has afforested about 800 hectares (2,000 acres) and carried out land rehabilitation and river training on some 4,000 hectares (10,000 acres). Further work will focus on the seven areas drained by the Rio Minho, Cane River, Rio Pedro, Negro-Johnson Rivers, Rio Nuevo, Lucea-Cabarita Rivers, and the Roaring River. These schemes involve the restoration of 70,000 hectares (174,000 acres), of which about 2,000 hectares (5,000 acres) will be reafforested. The Lucea-Cabarita project includes experiments with terraced agriculture.

About eighty small saw-mills are scattered throughout the interior; many encounter problems in securing enough lumber to guarantee even their modest levels of production. The value of Jamaica's timber output barely exceeds £1·5 million. Imports of wood, lumber and cork cost double this figure; many of the commodities are bulky, heavy and expensive to handle. In addition to timber for construction, a local demand exists for citrus boxes, transmission poles, matches and furniture. By 1990 it is estimated that about 40,000 hectares (100,000 acres) of forest will be needed to make Jamaica self-sufficient in soft woods alone. Forest reserves and land already in forest or ruinate could supply half the area required. But the remainder may have to be found in peasant farming districts where the slopes exceed 30 degrees. From the ecological point of view the shift to a more controlled and extensive use of marginal farm land is highly desirable. But people will be displaced and will need new land or new jobs. In the recent past neither land nor employment have been readily available.

Forestry industries can lead to substantial improvements in the infrastructure of even the most isolated rural districts. Electricity, roads and telephones, it is argued, will follow the activities of the Forestry Department. Indeed, the Forestry Department has a minor function as a road-building agency. But there is much evidence from other countries that roads do not stabilize the population of the settlement fringe; rather they draw the inhabitants down to the more financially rewarding core areas. Nevertheless, forestry can provide many jobs, both in wood-lot management and in manufacturing. One forester is needed for each unit of 10 hectares (25 acres), and timber-processing industries tend to be labour-intensive. The flexible nature of forest operations also makes it possible to engage workers on a seasonal basis, as well as full time. The Forestry Department employed more than 10,000 persons on a casual basis in 1969.

In recent years the forests have drawn increasing numbers of visitors. The ease and flexibility of travel by motor car have begun to give the mountains and forests an attractiveness previously enjoyed only by the beaches. The coolness of the mountains and the freedom to walk in a natural environment have a very definite appeal for Jamaica's urban dwellers. In 1970 a national parks committee was set up under the chairmanship of the Conservator of Forests to examine areas suitable for recreational purposes. Provisions for forest recreation have been rapidly improved to meet the growing demands of week-end visitors, especially day-trippers from Kingston. Trails have been set out and cabins and picnic places built. It is likely that demand for camping, hiking, and for scenic vistas will expand rapidly, and that the forested areas will soon develop modest resort functions. Initially, these will probably cater to Jamaicans; but eventually foreign tourists will want to visit the beautiful, forested interior. Both the Blue Mountains and the Cockpit Country are fairly accessible from the principal hotel areas.

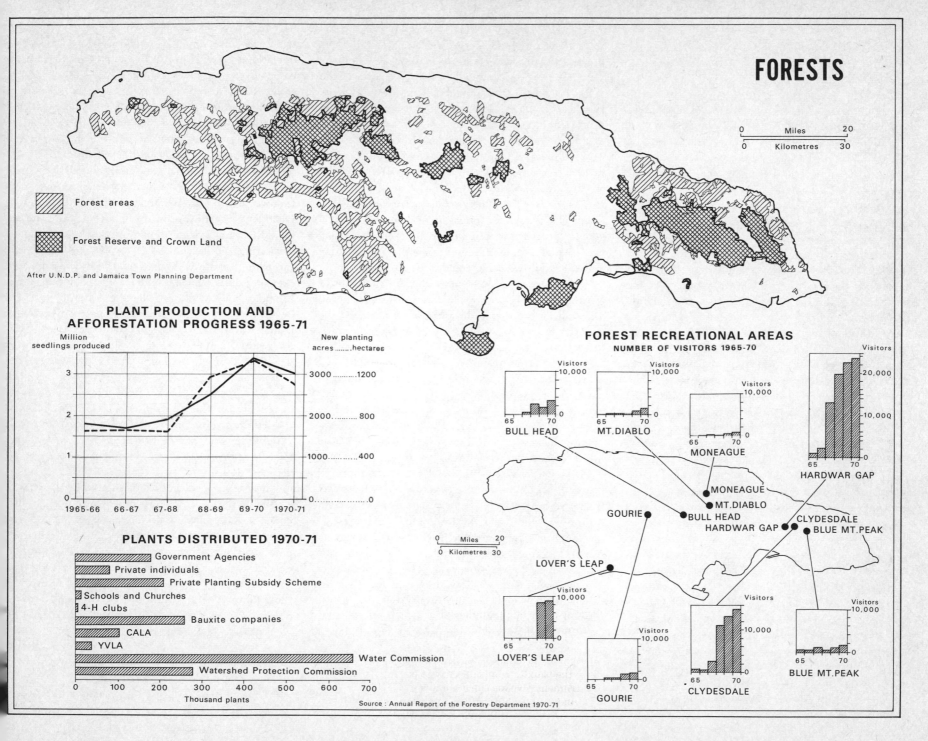

FORESTS

Forest areas

Forest Reserve and Crown Land

After U.N.D.P. and Jamaica Town Planning Department

0 Miles 20
0 Kilometres 30

PLANT PRODUCTION AND AFFORESTATION PROGRESS 1965-71

Million seedlings produced

New planting
acres .... hectares

3 .... 3000 1200
2 .... 2000 800
1 .... 1000 400
0 .... 0 0

1965-66   66-67   67-68   68-69   69-70   1970-71

PLANTS DISTRIBUTED 1970-71

Government Agencies
Private individuals
Private Planting Subsidy Scheme
Schools and Churches
4-H clubs
Bauxite companies
CALA
YVLA
Water Commission
Watershed Protection Commission

0   100   200   300   400   500   600   700
Thousand plants

FOREST RECREATIONAL AREAS
NUMBER OF VISITORS 1965-70

Visitors 10,000
BULL HEAD   65 70

Visitors 10,000
MT.DIABLO   65 70

Visitors 10,000
MONEAGUE   65 70

Visitors
20,000
10,000
HARDWAR GAP   65 70

MONEAGUE
MT.DIABLO
GOURIE   BULL HEAD   CLYDESDALE
HARDWAR GAP   BLUE MT.PEAK
LOVER'S LEAP

0 Miles 20
0 Kilometres 30

Visitors 10,000
LOVER'S LEAP   65 70

Visitors 10,000
GOURIE   65 70

Visitors
10,000
CLYDESDALE   65 70

Visitors 10,000
BLUE MT.PEAK   65 70

Source : Annual Report of the Forestry Department 1970-71

35 BAUXITE

Although the widespread occurrence of aluminium oxide was noted by the first geological survey of Jamaica in 1869, it was not until 1942 that the island's red-earths were identified as low grade (40–50 per cent) bauxite. The deposits contain about 20 per cent iron oxide, but very little silica. They lie in pockets averaging 3 to 9 m (10 to 30 ft) deep on the north and south flanks of the limestone plateau at altitudes of 300 to 600 m (1,000 to 2,000 ft). There is little or no overburden, and open-cast mining has been easy to initiate. The island's reserves amount to about 500 million tonnes, or half the known resources of the Americas. North American companies have been buying land and acquiring options since 1944, and Alcan, Alcoa, Reynolds and Kaiser have extensive operations. The industry is of strategic importance to the USA since bauxite converts to alumina and ultimately to aluminium, which is widely employed in the construction and aircraft industries. Bauxite is also used in abrasives, chemicals, cement, glass and oil.

Reynolds and Alcan began their Jamaican operations with Marshall Aid, and were soon joined by Kaiser. The industry developed rapidly between 1952 and 1960, bauxite's contribution to the island's exports rising from 2 per cent to over 20 per cent. Two alumina plants were constructed by Alcan at Ewarton (244,000 tonnes : 240,000 tons) and Kirkvine (488,000 tonnes : 480,000 tons) to process all the company's bauxite, and by 1960 their output accounted for almost 30 per cent of the island's exports. Subsequent fluctuations in production have reflected us military activity and stockpiling policy, and the opening of new mines by Alcoa. Output of bauxite and alumina substantially expanded in the late 1960s; the industry became the leading contributor to the Gross Domestic Product in 1969, and in the same year accounted for 57 per cent of Jamaica's exports by value.

Each of the operating companies is supra-national and vertically integrated. While mining and drying of the bauxite are carried out in Jamaica, chemical treatment of the ore with caustic soda to produce alumina was originally concentrated at the Gulf ports of the USA. The smelting of aluminium requires very large supplies of power, and this stage is carried out in Canada, the USA and Scandinavia, often using hydro-electricity. Alcan was the first, and for many years the only, company to produce alumina in Jamaica. The critical factor from the Jamaican point of view is the large increase in value added at each stage in processing; to secure the same gross domestic product as is yielded by 30 tonnes (30 tons) of dried bauxite, only 8 tonnes (8 tons) is required if mining and beneficiating are carried out, and the introduction of smelting reduces requirements to 2·4 tonnes (2·4 tons).

Jamaica has been quite successful in its attempt to get the companies to install alumina plant and expand the scale of processing. In 1968 Alcan increased the capacity of its two works to a total 1,219,000 tonnes (1,200,000 tons), and in 1969 Aluminium Partners of Jamaica, a consortium of Kaiser, Reynolds, and Anaconda started production at Nain with an installed capacity of 965,000 tonnes (950,000 tons). Smaller works were opened by Alcoa at Halse Hall, and by Revere at Maggotty in 1971. However, a major disappointment occurred in 1969 when Alcoa announced plans to construct a smelter in Puerto Rico.

Although Jamaica is the world's largest producer of bauxite, it exercises no direct control over the price. Exports are transferred from one branch of the company to another, and the firms cannot be taxed by deducting cost from revenue. At first the government simply accepted the corporations' valuations, and Jamaica earned a very low revenue (£0·13 per tonne) for the first five years of operations. In 1957 half the payment of income tax and royalty was tied to the market price of aluminium. The average yield to the government increased by 500 per cent. No allowances were made for changes in the quality of ore or for changes in production costs. However, negotiations with the bauxite companies have substantially boosted government revenue since 1969.

Bauxite and alumina are important growth-industries, and Jamaica derives numerous benefits from the operations. More than half the income of the railway comes from bauxite and alumina, the bulk loader at Ocho Rios is also used for sugar, and the companies are important land-owners and agricultural innovators. Nevertheless, these industries tend to form enclaves within the Jamaican economy. Most of the companies have built alumina plant and developed their own specialized ports; some have constructed their own railways; and Reynolds have completed an overhead tramway which links the mines to their bulk loader at Ocho Rios. Alumina plant are imported; there are no forward linkages with aluminium smelting and pre-fabricating; no caustic soda is produced in Jamaica; and while bauxite is exported to the Bahamas for the cement industry, none is used locally for this purpose. Labour requirements are slight compared with the capital involved. Only 3,000 were engaged directly in mining in the late 1950s, and each job cost £100,000 to create. Numbers rose in the late 1960s, reaching 9,900 in 1969, but construction work was largely responsible. The average bauxite worker receives over £20 per week, or five times the amount earned in agriculture. This has resulted in pockets of inflation and has incited discontent among other workers.

If the current rate of bauxite extraction is maintained, reserves may be exhausted in two or three decades. Rehabilitation is being carried out where mining has stopped, but the capability of the land is usually diminished. Although the companies receive a depletion allowance, it is the Jamaican government which will eventually suffer the greatest loss. The corporations will transfer their activities to Australian concessions. Some Jamaican economists argue that the other Caribbean producers – Guyana and Surinam – should join Jamaica in formulating a regional bauxite policy. The majority of shares should be taken over by government, in Guyanese fashion, and the industry integrated regionally rather than corporately. Extraction rates should be cut, regional smelters established, and other industrial linkages created.

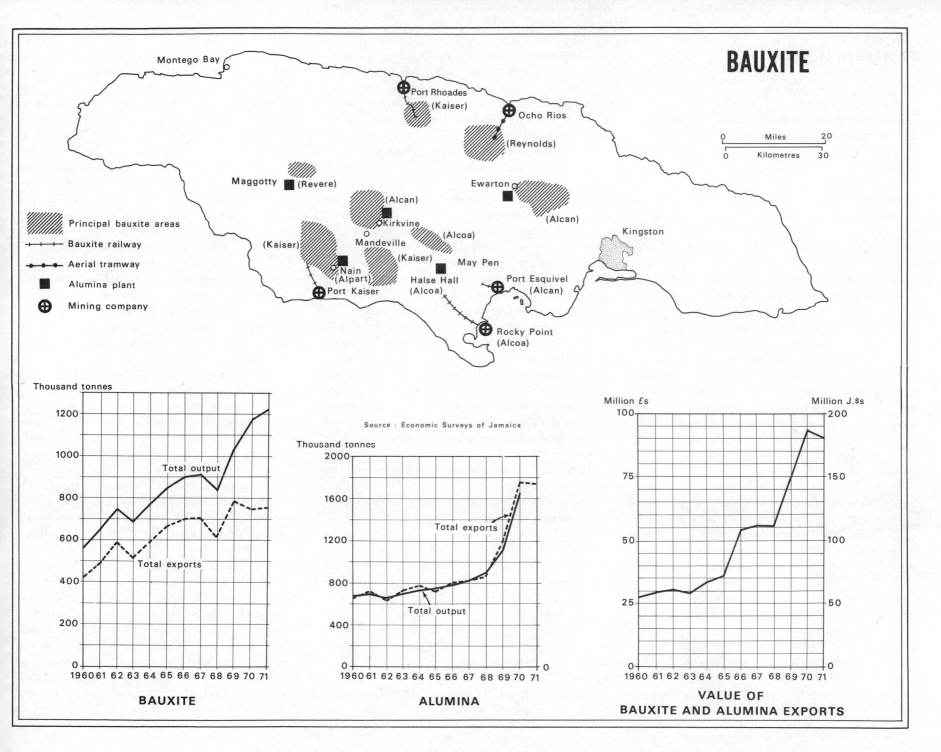

BAUXITE

Montego Bay

Port Rhoades
(Kaiser)

Ocho Rios

(Reynolds)

Maggotty (Revere)

(Alcan)

Ewarton

Kirkvine

(Alcoa)

(Alcan)

(Kaiser)

Mandeville

Kingston

(Kaiser)

May Pen

Nain
(Alpart)

Halse Hall
(Alcoa)

Port Esquivel
(Alcan)

Port Kaiser

Rocky Point
(Alcoa)

Miles 20

Kilometres 30

Principal bauxite areas

Bauxite railway

Aerial tramway

Alumina plant

Mining company

Thousand tonnes

1200

1000

800 — Total output

600

400 — Total exports

200

0

1960 61 62 63 64 65 66 67 68 69 70 71

BAUXITE

Source : Economic Surveys of Jamaica

Thousand tonnes

2000

1600

Total exports

1200

800

Total output

400

0

1960 61 62 63 64 65 66 67 68 69 70 71

ALUMINA

Million £s   Million J.$s
100   200

75   150

50   100

25   50

0   0

1960 61 62 63 64 65 66 67 68 69 70 71

**VALUE OF
BAUXITE AND ALUMINA EXPORTS**

36 MANUFACTURING

The absence of raw materials such as coal and iron-ore, lack of cheap supplies of power, and the adverse influence of British colonial policy, inhibited the development of manufacturing industry in Jamaica. The domestic market was limited by the small size of the population and low *per capita* income. Local entrepreneurs traditionally invested in commerce rather than industry. But by the end of the Second World War a number of manufacturing activities were in evidence. Factories either transformed the island's agricultural output or produced a modest range of unsophisticated consumer goods engendered by wartime import substitution. Grinding of sugar cane remained the largest factory activity in Jamaica, but light industries produced boots and shoes, aerated beverages, beer, cornmeal, copra, edible oils, cigarettes, matches, ice and bread. In Kingston one firm constructed heavy machinery for the sugar factories, and there were a few companies producing rum and cigars of high quality for local consumption and export. The share of manufacturing in the total product of the economy was only 6·5 per cent in 1938; by 1950 it had risen to 11·3 per cent.

Industrial activity has developed rapidly since 1950. Net output of manufacturing increased from £8 million in 1950 to £56 million in 1968, a rate of growth of 7·6 per cent each year at constant prices. The manufacturing sector (13·8 per cent) exceeded agriculture (13·4 per cent) in its contribution to the Gross Domestic Product in 1959, and in 1963 manufacturing (15·2 per cent) surpassed distribution (15·0 per cent) to take top place. However, these statistics treat sugar milling as manufacturing. The acceleration in industrial activity after 1950 was primarily due to encouragement given by the government. Textiles were stimulated in 1947, and a cement monopoly was approved in 1948. An Industrial Development Corporation was set up in 1952, and a variety of tax incentives were offered to local and foreign manufacturers. Furthermore, import duties on steel, iron, non-ferrous metals, crude rubber and leather were reduced to facilitate the creation of new secondary industries. Import licences and quotas were employed to secure the market in footware and edible oils for local manufacturers.

Between 1950 and 1968 the industrial groups experiencing the fastest growth in annual output were cement and clay products (11·3 per cent), textiles and garments (10·7 per cent), metal products (9·6 per cent), food and beverages (7·9 per cent), furniture and fixtures (7·1 per cent). The rise in the production of cement, tiles and building blocks reflected the demands of the construction sector, while the expansion in the output of furniture and fixtures was related to residential development and hotel construction. In view of expenditure patterns in Jamaica, the food and clothing industries were the most feasible in the early stages of industrialization. Metal products developed rapidly under the incentive programme, and recorded a rate of growth far in excess of agriculturally-based industries such as sugar, rum and tobacco. By the late 1960s metal products were the second largest contributor to the gross product from manufacturing; and the non-food and drink sectors together accounted for almost half the value of industrial output. About 50 per cent of the growth in manufacturing was due to import substitution.

The Factory Inspectorate investigates conditions in all manufacturing enterprises employing ten or more persons. Data collected by this body reveal the increase in factories, diversification of output, and high degree of industrial concentration in Kingston and St Andrew.

Inspected factories increased from 627 in 1951 to 924 in 1961 and 1149 in 1970. The food sector, which was outstanding in 1951, was broken into more detailed products at later periods; as time passed, manufacturers of beverages and tobacco declined. Firms producing wood and paper expanded to 1960, then contracted slightly; so, too, did leather manufacturers. Major growth in factory numbers after 1960 occurred in basic metals and machinery, non-metallic products, transport equipment, chemicals, clothing and textiles.

By 1970 a heavy concentration of manufacturing had taken place in Kingston. About 60 per cent of manufacturing enterprises and 66 per cent of factory employment was located in the capital. A further 10 per cent of all factories was situated in St Catherine and 15 per cent of employees. Over three-quarters of manufacturing activity and almost all of the non-agriculturally based factories were located in the contiguous parishes of Kingston, St Andrew, and St Catherine. In the corporate area a relatively wide range of factories and jobs were available, and this was especially so in St Andrew, where the Industrial Development Corporation had established an industrial estate. In contrast, the rural parishes produced food, wood and bakery products; manufacturing employment was heavily dependent on sugar factories.

The agglomeration of factories in and around the capital increased throughout the period 1960 to 1970. The most rapidly industrializing areas, as measured by the increase in the number of factories, were St Andrew (207), Kingston (46) and St Catherine (21). An identical ranking applies to job creation. Kingston contains the island's only substantial market and reservoir of capital. The indifferent quality of country roads inhibits decentralization; and educational and manual skills are centred on the city.

Three more regional features deserve attention: the growth of factory operations at the eastern and western extremities of the island, which reflects government help for two of Jamaica's most backward areas; the absolute decline of industrial activities in St Elizabeth; and the shrinkage of industrial employment in St Elizabeth, Trelawny and Clarendon.

Comparison between material from the Factory Inspectorate and the census of population is instructive. In 1960 only half the workers in Kingston who described themselves as engaged in manufacturing were employed in factories having ten or more people. For Jamaica as a whole the proportion was one-third. Petty manufacturing for men and work as seamstresses for women loom large on the industrial scene.

MANUFACTURING

Source : Reports of Factory Inspectorate

FACTORIES AND EMPLOYMENT BY INDUSTRIAL GROUPS BY PARISHES 1970

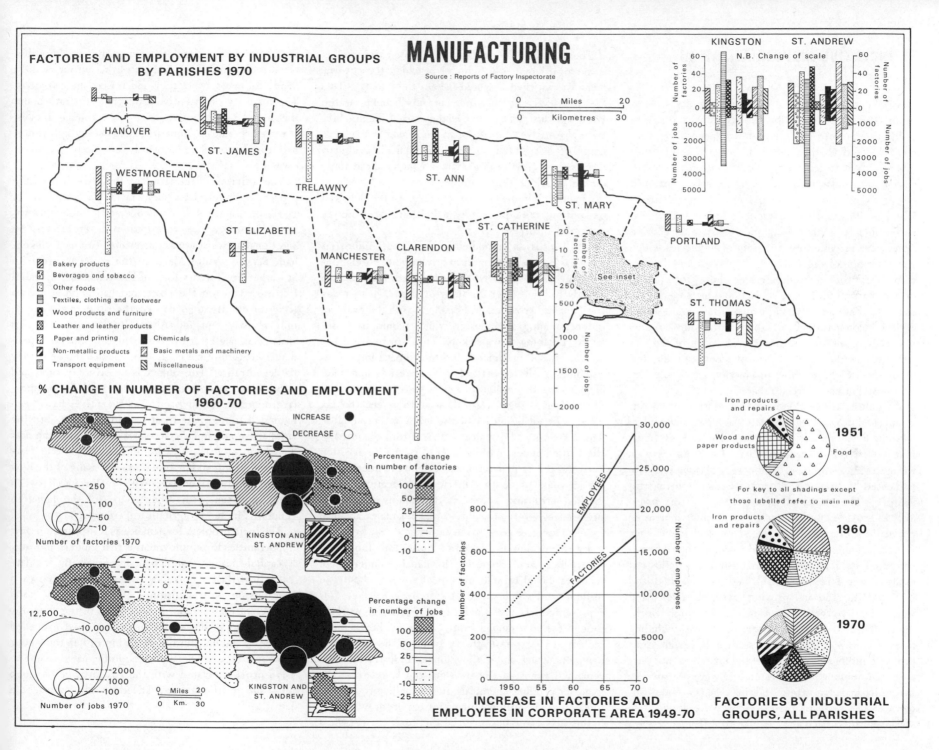

HANOVER

ST. JAMES

WESTMORELAND

TRELAWNY

ST. ANN

ST. MARY

ST ELIZABETH

MANCHESTER

CLARENDON

ST. CATHERINE

PORTLAND

See inset

ST. THOMAS

Miles 0 — 20
Kilometres 0 — 30

KINGSTON   ST. ANDREW

N.B. Change of scale

Number of factories — 60 / 40

Number of jobs — 1000 / 2000 / 3000 / 4000 / 5000

Number of factories — 20 / 10

Number of jobs — 250 / 500 / 1000 / 1500 / 2000

Key:
- Bakery products
- Beverages and tobacco
- Other foods
- Textiles, clothing and footwear
- Wood products and furniture
- Leather and leather products
- Paper and printing
- Non-metallic products
- Transport equipment
- Chemicals
- Basic metals and machinery
- Miscellaneous

% CHANGE IN NUMBER OF FACTORIES AND EMPLOYMENT 1960-70

INCREASE ●
DECREASE ○

Percentage change in number of factories
100 / 50 / 25 / 10 / 0 / -10

Number of factories 1970
250 / 100 / 50 / 10

KINGSTON AND ST. ANDREW

Percentage change in number of jobs
100 / 50 / 25 / 10 / 0 / -10 / -25

Number of jobs 1970
12,500 / 10,000 / 2000 / 1000 / 100

Miles 0 — 20
Km. 0 — 30

KINGSTON AND ST. ANDREW

INCREASE IN FACTORIES AND EMPLOYEES IN CORPORATE AREA 1949-70

EMPLOYEES

FACTORIES

Number of factories: 200 / 400 / 600 / 800

Number of employees: 5,000 / 10,000 / 15,000 / 20,000 / 25,000 / 30,000

1950 / 55 / 60 / 65 / 70

FACTORIES BY INDUSTRIAL GROUPS, ALL PARISHES

Iron products and repairs
Wood and paper products
Food

1951

For key to all shadings except those labelled refer to main map

Iron products and repairs

1960

1970

37 INCENTIVE INDUSTRIALIZATION

In an attempt to diversify the economy and create additional employment, the post-war Jamaican government decided to throw British imperial policy into reverse, and to encourage local entrepreneurs to engage in manufacturing. Copying techniques evolved during 'Operation Bootstrap' in the neighbouring island of Puerto Rico, a Pioneer Industry Law was passed in 1949. Income tax and import duty concessions were provided for a variety of industries which were not already established in the island. Manufacturers were allowed to import free of duty for a period of five years all building materials and machinery used in the factory; and for tax purposes they could set off against income their capital expenditure on building materials, plant and machinery. One-fifth of the expenditure could be set off against income for any five of the first eight years of production and equivalent sums distributed tax free to share-holders.

An Industrial Development Corporation (IDC) was established in 1952 'to stimulate, facilitate, and undertake the development of industry.' The Corporation's first annual report revealed that 'its origins lay in the growing awareness of the very serious problem presented by pressure of population on existing resources.' The object of industrialization was primarily to provide employment for the rapidly increasing population. Emphasis was placed on social efficiency rather than on economic considerations. The IDC concentrated its activities in the capital. An industrial estate of 300 acres was established on reclaimed land in West Kingston and provided with electricity and water. The IDC granted direct loans to supply working capital, and offered a variety of services including market surveys and feasibility studies. In certain cases factory buildings were constructed for rental. But only a limited number of local capitalists were prepared to invest in manufacturing, and in 1956 two new incentive laws were prepared. These were designed to appeal more particularly to investors from overseas.

The Industrial Incentives Law enabled concessions to be awarded to any industry provided the government was satisfied it would benefit the country. This law provided for the same customs benefits as the Pioneer Industry Law, but in the case of income tax, two alternative concessions. Moreover, dividends could be distributed tax free provided the recipient was living in Jamaica or a country which did not apply double taxation. Where tax would have to be paid in the investor's home country as a result of the Jamaican exemption, the concession was withheld and the tax collected locally.

The legislation embodied in the Export Industries Law was potentially the most attractive to foreign investors, and especially to established firms which already had an outlet for their products. In this way the Jamaican government hoped to avoid the problem of encouraging an industry which would have difficulty breaking into markets. These firms were not allowed to sell in Jamaica, but their initial imports of machinery, all imports of raw materials and fuel, and exports of finished products were exempt duty. Furthermore, they were allowed to select the tax reliefs offered by either of the other incentive laws. The proximity of Jamaica to the eastern seaboard of the United States, its low level of wages, its position between the capital resources of North America and the markets of South America, its location in the sterling area and access to Commonwealth tariff preferences, were thought to make Jamaica an ideal location for 'free port' manufacturing.

By the beginning of 1970 almost 200 'footloose' enterprises were operating in Jamaica under these schemes. Fixed capital investment stood at about £30 million, and employment at just over 13,000. This represented an investment of £2,300 per worker, though the sum ranged from £9,000 in the chemical industry to £250 in leather products. The number of firms operating under the Pioneer Industry Law has remained almost stationary since the late 1950s: the majority produce chemicals, non-metallic products or food. Factories manufacturing for export grew rapidly in the early 1960s but received a set back in 1963 when

the United States raised its tariff on imported textiles. Nevertheless, clothing dominates the output of these firms, followed by leather and miscellaneous goods. The majority of incentive enterprises operate under the industrial incentive law, and produce metals, plastics, chemicals, containers and packaging. Almost half the factories are entirely or partly Jamaican-owned.

The activities of the IDC have greatly enhanced the process of industrial agglomeration in Kingston. In 1970, out of the 198 firms operating under government incentives 147 were located in the capital. An additional 24 were situated at Spanish Town – Twickenham Park – White Marl, in the adjacent parish of St Catherine. Twenty-four of the remaining 27 rural factories were on the coast, but had good access to Kingston or Montego Bay via the main road system; only at May Pen and Above Rocks were factories situated in the interior. Nevertheless, since independence an attempt has been made to encourage industry to decentralize. The object is to diversify rural and small-town employment and create work for prospective migrants to Kingston. Tax incentives have been extended to 10 years to attract investments into the rural areas, and industrial estates have been created at Twickenham Park, Yallahs, Eleven Miles, Old Harbour and Montego Bay Freeport. But many of the new firms are industrial enclaves with few linkages between them; and ties with other sectors of the Jamaican economy, including agriculture, are rare.

The basic problem for Jamaica as it searches for new opportunities for employment is that modern industry is capital- rather than labour-intensive. By the late 1960s less than 1,000 jobs were being created each year. Assuming a multiplier effect of 2, the total number of jobs created in all sectors of the economy through the incentive sytem cannot have exceeded 2,000 per annum. But the yearly increase in the labour force was 10,000. Nevertheless, in the period 1960 to 1970 firms associated with the IDC provided 10,000 jobs out of the 15,000 added in all factories in Jamaica.

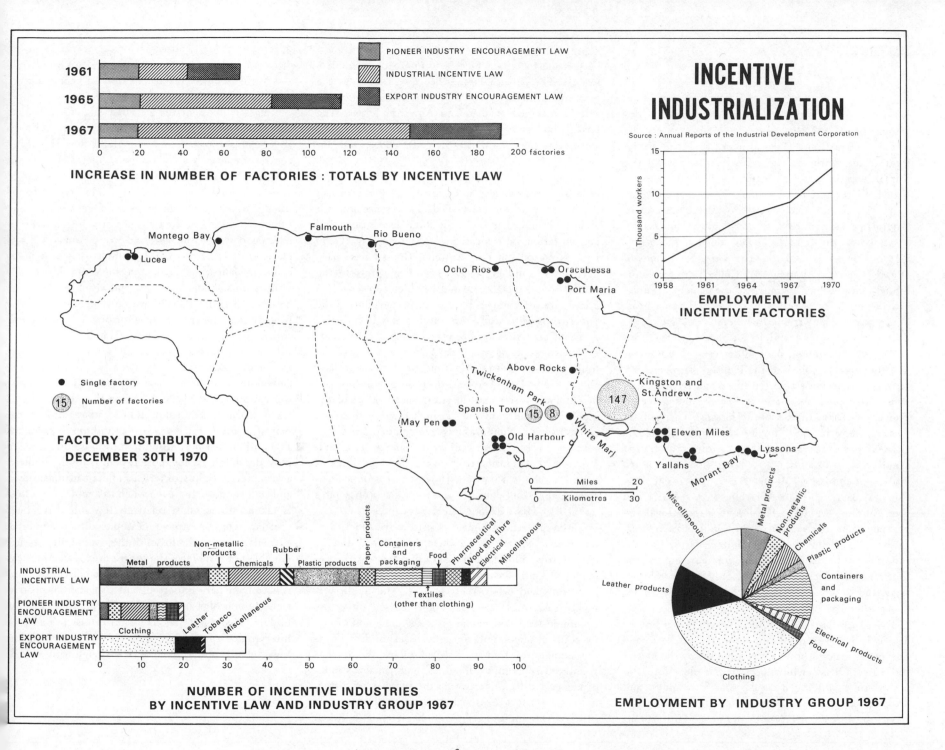

INCENTIVE INDUSTRIALIZATION

Source : Annual Reports of the Industrial Development Corporation

PIONEER INDUSTRY ENCOURAGEMENT LAW

INDUSTRIAL INCENTIVE LAW

EXPORT INDUSTRY ENCOURAGEMENT LAW

1961

1965

1967

0 20 40 60 80 100 120 140 160 180 200 factories

INCREASE IN NUMBER OF FACTORIES : TOTALS BY INCENTIVE LAW

EMPLOYMENT IN INCENTIVE FACTORIES

Thousand workers

15

10

5

0

1958 1961 1964 1967 1970

FACTORY DISTRIBUTION DECEMBER 30TH 1970

Montego Bay
Lucea
Falmouth
Rio Bueno
Ocho Rios
Oracabessa
Port Maria
Above Rocks
Twickenham Park
Kingston and St.Andrew
147
Spanish Town 15 8
May Pen
White Marl
Old Harbour
Eleven Miles
Yallahs
Morant Bay
Lyssons

● Single factory

(15) Number of factories

Miles 0 20
Kilometres 0 30

INDUSTRIAL INCENTIVE LAW

PIONEER INDUSTRY ENCOURAGEMENT LAW

EXPORT INDUSTRY ENCOURAGEMENT LAW

Metal products
Non-metallic products
Chemicals
Rubber
Plastic products
Paper products
Containers and packaging
Food
Pharmaceutical
Wood and fibre
Electrical
Miscellaneous
Textiles (other than clothing)
Clothing
Leather
Tobacco
Miscellaneous

0 10 20 30 40 50 60 70 80 90 100

NUMBER OF INCENTIVE INDUSTRIES BY INCENTIVE LAW AND INDUSTRY GROUP 1967

Miscellaneous
Metal products
Non-metallic products
Chemicals
Plastic products
Leather products
Containers and packaging
Electrical products
Food
Clothing

EMPLOYMENT BY INDUSTRY GROUP 1967

85

38 TOURISM

Jamaica possesses many natural advantages for the development of tourism. Sun, sand and sea are its principal attractions. These are critical factors in the location and rhythm of the industry, which is coastal, primarily associated with white beaches, and seasonal – the hot, wet months are avoided by visitors. Furthermore, the island is close to the world's largest pool of English-speaking tourists, the residents of the USA.

A modest tourist industry developed at the beginning of this century. By the 1920s the coral sands of Doctor's Cave at Montego Bay had achieved a minor reputation, but Port Antonio was the principal centre, and the majority of tourists arrived by banana boat. Visitors to Jamaica trebled between 1929 and 1938. The war intervened, and it was not until the late 1940s that the numbers once more rose above 60,000. The subsequent growth of the industry has been very rapid: 93,000 tourists visited the island in 1950, and figures for 1960 and 1969 were 225,000 and 375,000. The composition of the traffic has also changed. In 1950 74 per cent stayed for less than three nights; by 1969 63 per cent were long-stay visitors. The tourist area forms a discontinuous ribbon along the north coast, encompassing Montego Bay, Discovery Bay, Runaway Bay, Ocho Rios, Oracabessa, Port Maria, and Port Antonio. Montego Bay has an international airport and acts as the hub of the 'gold coast'. International flights link it to the United States, Canada, and the United Kingdom, and 70 per cent of the tourists arrive by air. Miami is only ninety minutes away, and New Yorkers can reach Montego Bay in less than four hours.

The expansion of the hotel industry has depended heavily on government investment, initiative and subsidy. A major stimulus was provided by the Hotels Aid Law of 1944 which permits the duty-free importation of building materials and furnishings, and provides accelerated depreciation allowances. The Hotels Incentive Law (1968) granted additional incentives, including tax holidays. Efforts have also been made to attract increasing numbers of holiday-makers. The Jamaica Tourist Board was set up by the government in 1955, and maintains offices in London and in several Canadian and American cities. The board's budget rose to £1,500,000 in the late 1960s, and promotional activities include widespread advertising.

Accommodation is provided by hotels, guest houses, resort cottages and apartments. Just over half the capacity is foreign-owned. Hotels account for almost three-quarters of the total bed-space, and concentrations are located at Montego Bay, Ocho Rios, Kingston and Port Antonio. Guest houses have declined in number since 1957. They pre-date the tourist boom, and are situated in older centres, often inland. Resort cottages became important during the 1960s, especially near Port Antonio and Ocho Rios. A recent departure has been the leasing of apartments in Kingston and Montego Bay. Over one-fifth of the tourists are on cruises. They anchor at Montego Bay, Kingston and Port Antonio, sleep on board ship, and buy at local stores and duty-free shops. Most of the hotels are small, and only eight had more than 100 rooms in 1965. None was large enough to house a convention on the American scale. Efforts have subsequently been made to provide these facilities at Rose Hall and in Kingston. However, it is difficult to match supply and demand, and room occupancy rates on the island have dropped to 50 per cent.

Three-quarters of Jamaica's visitors are Americans, the most important sources being New York, Illinois, New Jersey, Florida and California. Among the remainder, Canadians are most numerous, followed by Europeans and other West Indians. The industry is highly susceptible to fluctuations caused either by economic recession in the visitor's home country or by political uncertainty in Jamaica. In the late 1950s the number of tourists levelled off as the US encountered economic difficulties, and Jamaica's independence led to a decrease in the number of visitors in the early 1960s. Seasonal variation is also characteristic of the industry, hotel jobs ranging between 6,300 and 4,700. Tourist arrivals concentrate in the dry months between December and March and July and August, but this maldistribution has been gradually reduced by lowering tariffs.

Kingston is essentially a tourist stop for shopping and sight-seeing *en route* to the north coast. Montego Bay possesses restaurants and clubs, but the other centres depend heavily on golf, tennis and beach facilities. Glass-bottomed boats take visitors out to view the coral reef, and sailing, skin-diving, spear-fishing, water-skiing and deep-sea fishing are available. Limousines can be rented and cars hired, but Jamaicans drive on the left, and many Americans stay close to their hotels. Greater emphasis is now being given to Jamaica's scenic interior. Mini-buses take visitors on sight-seeing tours, and visits to plantation houses and to Port Royal are now included in many itineraries. The more adventurous can go pony-trekking, and rafting on the Rio Grande.

Tourism surpassed sugar as a foreign exchange earner in 1965 and has subsequently replaced bauxite and alumina in first place. As an invisible export tourism makes good the deficit on the island's visible trade balance. Estimated tourist expenditure rose from £10 million in 1959 to £23 million in 1965 and £39 million in 1969. In addition to those directly employed in hotels, many more benefit from the industry as chauffeurs, shop-workers, handicraft manufacturers and stall vendors. But even when this multiplier effect is taken into account, relatively few jobs have been created. The investment cost per direct employee exceeds £2,000. The losses to the community are less tangible but insidious. The tourist area is an American enclave and currency is the dollar; 70 per cent of food requirements are imported, and a substantial proportion of the profits are repatriated. While the Jamaican middle class regret the alienation of beaches and the interference of tourism with the environment, the lower class is resentful of the rich foreign whites.

TOURISM

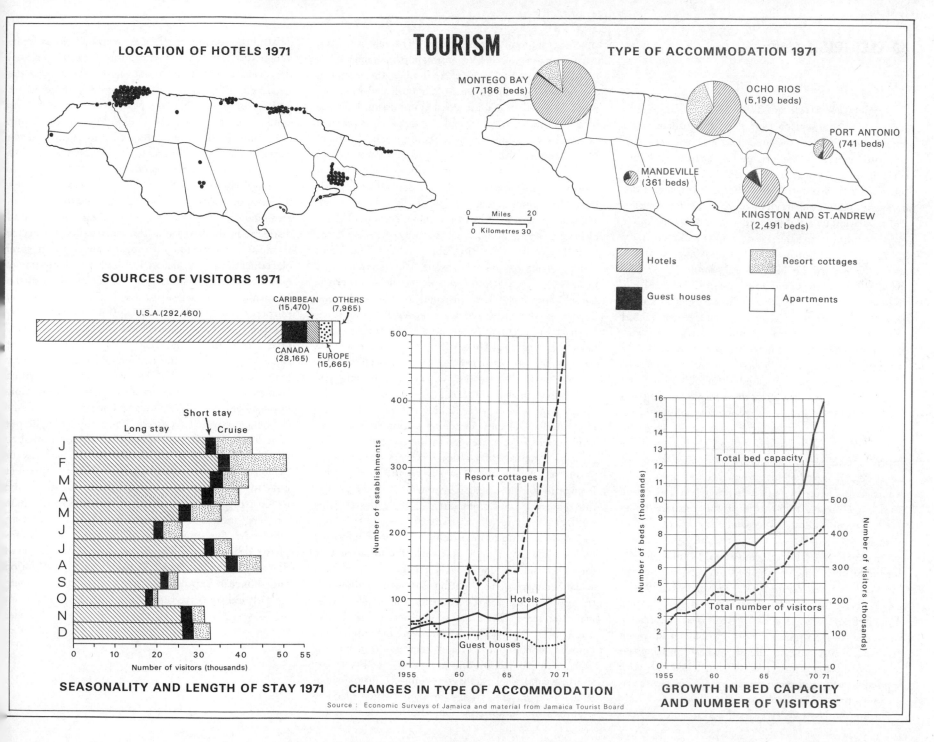

LOCATION OF HOTELS 1971

TYPE OF ACCOMMODATION 1971

MONTEGO BAY
(7,186 beds)

OCHO RIOS
(5,190 beds)

PORT ANTONIO
(741 beds)

MANDEVILLE
(361 beds)

KINGSTON AND ST.ANDREW
(2,491 beds)

0 Miles 20
0 Kilometres 30

Hotels   Resort cottages

Guest houses   Apartments

SOURCES OF VISITORS 1971

U.S.A.(292,460)

CARIBBEAN
(15,470)

OTHERS
(7,965)

CANADA
(28,165)

EUROPE
(15,665)

Short stay

Long stay   Cruise

J F M A M J J A S O N D

Number of visitors (thousands)
0 10 20 30 40 50 55

SEASONALITY AND LENGTH OF STAY 1971

Number of establishments
500
400
300
200
100
0

Resort cottages

Hotels

Guest houses

1955 60 65 70 71

CHANGES IN TYPE OF ACCOMMODATION

Number of beds (thousands)
16
15
14
13
12
11
10
9
8
7
6
5
4
3
2
1
0

Total bed capacity

Total number of visitors

Number of visitors (thousands)
500
300
100
0

1955 60 65 70 71

**GROWTH IN BED CAPACITY
AND NUMBER OF VISITORS**

Source : Economic Surveys of Jamaica and material from Jamaica Tourist Board

39 ELECTRICITY

The generation of electricity is in the hands of the Jamaican Public Service Company, a Canadian-based organization which was incorporated in 1923. The company operates under an exclusive All-Island Electric Licence which was granted in 1966 and is tenable for twenty-five years. The performance of the company and rates charged by it are subject to scrutiny and regulation by a Public Utility Commission. About 60 per cent of the island's requirements of electricity are met by the company, and the remainder is generated privately by the bauxite and alumina concerns, the cement industry and sugar estates. Demand has risen very rapidly since 1950 and more especially since 1960. Growth in private consumption has been caused primarily by expansion of mineral operations: bauxite and alumina accounted for two-thirds of the privately generated total in 1965, rising to over four-fifths in 1969. Public output increased threefold during the 1960s and reflected the growth of manufacturing and tourism, and the expansion of residential consumption.

The economic development of Jamaica since the Second World War has created an urgent need for improvements in the generation and distribution of electricity. In 1950 about 90 per cent of the island's requirements were supplied by the Jamaica Public Service Company, two-thirds of the capacity being accounted for by four hydro-electric stations. There were less than 30,000 consumers, and the grid was rudimentary. A 69 kV transmission line linked Kingston and Spanish Town to the hydro-electric stations at Bog Walk, Upper White River, Lower White River, and Roaring River. Claremont, Brown's Town and Old Harbour were attached to this system; Lucea, Montego Bay, Falmouth, Port Antonio and Black River each had a small diesel generator; Kingston possessed a steam-powered station bunkered with imported coal; and the remainder of the island was without a public supply of power and light.

During the last twenty years this situation has been almost completely transformed. The entire south coast is linked by a 69 kV transmission line, and a similar connection has been carried along the northern coast from Roaring River to Falmouth and Montego Bay. The north and south coast transmission lines are linked via Savanna-la-Mar and Bogue, and it is planned eventually to complete the circuit through Portland and St Thomas. The grid covers 700 kilometres (430 miles), and only to the south-east of Kingston and southwest of Old Harbour does it depend on a 33 kV line. Uneconomic generating units have been closed and small towns have lost their diesel stations; hydro-electric power is no longer produced at Roaring River or at Bog Walk on the Rio Cobre, and the Gold Street plant in Kingston has been shut. New stations have been set up at strategic intervals on the south coast. Diesel units have been installed at Mandeville and Savanna-la-Mar; hydro-electric power has been harnessed at Maggotty Falls; steam and gas-turbine units have been located at Hunt's Bay, Kingston; and three large, steam-powered generators have been brought into service at Old Harbour. Old Harbour has emerged as the nexus of the grid, and 138 kV transmission lines radiate to the Tredegar switching station in St Catherine and the Duhaney switching station in Kingston. This system will be extended by the construction of an eighty kilometre (fifty-mile) link between the Parnassus sub-station and Duncans on the north coast. Eventually the line will be carried to Montego Bay, thus ensuring power not only for the industrializing south coast, but for the tourist areas, too.

The generation of electricity based upon imported combustible materials has provided the infrastructure for social and economic development. The spread of social benefits, such as lighting, has been paralleled by the possibilities for decentralization, especially of manufacturing. However, supply and demand have often been poorly articulated. In the mid-1960s demand increased by 42 per cent while generating capacity expanded by only 14 per cent. Electricity shortages and blackouts were common, and the situation was aggravated by the drought, which placed a premium on pump-irrigation, and by strikes, which delayed the opening of the Old Harbour No. 2 Unit. When this came into operation in 1970 it increased the island's capacity by about one-third. In 1972 the Jamaica Public Service Company was granted a rate increase of 30 per cent, the first for twenty years. The company is to invest £140 million by 1982 to expand the island's generating system to one million megawatts. Capacity will have to be doubled every five years to keep ahead of projected demand.

Transmission lines follow the main roads and link the largest towns: distribution lines serve the urban areas and carry light and power into the remoter rural districts. In the late 1960s the Jamaica Public Service Company was spending £500,000 annually on rural electrification, but financial difficulties temporarily curtailed the scheme in 1970. About one-fifth of the population have access to electricity for domestic purposes. Future projects are planned for Portland, Westmoreland and Hanover, at the eastern and western extremities of the island. A major development since 1957 has been the conversion of the frequency from 40 to 50 hertz. This has been carried out with a loan from the Commonwealth Development Corporation and the Royal Bank of Canada, and the cost is being recovered from consumers by an eight per cent surcharge. The conversion has been essential to the modernization of the system. By the early 1950s manufacturers were producing 40 hertz equipment only to special order: it was difficult to obtain and expensive. Jamaican consumers often had to purchase 50 hertz motors which worked at only 80 per cent efficiency. The importance of the conversion is emphasized by the doubling of customers and trebling of demand during the 1960s. Despite rural electrification and suburban expansion, commercial, industrial and agricultural concerns remain the largest consumers.

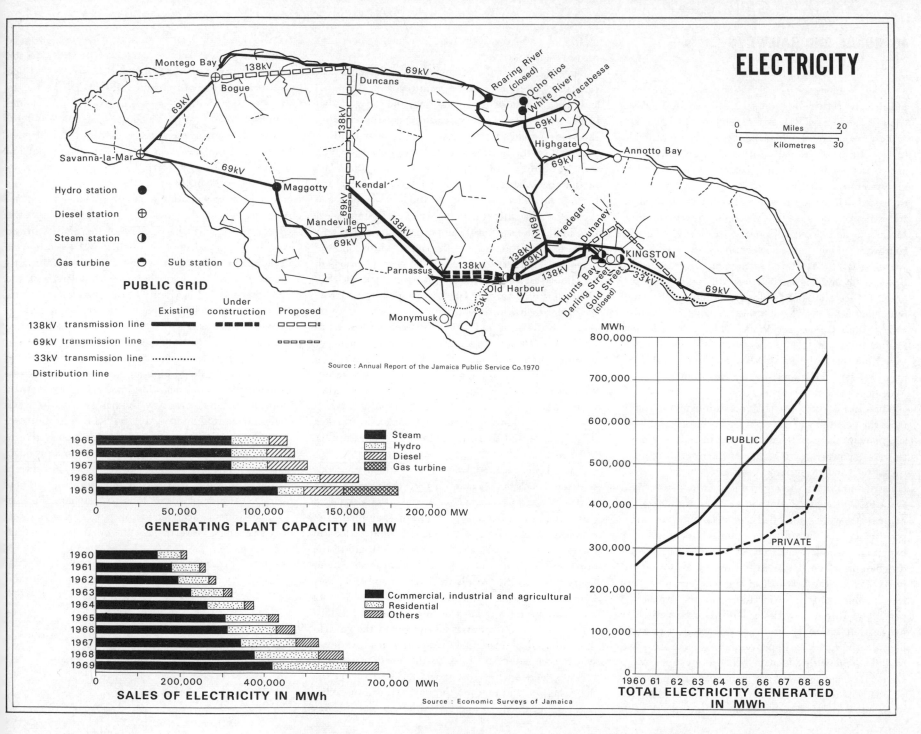

ELECTRICITY

Hydro station ●
Diesel station ⊕
Steam station ◖
Gas turbine ◗   Sub station ○

PUBLIC GRID

	Existing	Under construction	Proposed
138kV transmission line			
69kV transmission line			
33kV transmission line			
Distribution line			

Source : Annual Report of the Jamaica Public Service Co. 1970

Steam
Hydro
Diesel
Gas turbine

0   50,000   100,000   150,000   200,000 MW

GENERATING PLANT CAPACITY IN MW

Commercial, industrial and agricultural
Residential
Others

0   200,000   400,000   700,000 MWh

SALES OF ELECTRICITY IN MWh

Source : Economic Surveys of Jamaica

MWh
800,000
700,000
600,000
500,000
400,000
300,000
200,000
100,000
0

PUBLIC

PRIVATE

1960 61 62 63 64 65 66 67 68 69
TOTAL ELECTRICITY GENERATED IN MWh

40 ROADS AND RAILWAYS

Jamaica is relatively well-served with routeways. Class A and class B roads extend over 4,200 km (2,600 mls), and parochial roads provide a motorable surface for an additional 5,100 km (3,200 mls). The network is densest on the coastal periphery and is integrated by an A-class road which virtually encircles the island. This road turns inland between Black River and Kingston and links up the largest towns. The Blue Mountains and Cockpit Country are devoid of major routeways. Much of the terrain is impassable for vehicles, and the scattered settlements are reached by bridle paths and tracks. North-south routes cross the grain of the relief and are few in number. The most important is the road from Spanish Town to Ocho Rios and St Ann's Bay via Bog Walk, which crosses Mount Diablo at 540 m (1,800 ft). Other high-level routes join Kingston and Annotto Bay via Stony Hill (400 m : 1,350 ft), and Savanna-la-Mar and Montego Bay via Mackfield (300 m : 1,000 ft).

The class A roads existed in a rudimentary fashion from the beginning of the eighteenth century and were supplemented by estate roads which linked the plantations to the nearest port. Some of the interior roads at the eastern and western extremities of the island were constructed during the eighteenth century campaigns against the maroons. From the 1750s to the 1850s the main roads were controlled and maintained by turnpike trusts, but the tolls were numerous and the fees expensive. Goods were frequently carried by coastal droghers between the estate wharves and the official ports. During the first half of the nineteenth century the smaller roads deteriorated, and the expanding peasantry were left with inadequate access to their markets. It was only after 1865 that effective steps began to be taken to improve and extend roads, and to link them with adequate bridges. By 1882 there were 1,200 km (750 mls) of main road and 4,800 km (3,000 mls) of parochial road. In 1909 one kilometre of metalled road existed for every three square kilo-metres of area; this ratio has subsequently been improved by 100 per cent.

Since the end of the Second World War modifications have been made to the main roads on the north and south coasts of the island, and the network has been extended between Lucea and Negril to open up the sandy beaches for tourism. The heaviest traffic is recorded on the north and south coastal routes which meet at Spanish Town on their way to Kingston. The section between the capital and Spanish Town has become severely congested, and the highway between these two settlements is being widened to four lanes. Communications are still hampered by the ruggedness of the terrain, the width of the river mouths, and the height of flood waters. Some of the river crossings in St Thomas are little more than fords, and the Rio Cobre north of Spanish Town is spanned by a narrow flat bridge over which flood waters can rise. Moreover, road improvement and repair has been influenced as much by political considerations as by economic need. In some years over one hundred projects have been financed, the object being to create work for the unemployed, usually before the Christmas festivities. Poor surfaces and narrow roads, the rapid growth in the number of buses, trucks and cars, and cavalier driving, have led to rising accident- and death-rates in Jamaica.

The island is served by a railway which was constructed between 1843 and 1925, the greater part of it between 1885 and 1896. It consists of a standard gauge track, and extends for 333 km (207 mls). The principal lines connect Kingston and Montego Bay in the north-west and Kingston and Port Antonio in the north-east; a junction is located at Spanish Town. Spurs run from Bog Walk to Ewarton and from May Pen to Frankfield. Since its inception by a private company the railway has run into continual financial difficulties. The system was taken over by the government in 1879 and later sold to an American syndicate which completed the lines to the north coast. But receipts were so low that it was unable to meet the debt charges, and in 1900 the railway once more became government property. Although the railway seemed ideal for hauling bulky agricultural produce such as sugar and bananas, much of the track to the west of Porus runs through infertile areas. The line had to compete with coastal transport in the north-east between Annotto Bay and Port Antonio, and after 1920 road transport vied with the entire system.

The alignment of the railway network is conditioned by the 300 m (1,000 ft) contour. The high proportion of steep grades and sharp curves greatly increases operating costs by limiting the number of cars per train and by accelerating wear and tear on equipment. A report published in the early 1950s claimed that the cost of moving freight was one of the highest in the world; the annual operating deficit was £300,000. A decade later the railway was in a perilous state. Passenger traffic declined because of delays and the greater speed and flexibility of the private motor car. Receipts from freight increased, but only very slowly. Bauxite, bananas and sugar were the major commodities handled, but consumer goods imported through Kingston were forwarded by truck. Since 1963, however, congestion on the roads, the purchase of new rolling stock and diesel railcars, and the initiation of a daily, two-way return service between Kingston and Montego Bay and Kingston and Port Antonio, have lifted passenger figures back to the level achieved in the late 1950s. Agricultural products have been entirely switched to the roads, but several bauxite companies have feeder lines into the rail network, and their payments for the growing volume of ore and alumina account for 60 per cent of the railway's receipts. Nevertheless, the operating deficit has increased.

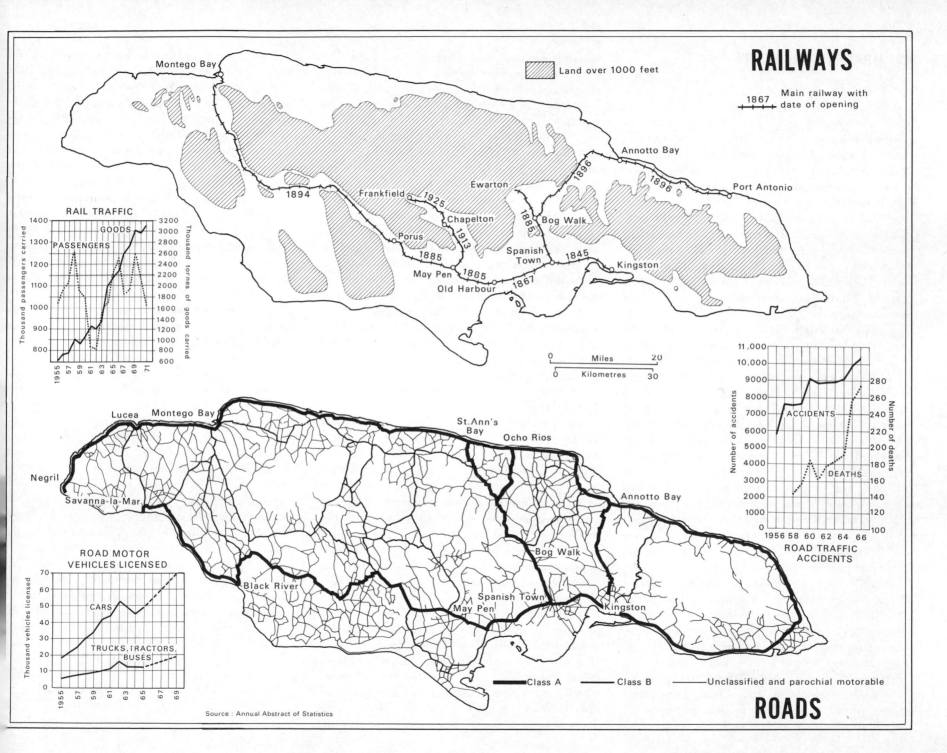

RAILWAYS

Land over 1000 feet

1867 Main railway with date of opening

Montego Bay

Annotto Bay

Port Antonio

Ewarton

Frankfield 1925

1896

1896

Chapelton

1894

1885

Bog Walk

Porus

1913

Spanish Town

1885

1845

Kingston

May Pen 1885

Old Harbour 1867

RAIL TRAFFIC

GOODS

PASSENGERS

Thousand passengers carried

1400
1300
1200
1100
1000
900
800

Thousand tonnes of goods carried

3200
3000
2800
2600
2400
2200
2000
1800
1600
1400
1200
1000
800
600

1955 57 59 61 63 65 67 69 71

Miles 0 — 20

Kilometres 0 — 30

ROAD TRAFFIC ACCIDENTS

Number of accidents

11,000
10,000
9000
8000
7000
6000
5000
4000
3000
2000
1000
0

ACCIDENTS

DEATHS

Number of deaths

280
260
240
220
200
180
160
140
120
100

1956 58 60 62 64 66

Lucea   Montego Bay

St. Ann's Bay

Ocho Rios

Negril

Savanna-la-Mar

Annotto Bay

Bog Walk

Black River

Spanish Town

May Pen

Kingston

ROAD MOTOR VEHICLES LICENSED

Thousand vehicles licensed

70
60
50
40
30
20
10

CARS

TRUCKS, TRACTORS, BUSES

1955 57 59 61 63 65 67 69

Class A   Class B   Unclassified and parochial motorable

ROADS

Source : Annual Abstract of Statistics

41 AIRPORTS AND PORTS

Jamaica's insularity and reliance upon tourism and overseas trade require a wide range of port and airport facilities. The earliest ports were created during the seventeenth and eighteenth centuries and served local coasters, the entrepôt trade with the Spanish Main, and above all the sugar industry. Sugar exports declined after emancipation as production faltered and plantations were amalgamated. But port activities were enlivened by the banana trade at the end of the nineteenth century and by the resuscitation of sugar after 1918. The development of the bauxite industry since 1950 has led to the construction of entirely new port installations.

Jamaica has twelve active ports and six legally recognized but inactive ones: Falmouth, Port Maria, Annotto Bay, Manchioneal, Oracabessa, and Lucea have all ceased operation in the last few years. Kingston possesses by far the biggest harbour and records a volume of shipping which exceeds that of all the other ports. It handles almost two thousand ships a year, nearly twice the figure of the eleven outports. Kingston's trade has grown steadily since the early 1960s, and about 80 per cent of the island's imports cross its wharves. The most important imports are general cargo, especially consumer durables, food, fuel, and machinery. But Kingston ships only about 5 per cent of Jamaica's bulky exports. Primary products are the concern of the outports, and Montego Bay is the only other port which handles general cargo.

Sugar is shipped through Savanna-la-Mar, Black River, Rocky Point and Kingston. Falmouth has recently closed, and the bulk loader at Ocho Rios handles most of the north coast's sugar exports. Bananas are shipped from Port Antonio and Montego Bay; sugar and bananas from Bowden. The smallest ports have shallow draughts and depend on lighterage. They are kept open by inertia and fears of small-town unemployment. Unlike these produce ports, the five bauxite terminals are modern in design, mechanized, heavily capitalized, and sited on deep anchorages. With the exception of the bulk loader at Ocho Rios, they handle only bauxite, and, in some cases, alumina.

International airports have been developed by the government since the Second World War, and both the Norman Manley Airport on the Palisadoes at Kingston and the Sir Donald Sangster Airport at Montego Bay are capable of taking jumbo jets. Scheduled internal flights link Kingston, Port Antonio, Ocho Rios and Montego Bay. A small airfield is available at the industrial estate in West Kingston, and smaller grass or dirt strips are maintained for occasional traffic by the large estates. Jamaica is strategically situated between North and South America, and most of the major West European and North American airlines have established regular flights to the island. Both international airports record large numbers of transit passengers, and Montego Bay has a substantial charter traffic based upon the tourist trade. Air freight is of negligible proportions compared with the volume of sea cargo, though some American-owned factories fly their high value-to-weight products to the United States market.

The provision of port facilities in Jamaica has traditionally been left to private investors. During the last decade two new schemes have been initiated. At Montego Bay a freeport and new harbour facilities were opened by private enterprise in 1968. This development is located on made ground and lies opposite the original port. In addition to the usual wharfage facilities, Montego Freeport contains a berth for cruise ships, a yacht club, apartments, a cold-storage for imports of frozen food, and an Esso tank farm. The old waterfront is now derelict and on the verge of redevelopment under government supervision.

The largest scheme for port improvement is located in Kingston, where the creation of Newport West has released the obsolete waterfront for redevelopment. The new port forms an integral part of a causeway across Hunts Bay which links the city with a new satellite at Portmore. Port improvements in Kingston have been badly needed. By the mid 1960s the proximity of the wharves to the central business district, the generation of heavy traffic flows, narrowness of the streets, frequency of intersections and use of donkey carts for haulage, had brought about the congestion of the entire commercial area. In the port itself, the handling of cargo was slow and hampered by the system of finger piers which, for more than two hundred and fifty years, had supplied berths for visiting ships. Furthermore, the prevailing south-easterly winds made the docking of vessels difficult.

With the demand of shipping for alongside berths and with the possibilities for containerization in mind, a Foreshore Development Corporation was set up by local capitalists to construct Newport West. The area to be developed lay adjacent to a main arterial road, the Marcus Garvey Drive, on the opposite side of which was located Kingston's industrial estate. Paradoxically, the distance of the site from the main ship channel proved an added advantage; material excavated from the harbour to secure a deep-water frontage was deposited seawards of the original coast, creating an area of made ground across which warehouses could be laid out. A similar procedure had been used previously by Esso while establishing their oil terminal and refinery in West Kingston.

By 1966 most of the wharf owners in the old port had created berths at Newport West, and the waterfront adjacent to the city centre was ready for redevelopment. Private property in the old port was rapidly exchanged for publicly-owned facilities at Newport East, and the government set up the Kingston Waterfront Redevelopment Company (later the Urban Development Corporation) to plan and carry out the project. The British firm of Shankland, Cox and Associates was invited to zone the waterfront for shops, offices, hotels, apartments, car parks, public open space, tourist facilities, and cultural activities. The first stage of the scheme was completed during 1973.

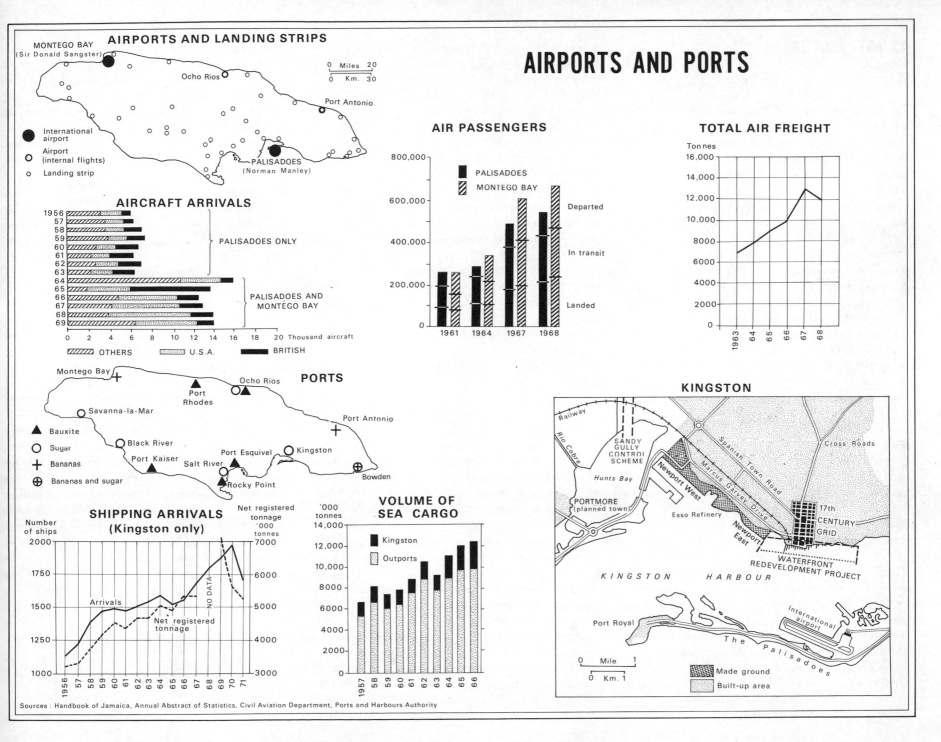

AIRPORTS AND PORTS

AIRPORTS AND LANDING STRIPS

MONTEGO BAY
(Sir Donald Sangster)

Ocho Rios

Port Antonio

PALISADOES
(Norman Manley)

● International airport
○ Airport (internal flights)
∘ Landing strip

0 Miles 20
0 Km. 30

AIRCRAFT ARRIVALS

1956
57
58
59
60
61
62
63
64
65
66
67
68
69

PALISADOES ONLY

PALISADOES AND MONTEGO BAY

0 2 4 6 8 10 12 14 16 18 20 Thousand aircraft

▨ OTHERS   ▦ U.S.A.   ■ BRITISH

AIR PASSENGERS

800,000

600,000

400,000

200,000

0

■ PALISADOES
▨ MONTEGO BAY

Departed

In transit

Landed

1961   1964   1967   1968

TOTAL AIR FREIGHT

Tonnes

16,000
14,000
12,000
10,000
8000
6000
4000
2000
0

1963 64 65 66 67 68

PORTS

Montego Bay

Ocho Rios

Port Rhodes

Savanna-la-Mar

Port Antonio

▲ Bauxite
○ Sugar
+ Bananas
⊕ Bananas and sugar

Black River

Port Kaiser

Salt River

Port Esquivel

Kingston

Rocky Point

Bowden

SHIPPING ARRIVALS
(Kingston only)

Number of ships

2000

1750

1500

1250

1000

Net registered tonnage
'000 tonnes

7000

6000

5000

4000

3000

Arrivals

Net registered tonnage

NO DATA

1956 57 58 59 60 61 62 63 64 65 66 67 68 69 70 71

VOLUME OF SEA CARGO

'000 tonnes

14,000

12,000

10,000

8000

6000

4000

2000

0

■ Kingston
▨ Outports

1957 58 59 60 61 62 63 64 65 66

KINGSTON

Railway

Rio Cobre

SANDY GULLY CONTROL SCHEME

Hunts Bay

Newport West

PORTMORE (planned town)

Esso Refinery

Newport East

Spanish Town Road

Marcus Garvey Drive

Cross Roads

17th CENTURY GRID

WATERFRONT REDEVELOPMENT PROJECT

KINGSTON   HARBOUR

Port Royal

International airport

The Palisadoes

0 Mile 1
0 Km. 1

▨ Made ground
░ Built-up area

Sources : Handbook of Jamaica, Annual Abstract of Statistics, Civil Aviation Department, Ports and Harbours Authority

42 EXTERNAL TRADE

Jamaica has an open economy, and is heavily dependent on exports of primary products and imports of manufactured goods and food. Overseas trade has influenced the economic development of the island, and helped to determine its orientation towards the outside world.

Before the Second World War the United Kingdom was Jamaica's most important trading partner. It received just under 60 per cent of the colony's exports and provided almost 33 per cent of imports. Canada ranked second for exports, the United States second for imports. A drastic redirection of trade took place after 1945, and by the late 1960s the United Kingdom's share of Jamaica's exports dropped to 24 per cent, and its contribution to imports fell to 20 per cent. The United States emerged as the island's major trading partner, and accounted for approximately 40 per cent of both exports and imports. Canada remained in third position behind the United Kingdom, though its relative contribution to Jamaica's trade sank quite considerably.

Factors affecting these shifts were a policy of trade liberalization between the Stirling and Dollar Areas, aggressive salesmanship by North Americans, and above all the rapid growth of the bauxite and alumina industries. Bauxite and alumina supply over half Jamaica's exports: both industries are American- and Canadian-owned, and account for 64 per cent of exports to the United States, and 75 per cent of those to Canada. In contrast, exports to the United Kingdom have remained predominantly agricultural, and levelled off during the 1960s. However, sugar and bananas are labour intensive and derive their viability from preferential entry to the British market. When the United Kingdom decided to devalue its currency in 1967, Jamaica rapidly followed suit.

Although the value of Jamaica's exports increased by over 50 per cent during the 1960s, the cost of imports from North America, in particular, raced ahead.

Attempts at import substitution have saved relatively little foreign exchange; incentive industries tend to be based on imports of fuel and raw materials. Moreover, the growth of national income has led to an even faster increase in imports of certain consumer goods.

A striking feature of the post-war period has been the expansion in the receipt of machinery and transport equipment. These items accounted for 16 per cent of imports in 1950, 28 per cent in 1968. Imports of construction materials, fuels and raw materials have also increased rapidly, and indicate the growth of the bauxite-alumina, tourist, and manufacturing industries. Imports of food, especially from the United States and Canada, increased in value from £4·9 million in 1950 to £28·9 million in 1968. This reflected the rapid growth of the population, the demands of the tourist industry, lagging domestic production, and growing consumer preferences for imported brands. A substantial increase has also taken place in the importation of consumer durables which account for about 40 per cent of consumer imports. The demand for motor cars, refrigerators, radios, televisions and other items of conspicuous consumption has risen rapidly, triggered by a hire-purchase boom in 1960.

Since 1968 a major development has been the formation of the Caribbean Free Trade Association (CARIFTA), whose object is to strengthen commercial links among the former British colonies in the West Indies. Traditionally, these units have been competitive monocultures, separately orientated towards the mother country. Ecology and economy have provided a poor basis for reciprocal trade among the islands. In the mid 1960s less than 5 per cent of Jamaica's overseas trade was with the South-Eastern Caribbean. Since then, however, Jamaica's exports have exceeded imports, and Jamaican manufacturers have been encouraged by CARIFTA to explore the island markets. Exports to the Windwards and Leewards of food, manufactured goods and chemicals have risen substantially, though imports from these territories remain negligible. Jamaica's exports to Guyana exceed the value of its rice imports, but the trade with Trinidad in

petroleum and manufactured goods outvalues Jamaican exports. From Jamaica's point of view, these gains are likely to be short-lived. Increased trade in the period immediately following the creation of CARIFTA has been due primarily to excess capacity in Jamaican industry.

Evidence suggests that the Jamaican economy has become even more reliant on overseas trade during the last two decades. But as trade has expanded, the gap between Jamaica's receipts and payments has widened. This has clearly been the case with regard to trade with the United Kingdom and United States; a similar pattern has slowly emerged in the case of commerce between Jamaica and Canada. Only the dollar earnings of the tourist industry have staved off a balance of payments crisis. The trade gap has been exacerbated by Jamaica's worsening terms of trade: primary products yield lower prices than manufactured articles. Apart from 1957 and 1969, when the value of bauxite and alumina exports was raised by negotiation, and 1963, when world sugar prices rocketed because of Cuba's economic problems, export prices for Jamaican produce have tended to level off since 1955. Worsening terms of trade have retarded the growth of real income as well as the expansion of real import capacity.

The small size and openness of the Jamaican economy have facilitated its penetration by foreign companies, and thereby heightened the island's dependence on overseas decision-makers. Jamaican producers feel themselves at the mercy of middlemen, markets and marketeers. Britain's membership of the European Common Market has caused apprehension in Jamaica, despite the United Kingdom's promise to secure trading concessions from its new partners for sugar and bananas exported from the Commonwealth Caribbean.

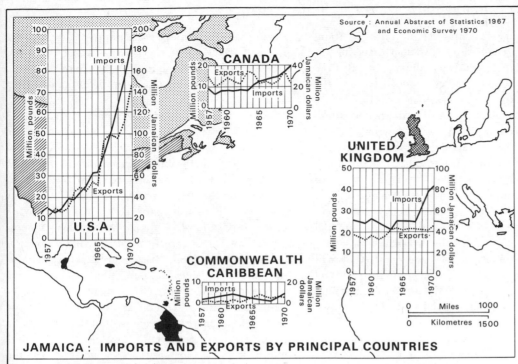

Source : Annual Abstract of Statistics 1967 and Economic Survey 1970

CANADA

Exports

Imports

Million pounds

Million Jamaican dollars

1957 1960 1965 1970

UNITED KINGDOM

Imports

Exports

Million pounds

Million Jamaican dollars

1957 1960 1965 1970

COMMONWEALTH CARIBBEAN

Imports

Exports

Million pounds

Million Jamaican dollars

1957 1960 1965 1970

Imports

Exports

U.S.A.

Million pounds

Million Jamaican dollars

1957 1965 1970

0 Miles 1000

0 Kilometres 1500

JAMAICA : IMPORTS AND EXPORTS BY PRINCIPAL COUNTRIES

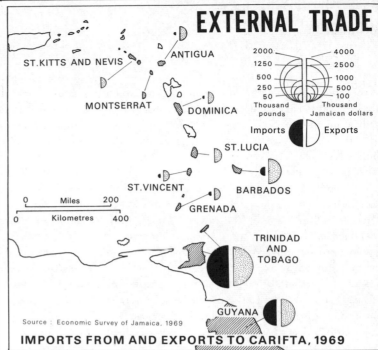

EXTERNAL TRADE

ST.KITTS AND NEVIS

ANTIGUA

MONTSERRAT

DOMINICA

ST.LUCIA

ST.VINCENT

BARBADOS

GRENADA

2000 4000
1250 2500
500 1000
250 500
50 100

Thousand pounds

Thousand Jamaican dollars

Imports Exports

0 Miles 200

0 Kilometres 400

TRINIDAD AND TOBAGO

GUYANA

Source : Economic Survey of Jamaica, 1969

IMPORTS FROM AND EXPORTS TO CARIFTA, 1969

VALUE OF DOMESTIC EXPORTS

Source : Economic Survey, Jamaica, 1969

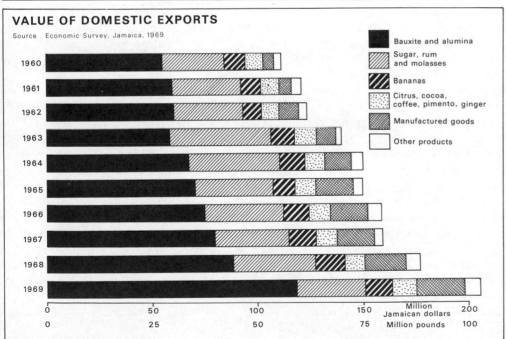

■ Bauxite and alumina

Sugar, rum and molasses

Bananas

Citrus, cocoa, coffee, pimento, ginger

Manufactured goods

□ Other products

1960
1961
1962
1963
1964
1965
1966
1967
1968
1969

0 50 100 150 Million Jamaican dollars 200

0 25 50 75 Million pounds 100

IMPORTS BY ECONOMIC FUNCTION

Source : Economic Survey, Jamaica, 1969

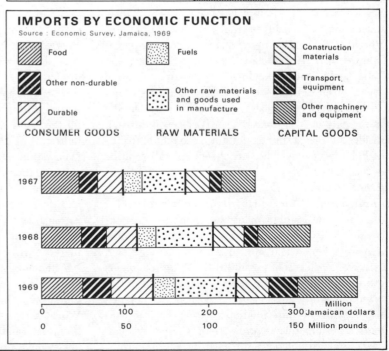

Food

Other non-durable

Durable

Fuels

Other raw materials and goods used in manufacture

Construction materials

Transport equipment

Other machinery and equipment

CONSUMER GOODS   **RAW MATERIALS**   **CAPITAL GOODS**

1967
1968
1969

0 100 200 300 Million Jamaican dollars

0 50 100 150 Million pounds

CONCLUSION

The preceding maps and text are primarily concerned with Jamaican society and economy during the first decade of independence. They do not adequately summarize the changes which have taken place since the People's National Party came to power in April 1972.

The new government, under the leadership of Michael Manley, has committed itself to creating social justice. But the government's determination to improve conditions among the lower class has been constrained by a number of economic difficulties. Economic growth slowed down in 1971, and a drop in tourism occurred in 1972. A price freeze has been necessary to curb inflation; the foreign transfer of funds has been curtailed to rectify the balance of payments; and at the beginning of 1973, the Jamaican dollar, which had floated with the pound, was devalued and pegged to the United States dollar.

Nevertheless, an attempt has been made to tackle Jamaica's problems in an energetic and rather unorthodox fashion. Unemployment has been selected as the major national problem. £5 million is being spent to alleviate conditions, and priority in work allocation is being given to those who have been longest without jobs. Labouring tasks have been carried out in the Sandy Gully in Kingston, roads have been improved, hillsides afforested, public buildings and schools painted. But this is only a palliative; efforts will soon be needed to create developments based on labour-intensive methods.

Agriculture is emerging as the cornerstone of a policy to create employment and economic growth. This sector is more susceptible than others to labour-intensive schemes and intermediate technology, and there are considerable possibilities for improvements both in export marketing and the substitution of imported foodstuffs. Agricultural experts have examined cattle feedlots in Cuba, and hopes are high for improvements in beef and dairy production. The government has set aside 50,000 acres for devotion to food crops,

and Project Food Farms has been put into operation, the Prime Minister himself spending a day digging with 4,000 volunteers. Through displays like this and 'put work into labour day' it is hoped to raise the status of agriculture and manual labour. Moreover, a National Farmers Union has been established to stimulate local activity, and the World Bank has been asked for funds to mobilize the agricultural sector.

Poor housing remains a major source of hardship. A National Housing Corporation has been set up to promote moderate- and middle-income projects. In Kingston, where the situation is at its worst, a number of locations have been selected for site and service schemes. These will be provided with water, electricity and sanitation. It is hoped that they will alleviate pressure on the tenements and yards. Site and service schemes may regulate the process of squatting, since occupants will be allowed to build their own houses.

Illiteracy has been revealed as a major problem: estimates place the number unable to read and write at 500,000. The government has called for 20,000 volunteers to eradicate illiteracy in four years. Schools in Kingston are so overcrowded that two have converted to a shift system. Moreover, the in-service training programme for teachers is being stepped up. Well-educated people remain in short supply. Insufficient school children get the two GCE A levels required to fill the Jamaican quota at the University of the West Indies. More than 2,000 posts in the civil service remain vacant because of the lack of trained candidates.

To facilitate these developments it is intended to lower the birth-rate to 25 per 1,000. The Minister of Health has talked publicly about the necessity for a national demographic policy, and some would like to see this include legalized abortion. One estimate puts illegal abortions at 10,000 cases per annum.

Although it has maintained tax incentives to investors and perpetuates a climate favourable to capitalism, the government has wooed the New World Group, admitted left-wing and black power literature, and removed the mandatory penalty for possessing ganja (cannabis). Moreover, the govern-

ment has adopted a much more positive attitude to the Eastern Caribbean than the Jamaica Labour Party, and has committed the island to membership of the Caribbean Common Market which evolved out of CARIFTA in July 1973.

This programme has received widespread support in Jamaica. Ten years ago poverty was disregarded by the upper and middle classes. Slum dwellers were stereotyped as idlers and the unemployed treated as parasites. The upper and middle classes believed that Jamaica was entering the 'take-off stage', and social scientists producing reports critical of the social and economic scene were castigated as trouble-makers. Now there is a greater awareness of the intractability and seriousness of Jamaica's problems. Black power activists, novelists, the New World Group, film makers, and a burgeoning crime wave, have spelled out the inadequacies of the present situation. Awareness is one thing, action another. Much will depend upon the people's response to government policy. Equally, it is important that the upper classes should appreciate the subtle but important cultural differences between themselves and the lower class. These differences may be crucial to developments in family planning, small farming, medicine and education, to name but a few of the relevant fields.

Jamaica's problems remain almost exactly as they were at independence: the creation of a national identity, a multi-racial concord, and a balance between disharmonious social and economic forces. Social justice will require both a reallocation of resources and a further decline of the birth-rate. It is also essential to lower the aspirations of all social classes to levels consistent with the resources of the island, and to instil in people's minds the idea that there is dignity in agricultural labour. Jamaica's history suggests that the island's entrenched inequalities – and their beneficiaries – will prevent the accomplishment of rapid and substantial change. But modest improvements may be achieved.

BIBLIOGRAPHY

This bibliography includes recent publications on the physical, social, economic and political aspects of Jamaica. Only the most outstanding pre-twentieth century material is cited. General works on the West Indies have been included if they contain a substantial amount on Jamaica or present arguments which are especially relevant to Jamaica. For further bibliographic guidance readers should refer to the following:

COMITAS, LAMBROS, *Caribbeana 1900–1965: a topical bibliography*, Seattle, University of Washington Press, 1968.

NORTON, ANN V. *A bibliography of the Caribbean area for geographers*, Kingston, Department of Geography, University of the West Indies, 3 vols., 1971.

Professor Comitas' guide is multidisciplinary and uses an excellent system of cross-referencing by topic and territory.

The principal social science journal containing work on Jamaica is *Social and Economic Studies*, published by the Institute of Social and Economic Research at the University of the West Indies in Kingston, Jamaica. Other major West Indian journals which are cited are *Caribbean Studies*, produced by the Institute of Caribbean Studies, University of Puerto Rico, Río Piedras; *Caribbean Quarterly*, which is edited from the Department of Extra-Mural Studies, University of the West Indies, Kingston, Jamaica; and *New World Quarterly*, issued by the New World Group in Kingston, Jamaica.

ABRAHAMS, PETER. *Jamaica: an island mosaic*, London, HMSO, 1957.

ADAMS, NASSAU A. 'An analysis of food consumption and food import trends in Jamaica, 1950–1963', *Social and Economic Studies*, vol. 17, 1968, pp. 1–22.

— 'Internal migration in Jamaica: an economic analysis', *Social and Economic Studies*, vol. 18, 1969, pp. 137–51.

— 'Import structure and economic growth in Jamaica, 1954–1967', *Social and Economic Studies*, vol. 20, 1971, pp. 235–66.

AHIRAM, E. 'Income distribution in Jamaica, 1958', *Social and Economic Studies*, vol. 13, 1964, pp. 333–69.

— 'Distribution of income in Trinidad–Tobago and comparison with distribution of income in Jamaica', *Social and Economic Studies*, vol. 15, 1966, pp. 103–25.

ALLEYNE, MERVYN. 'Communication and politics in Jamaica', *Caribbean Studies*, vol. 3, 1962, pp. 22–61.

ANDIC, FUAT M. & MATHEWS, T. G. (eds). *The Caribbean in transition: papers on social, political and economic development*, Proceedings of the Second Caribbean Scholars' Conference, 1964, Río Piedras, Institute of Caribbean Studies, 1965.

ANDRADE, JACOB A. P. M. *A record of the Jews in Jamaica from the English conquest to the present time*, Kingston, *Jamaica Times*, 1941.

*Annual report of the Jamaica industrial development corporation 1952– *, Kingston, Jamaica Industrial Development Corporation.

ARONSON, ROBERT L. 'Labour commitment among Jamaican bauxite workers', *Social and Economic Studies*, vol. 10, 1961, pp. 156–82.

ASPREY, G. F. & ROBBINS, R. G. 'The vegetation of Jamaica', *Ecological Monographs*, vol. 23(4), 1953, pp. 359–412.

ATSU, S. Y. *An economic study of the dairy industry of Jamaica*, St Augustine, Department of Agricultural Economics and Farm Management, University of the West Indies, 1970.

AUGIER, F. ROY. 'The consequences of Morant Bay: before and after 1865', *New World Quarterly*, vol. 2, no. 2, Croptime, 1966, pp. 21–42.

BACK, KURT W. & STYCOS, J. MAYONE. *The survey under unusual conditions: methodological facets of the Jamaican human fertility investigation*, Ithaca, New York, Society for Applied Anthropology, 1959.

BARRETT, LEONARD E. 'The Rastafarians: a study in messianic cultism in Jamaica', *Caribbean Monograph Series*, no. 6, Río Piedras, Institute of Caribbean Studies, 1968.

BECKFORD, GEORGE L. *The West Indian banana industry*, Kingston, Institute of Social and Economic Research, University of the West Indies, 1967.

— 'Toward rationalization of West Indian agriculture' in *Papers presented at the regional conference on devaluation*, Kingston, Institute of Social and Economic Research, University of the West Indies, 1968, pp. 147–54.

— (ed). 'Agricultural development and planning in the Caribbean', *Social and Economic Studies*, vol. 17, 1968, special number.

— *Persistent poverty*, London, Oxford University Press, 1972.

BECKWITH, MARTHA WARREN. *Black roadways: a study of Jamaican folk life*, Chapel Hill, University of North Carolina Press, 1929.

BELL, WENDELL. 'Equality and attitudes of elites in Jamaica', *Social and Economic Studies*, vol. 11, 1962, pp. 409–32.

— *Jamaican leaders: political attitudes in a new nation*, Berkeley, University of California Press, 1964.

BENNET, LOUISE. *Jamaica Labrish*, Kingston, Sangster's Book Stores, 1966.

BLAKE, JUDITH, with STYCOS, J. MAYONE & DAVIS, KINGSLEY. *Family structure in Jamaica: the social context of reproduction*, New York, Free Press, 1961.

BLAUT, JAMES M., *et al*. 'A study of cultural determinants of soil erosion and conservation in the Blue Mountains of Jamaica: progress report', *Social and Economic Studies*, vol. 8, 1959, pp. 403–20.

BLOCH, IVAN & ASSOCIATES. *Electricity load survey for Jamaica*, Portland, Oregon, 1957.

BOLLAND, O. N. 'Literacy in a rural area of Jamaica', *Social and Economic Studies*, vol. 20, 1971, pp. 28–51.

BRADLEY, C. PAUL. 'Mass Parties in Jamaica', *Social and Economic Studies*, vol. 9, 1960, pp. 375–416.

BRATHWAITE, EDWARD. 'Jamaica slave society, a review', *Race*, vol. IX, 1967–8, pp. 331–42.

— *The development of creole society in Jamaica, 1770–1820*, London, Oxford University Press, 1971.

BRENNAN, J. F. *The meteorology of Jamaica*, Kingston, Government Printing Office, 1936.

BREWSTER, HAVELOCK. 'Wage, price and productivity relations in Jamaica, 1957–62', *Social and Economic Studies*, vol. 17, 1968, pp. 107–32.

— 'Sugar-mechanizing: our life or death', *New World Quarterly*, vol. 5, nos. 1 and 2, Dead Season and Croptime 1969, pp. 55–7.

— 'Caribbean economic integration – problems and perspectives', *Journal of Common Market Studies*, vol. XI, June 1971, pp. 282–98.

— & THOMAS, CLIVE Y. *The dynamics of West Indian economic integration*, Kingston, Institute of Social and Economic Research, University of the West Indies, 1967.

BROOM, LEONARD. 'Urban research in the British Caribbean, a prospectus', *Social and Economic Studies*, vol. 1, no. 1, 1953, pp. 113–19.

— 'The social differentiation of Jamaica', *American Sociological Review*, vol. 19, 1954, pp. 115–25.

— 'Urbanization and the plural society' in RUBIN, VERA, *op. cit.*, 1960, pp. 880–86.

BROWN, G. ARTHUR. 'Economic development and the private sector', *Social and Economic Studies*, vol. 7, no. 3, 1958, pp. 103–14.

— 'Sugar without emotion', *New World Quarterly*, vol. 5, nos. 1 and 2, Dead Season and Croptime 1969, pp. 40–41.

BROWN, SAMUEL E. 'Treatise on the Ras Tafari movement', *Caribbean Studies*, vol. 6, 1966, pp. 39–40.

BUCKMIRE, G. E. 'The emergence and resilience of the Jamaican peasantry', *Fifth West Indies Agricultural Economics Conference*, St Augustine, 1970.

BURN, W. L. *Emancipation and apprenticeship in the British West Indies*, London, Jonathan Cape, 1937.

CALLENDER, C. V. 'The development of the capital market institutions of Jamaica', supplement to *Social and Economic Studies*, vol. 14, 1965.

CARGILL, MORRIS (ed). *Ian Fleming introduces Jamaica*, London and Jamaica, Andre Deutsch and Sangster's Book Stores, 1965.

CASSIDY, FREDERIC G. *Jamaica talk: three hundred years of the English language in Jamaica*, London, Macmillan, 1961.

Census of Jamaica 1844, 1860, 1871, 1881, 1891, 1911, 1921, Kingston, Government Printing Office.

Census of Jamaica 1943, population, housing and agriculture, Kingston, Central Bureau of Statistics, Government Printing Office, 1945.

Census of Jamaica 1960, Kingston, Department of Statistics, vols. 1 and 2, 1963–4.

Census of Jamaica 1970: preliminary report, Kingston, Department of Statistics, 1971.

CHAPMAN, V. J. 'The botany of the Jamaica shoreline' in 'Sand cays and mangroves in Jamaica', Report of the Cambridge University Jamaica Expedition, 1939, *Geographical Journal*, vol. XCVI, 1940, pp. 305–28.

CHEN-YOUNG, PAUL. 'The costs of locating an apparel industry in Puerto Rico and Jamaica', *Caribbean Studies*, vol. 8, no. 1, 1968, pp. 3–30.

CLARKE, COLIN G. 'Population pressure in Kingston, Jamaica: a study of unemployment and overcrowding', *Transactions of the Institute of British Geographers*, vol. 38, 1966, pp. 165–82.

— 'Problemas de planeación urbana en Kingston, Jamaica', in *La geografía y los problemas de población*, Union Geografica Internacional, Conferencia Regional Latinoamericana, Tomo I, Mexico, Sociedad Mexicana de Geografía y Estadística, 1966, pp. 411–31.

— 'Aspects of the urban geography of Kingston, Jamaica', D.Phil. thesis, Oxford, 1967.

— 'An overcrowded metropolis: Kingston, Jamaica' in PROTHERO, R. MANSELL, KOSINSKI, LESZEK & ZELINSKY, WILBUR, *Geography and a crowding world*, New York and London, Oxford University Press, 1970 and 1971.

— 'The development and redevelopment of the waterfront in Kingston, Jamaica', *Geography*, vol, 56, 1971, pp. 237–40.

— *Kingston, Jamaica: urban growth and social change, 1692–1962*, Berkeley, University of California Press, 1974.

CLARKE, EDITH. 'Land tenure and the family in four selected communities in Jamaica', *Social and Economic Studies*, vol. 1, no. 4, 1953, pp. 81–118.

— *My mother who fathered me: a study of the family in three selected communities in Jamaica*, London, George Allen & Unwin, 1957, second edition, 1966.

CLARKE, S. ST. A. *The competitive position of Jamaica's agricultural exports*, Kingston, Institute of Social and Economic Research, University of the West Indies, 1962.

COHEN, YEHUDI A. 'The social organization of a selected community in Jamaica', *Social and Economic Studies*, vol. 2, no. 4, 1954, pp. 104–33.

— 'Four categories of interpersonal relations in the family and community in a Jamaican village', *Anthropological Quarterly*, vol. 3, no. 4, 1955, pp. 121–47.

— 'Character formation and social structure in a Jamaican community', *Psychiatry*, vol. 18, 1955, pp. 275–96.

— 'Structure and function: family organization and socialization in a Jamaican community', *American Anthropologist*, vol. 58, 1956, pp. 664–86.

COLLINS, SIDNEY. 'Social mobility in Jamaica with reference to rural communities and the teaching profession', *Transactions of the Third World Congress of Sociology*, vol. 3, 1956, pp. 267–75.

COLLINS, W. G. 'Aerial photography applied to tropical land use', *Chartered Surveyor*, Nov., 1966.

COMITAS, LAMBROS. 'Occupational multiplicity in rural Jamaica', in GARFIELD, VIOLA E. & FREIDL, ERNESTINE, *Symposium on Community Studies in Anthropology*, 1964, pp. 41–50.

COMMONWEALTH ECONOMIC COMMITTEE. 'Jamaica', *Commonwealth development and its financing*, no. 8, London, H M S O, 1964.

CORNISH, VAUGHAN. 'The Jamaica earthquake, 1907', *Geographical Journal*, vol. XXXI, 1908, pp. 245–71.

CRATON, MICHAEL & WALVIN, JAMES. *A Jamaican Plantation: the history of Worthy Park, 1670–1970*, London, W. H. Allen, 1970.

CRONON, EDMUND DAVID. *Black Moses: the story of Marcus Garvey and the Universal Negro Improvement Association*, Madison, University of Wisconsin Press, 1964.

CUMPER, GEORGE E. *The social structure of Jamaica*, Kingston, University College of the West Indies, Extra-Mural Department, 1949.

— 'A modern Jamaican sugar estate', *Social and Economic Studies*, vol. 3, no. 2, 1954, 119–60.

— 'Labour supply and demand in the Jamaican sugar industry, 1830–1950', *Social and Economic Studies*, vol. 2, no. 4, 1954, pp. 37–86.

— 'Population movements in Jamaica, 1830–1950', *Social and Economic Studies*, vol. 5, 1956, pp. 261–80.

— 'The Jamaican family, village and estate', *Social and Economic Studies*, vol. 7, 1958, pp. 76–108.

— 'Tourist expenditure in Jamaica, 1958', *Social and Economic Studies*, vol. 8, 1959, pp. 287–310.

— (ed). *The economy of the West Indies*, Kingston, Institute of Social and Economic Research, University College of the West Indies, 1960.

— (ed). *Report of the conference on social development held at the University College of the West Indies, 1961*, Kingston, Standing Committee on Social Services, 1961.

— 'Preliminary analysis of population growth and social characteristics in Jamaica', *Social and Economic Studies*, vol. 12, 1963, pp. 393–431.

— 'A comparison of statistical data on the Jamaican labour force, 1953–1961', *Social and Economic Studies*, vol. 13, 1964, pp. 430–40.

— 'The fertility of common-law unions in Jamaica', *Social and Economic Studies*, vol. 15, 1966, pp. 189–202.

CUMPER, GLORIA. 'New pattern for Kingston', *Geographical Magazine*, vol. XL, no. 7, 1967, pp. 588–98.

CUNDALL, FRANK. *Historic Jamaica*, Kingston, Institute of Jamaica, 1915.

CURTIN, PHILIP D. *Two Jamaicas: the role of ideas in a tropical colony, 1830–1865*, Cambridge, Harvard University Press, 1955.

DAVENPORT, C. B. & STAGGERDA, M. 'Race crossing in Jamaica', Washington, *Carnegie Institution Publication*, no. 395, 1929.

DAVENPORT, WILLIAM. 'The family system of Jamaica', *Social and Economic Studies*, vol. 10, 1961 (special number on 'Caribbean Social Organization', edited by MINTZ, SIDNEY W. & DAVENPORT, WILLIAM), pp. 420–54.

DAVISON, BETTY. 'No place back home: a study of Jamaicans returning to Kingston, Jamaica', *Race*, vol. IX, 1967–8, pp. 499–509.

DAVISION, R. B. *West Indian migrants*, London, Oxford University Press for the Institute of Race Relations, 1962.

— *Black British: immigrants to England*, London, Oxford University Press for the Institute of Race Relations, 1966.

— 'Labour shortage and labour productivity in the Jamaican sugar industry', Kingston, Institute of Social and Economic Research, University of the West Indies, no date.

DELATRE, R. *A guide to Jamaican reference material in the West Indies reference library*, Kingston, Institute of Jamaica, 1965.

DEMAS, WILLIAM G. *The economics of development in small countries with special reference to the Caribbean*, Montreal, McGill University Press for the Centre for Developing-Area Studies, 1965.

'Demographic and housing statistics', Public Health Department, Kingston and St Andrew Corporation, 1960 and 1967, manuscript.

DEPARTMENT OF STATISTICS. *Report on a sample survey of population, 1953*, Kingston, Government Printing Office, 1957.

— *A survey of housing conditions in Trench Town*, Kingston, 1968.

— *A survey of housing conditions in Delacree Pen*, Kingston, 1970.

DUNCAN, NEVILLE. 'The political process and attitudes in a Jamaican parish council', *Social and Economic Studies*, vol. 18, 1970, pp. 89–113.

DUNCKER, SHEILA J. 'The free coloured and their fight for civil rights in Jamaica, 1800–1830', M.A. thesis, University of London, 1961.

DUNLOP, W. R. 'Queensland and Jamaica: a comparative study in geographical economics', *Geographical Review*, vol. 16, 1926, pp. 548–67.

EBANKS, G. EDWARD. 'Differential internal migration in Jamaica', *Social and Economic Studies*, vol. 17, 1968, pp. 197–214.

— & JACOBS, L. M. 'Jamaique', *Profils Demographiques*, Juillet, 1971, pp. 1–11.

Economic survey of Jamaica 1958– , Kingston, Central Planning Unit.

EDWARDS, BRYAN. *The history, civil and commercial, of the British colonies in the West Indies*, 5 vols., London, 1788–1819.

EDWARDS, DAVID T. 'An economic study of agriculture in the Yallahs Valley area of Jamaica', *Social and Economic Studies*, vol, 3, nos. 3–4, 1955, pp. 316–41.

— *An economic study of small farming in Jamaica*, Kingston, Institute of Social and Economic Research, University College of the West Indies, 1961.

— 'An economic view of agricultural research in Jamaica', *Social and Economic Studies*, vol. 10, 1961, pp. 306–39.

EISNER, GISELA. *Jamaica, 1830–1930: a study in economic growth*, Manchester, University Press, 1961.

ELLIS, ROBERT A. 'Colour and class in a Jamaican market town', *Sociology and Social Research*, vol. 41, 1957, pp. 354–60.

ERICKSEN, E. GORDON. *The West Indies population problem*, Lawrence, University of Kansas Publications, 1962.

EWBANK AND PARTNERS LTD. *Report on the Harbour of Kingston*, Toronto, 1961.

EYRE, L. ALAN. *Land and population in the sugar belt of Jamaica*, Kingston, Department of Geology and Geography, University of the West Indies, Occasional Papers in Geography, no. 1, 1965.

— *Geographic aspects of population dynamics in Jamaica*, Boca Raton, Florida, Atlantic University Press, 1972.

— 'The shantytowns of Montego Bay, Jamaica', *Geographical Review*, vol. 62, 1972, pp. 394–413.

FABER, F. 'A "swing" analysis of the Jamaican election of 1962', *Social and Economic Studies*, vol. 13, 1964, pp. 302–13.

FERMOR, JOHN H. 'The climates of Jamaica', in *Essays on Jamaica*, Kingston, Jamaican Geographical Society, Geology and Geography Department, University of the West Indies, 1970, pp. 30–33.

— 'The weather during northers at Kingston, Jamaica', *Journal of Tropical Geography*, vol. 31, 1971, pp. 31–37.

FIGUEROA, JOHN J. *Society, schools and progress in the West Indies*, Oxford, Pergamon Press, 1971.

FINCH, T. F. 'Soil survey of the area administered by the Yallahs Valley Land Authority', and 'A land-capability classification for the Yallahs Valley Area', both reprinted from *The farmer's guide*, by the Jamaica Agricultural Society, Kingston, no date.

Five year independence plan 1963–68: a long-term development plan for Jamaica, Kingston, Government Printing Office, 1963.

FLOYD, BARRY N. 'Jamaica', *Focus*, vol. XIX, no. 2, 1968.

— 'Rural land use in Jamaica', in *Essays on Jamaica*, Kingston, Jamaican Geographical Society, Geology and Geography Department, University of the West Indies, 1970, pp. 10–29.

— 'Rural land development in Jamaica', *Area*, no. 1, pp. 7–11.

— 'Agricultural innovation in Jamaica: the Yallahs Valley Land Authority', *Economic Geography*, vol. 46, 1970, pp. 63–77.

— 'Agriculture in Jamaica', *Geography*, vol. 57, 1972, pp. 32–36.

FONAROFF, L. SCHYLER. 'Ecological parameters of the kwashiorkor-marasmus syndrome in Jamaica', Berkeley, Department of Geography, University of California, ONR Contract Nonr-3656(83), Project NR 388 067, 1968.

FORESTRY DEPARTMENT. *Annual report notes*, Kingston, 1971, mimeo.

FOUND, W. C. 'A multivariate analysis of farm output in selected land-reform areas of Jamaica'', *Canadian Geographer*, vol. XII, no. 1, 1968, pp. 41–51.

FRANCIS, O. C. *The people of modern Jamaica*, Kingston, Department of Statistics, 1963.

FROUDE, JAMES ANTHONY. *The English in the West Indies, or, the bow of Ulysses*, London, Longmans, Green, 1888.

GARDNER, WILLIAM JAMES. *A history of Jamaica*, London, Elliot Stock, 1873.

GARVEY, AMY JACQUES. *Garvey and Garveyism*, London, Collier-Macmillan, 1970.

GIRVAN, NORMAN. *The Caribbean bauxite industry*, Kingston, Institute of Social and Economic Research, University of the West Indies, 1967.

— 'Bauxite: why we need to nationalize and how to do it', *New World Pamphlet*, no. 6, 1971.

— *Foreign capital and economic underdevelopment in Jamaica*, Kingston, Institute of Social and Economic Research, University of the West Indies, 1972.

— & JEFFERSON, OWEN (eds). *Readings in the political economy of the Caribbean*, Kingston, New World, 1971.

GLASSMER, MARTIN IRA. 'The foreign relations of Jamaica and Trinidad and Tobago, 1960–65, *Caribbean Studies*, vol. 10, 1970, pp. 116–54.

GORDON, HORACE. *Preliminary report of a socio-economic survey of parts of West Kingston*, Kingston, Jamaica Social Welfare Commission, 1961, typescript.

GORDON, SHIRLEY C. *A century of West Indian education: a source book*, London, Longmans, 1963.

GORDON, W. E. 'Imperial policy decisions in the economic history of Jamaica, 1664–1934', *Social and Economic Studies*, vol. 6, 1957, pp. 1–28.

HALL, DOUGLAS G. 'The apprenticeship period in Jamaica, 1834–1838', *Caribbean Quarterly*, vol, 3, 1953, pp. 142–66.

— 'The social and economic background to sugar in slave days (with special reference to Jamaica)', *Caribbean Historical Review*, nos. III-IV, 1954, pp. 149–69.

— *Free Jamaica 1838–1865: an economic history*, New Haven, Yale University Press, 1959.

— 'Slaves and slavery in the British West Indies', *Social and Economic Studies*, vol. 11, 1962, pp. 305–18.

— 'Absentee-proprietorship in the British West Indies to about 1850', *Jamaica Historical Review*, vol. IV, 1964, pp. 15–35.

— 'The colonial legacy in Jamaica', *New World Quarterly*, vol. 4, no. 3, High Season 1968, pp. 7–22.

— 'The ex-colonial society in Jamaica', in EMANUEL DE KADT, *Patterns of foreign influence in the Caribbean*, London, Oxford University Press, 1972, pp. 23–48.

HALL, MARSHALL. 'An analysis of the determinants of money wage changes in Jamaica 1958–64', *Social and Economic Studies*, vol. 17, 1968, pp. 133–46.

HAMILTON, B. L. ST JOHN. *Problems of administration in an emergent nation: a case study of Jamaica*, New York, Frederick A. Praeger, 1964.

Handbook of Jamaica 1960 and 1966, Kingston, Government Printing Office, 1961 and 1967.

HAREWOOD, JACK. *Human resources of the Commonwealth*

Caribbean, Kingston, Institute of Social and Economic Research, University of the West Indies, 1970.

HARRIS, D. J. 'Econometric analysis of household consumption in Jamaica', *Social and Economic Studies*, vol. 13, 1964, pp. 471–87.

HARRIS, R. N. S. & STEER, E. S. 'Demographic-resource push in rural migration: a Jamaican case-study', *Social and Economic Studies*, vol. 17, 1969, pp. 398–406.

HART, RICHARD. *The origin and development of the people of Jamaica*, Kingston, Education Department, Trades Union Congress, 1952.

— 'The life and resurrection of Marcus Garvey, *Race*, vol. IX, 1967, pp. 217–38.

HENRIQUES, FERNANDO. 'The social structure of Jamaica (with special reference to racial distinctions), D.Phil. thesis, Oxford, 1948.

— 'West Indian family organization', *Caribbean Quarterly*, vol. 2, 1952, originally published in *American Journal of Sociology*, vol. 55, no. 1, 1949, pp. 30–37.

— 'Colour values in Jamaican society', *British Journal of Sociology*, vol. 2, 1951, pp. 115–21.

— *Family and colour in Jamaica*, London, Eyre & Spottiswoode, 1953; 2nd edn., London, MacGibbon & Kee, 1968.

— *Jamaica, land of wood and water*, London, MacGibbon & Kee, 1957.

HICKS, J. R. & U. K. *Report on finance and taxation in Jamaica*, Kingston, Government Printing Office, 1955.

HIGMAN, BARRY W. 'Some demographic characteristics of slavery in Jamaica about 1832', Kingston, Department of History, University of the West Indies, Postgraduate Seminars, March, 1969.

— 'Slave population and economy in Jamaica at the time of emancipation', Ph.D. thesis, University of the West Indies, 1970.

HIRSCH, G. P. 'Jamaica – a regional approach', *Regional Studies*, vol. 1, 1967, pp. 47–63.

HOGG, DONALD W. 'The convince cult in Jamaica', *Yale University Publications in Anthropology*, no. 58, 1960, 24 p.

HOYT, ELIZABETH E. 'Voluntary unemployment and unemployability in Jamaica', *British Journal of Sociology*, vol. 11, 1960, pp. 129–36.

HUBBARD, RAYMOND. 'The spatial pattern and market areas of urban settlement in Jamaica', Kingston, Department of Geography, University of the West Indies, 1970.

— 'Some graph-theoretic properties of the Jamaican road network', Kingston, Department of Geography, University of the West Indies, 1971.

HUGGINS, H. D. *Aluminium in changing societies*, London, Andre Deutsch, 1965.

HUGHES, COLIN A. 'Adult suffrage in Jamaica, 1944–55', *Parliamentary Affairs*, vol. 8, 1955, pp. 344–52.

HUGHES, MARJORIE. *The fairest island*, London, Victor Gollancz, 1962.

HURWITZ, SAMUEL J. & EDITH F. *Jamaica: a historical portrait*, London, Pall Mall, 1972.

IMPERIAL COLLEGE OF TROPICAL AGRICULTURE, ST AUGUSTINE. *Soil and land-use surveys for the parishes of Jamaica*, Trinidad, various dates.

INNIS, DONALD Q. 'The efficiency of Jamaican peasant land use', *Canadian Geographer*, vol. 5, 1961, pp. 19–23.

INTERNATIONAL BANK FOR RECONSTRUCTION AND DEVELOPMENT. *The economic development of Jamaica*, Baltimore, Johns Hopkins Press, 1952.

Jamaica, an economic survey, London, Barclays Bank, 1959.

JAMAICA INDUSTRIAL DEVELOPMENT CORPORATION. *A review of industrial development in Jamaica*, West Indies, Kingston, 1961.

JAMAICA PUBLIC SERVICE CO. LTD. *Annual Report*, Kingston, 1970.

JAMAICA TOWN PLANNING DEPARTMENT (PHYSICAL PLANNING UNIT) AND THE UNITED NATIONS DEVELOPMENT PROGRAMME, *National Physical Plan for Jamaica 1970–1990*, vol. 1, Kingston, Government Printing Office, 1971.

— *National Atlas of Jamaica*, vol. II, Kingston, Government Printing Office, 1971.

JEFFERSON, OWEN. 'Some aspects of the post-war economic development of Jamaica', *New World Quarterly*, vol. 3, no. 3, High Season 1967, pp. 1–11.

— *The post-war economic development of Jamaica*, Institute of Social and Economic Research, University of the West Indies. 1972.

KAPP, KIT S. *The printed maps of Jamaica*, Kingston, Bolivar Press, 1968.

KATZIN, MARGARET. 'The Jamaican country higgler', *Social and Economic Studies*, vol. 8, 1959, pp. 421–35.

— 'The business of higglering in Jamaica', *Social and Economic Studies*, vol. 9, 1960, pp. 297–331.

KERR, MADELINE. *Personality and conflict in Jamaica*, Liverpool, University Press, 1952 and London, Collins, 1963.

KERTON, R. R. 'The unemployability hypothesis and the effective supply of effort', *Social and Economic Studies*, vol. 29, 1971, pp. 134–50.

KINGSTON & ST ANDREW CORPORATION. *Official souvenir album of the city of Kingston*, Kingston, 1964.

KIRKWOOD, R. 'A farm production policy for Jamaica', Kingston, Sugar Manufacturers' Association, 1968.

KITZINGER, SHEILA. 'The Ras Tafari brethren of Jamaica', *Comparative Studies in Society and History*, vol. IX, 1966, pp. 33–9.

KNOWLES, W. H. 'Social consequences of economic change in Jamaica', *Annals of the American Academy of Political and Social Science*, vol. 305, 1956, pp. 134–44.

— *Trade union development and industrial relations in the British West Indies*, Berkeley, University of California Press, 1959.

KRUIJER, G. J. & NUIS, A. *Report on an evaluation of the farm development scheme*, Kingston, Government Printer, 1960.

LANGTON, K. P. 'Political partisanship and political socialisation in Jamaica', *British Journal of Sociology*, vol. 17, 1966, pp, 419–29.

LE PAGE, R. B. & DE CAMP, DAVID. *Jamaican Creole*, London, Macmillan, 1960.

LEWIS, GORDON K. *The growth of the modern West Indies*, London, MacGibbon and Kee, 1968.

LEWIS, JAMES O'NEIL. 'A comparison of the economic development of Puerto Rico, Jamaica and Trinidad, 1939–53', B.Litt. thesis, Oxford, 1956.

LEWIS, S., & MATHEWS, T. G. (eds). *Caribbean integration: papers on social, political and economic integration*, Proceedings of the Third Caribbean Scholars' Conference, 1966, Río Piedras, Institute of Caribbean Studies, Puerto Rico, 1967.

LEWIS, W. A. 'The industrialization of the British West Indies', *Caribbean Economic Review*, vol. 2, 1950, pp. 1–61.

— 'Economic development with unlimited supplies of labour', *Manchester School of Economic and Social Studies*, vol. 22, 1954, pp. 139–91.

LIND, ANDREW W. 'Adjustment patterns among the Jamaican Chinese', *Social and Economic Studies*, vol. 7, 1958, pp. 144–64.

LIVINGSTONE, W. P. *Black Jamaica: a study in evolution*, London, 1899.

LONG, ANTON V. *Jamaica and the new order, 1827–1847*, Kingston, Institute of Social and Economic Research, Special Series, no. 1, 1956.

LONG, EDWARD. *The history of Jamaica, or, general survey of the ancient and modern state of that island*, 3 vols., London, T. Lowndes, 1774.

LOVEJOY, R. M. 'The burden of Jamaican taxation 1958', *Social and Economic Studies*, vol. 12, 1963, pp. 452–58.

LOWENTHAL, DAVID. 'The West Indies chooses a capital', *Geographical Review*, vol. 48, 1958, pp. 336–64.

— 'The range and variation of Caribbean societies, *Annals New York Academy of Sciences*, vol. 83, 1960, pp. 786–95.

— (ed). *The West Indies Federation: perspectives on a new nation*, New York, Columbia University Press for the American Geographical Society and Carleton University, 1961.

— 'Race and colour in the West Indies' in 'Colour and race', *Daedalus*, vol. 96, no. 2, 1967, pp. 580–626.

— 'Black power in the Caribbean', *Race Today*, vol. 2, no. 3, 1970, pp. 94–5.

— *West Indian Societies*, London, Oxford University Press for the Institute of Race Relations in collaboration with the American Geographical Society, New York, 1972.

LYNCH-CAMPBELL, H. *The Chinese in Jamaica*, Kingston, 1957.

MACMILLAN, W. M. *Warning from the West Indies: a tract for Africa and the Empire*, London, Faber & Faber, 1938.

McCULLOCH, C. S. 'Some ideas on the sociology of small farming in Jamaica', *Fifth West Indies Agricultural Economics Conference*, St Augustine, 1970, pp. 47–51.

McFARLANE, DENNIS. 'The future of the banana industry in the West Indies', *Social and Economic Studies*, vol. 13, 1964, pp. 38–93.

McINTYRE, ALISTER. 'Some issues of trade policy in the West Indies, *New World Quarterly*, Croptime, 1966, pp. 1–20.

McKENZIE, H. I., ALLEYNE, S. I. & STANDARD, K. L. 'Reported illness and its treatment in a Jamaican community', *Social and Economic Studies*, vol. 16, 1967, pp. 242–79.

McLEOD, DONALD. 'The personal income tax in Jamaica', *Social and Economic Studies*, vol. 18, 1969, pp. 254–63.

MANHERTZ, HUNTLEY. 'An exploratory econometric model for Jamaica', *Social and Economic Studies*, vol. 20, 1971, pp. 198–226.

MANLEY, DOUGLAS R. 'Mental ability in Jamaica', *Social and Economic Studies*, vol. 12, 1963, pp. 51–71.

— 'The Jamaica school certificate examination, 1962', *Social and Economic Studies*, vol. 18, 1969, pp. 54–71.

MANLEY, MICHAEL. 'Overcoming insularity in Jamaica', *Foreign Affairs*, vol. 48, 1970, pp. 100–110.

— *The politics of change: a Jamaican testament*, London, André Deutsch, 1974.

MATHEWS, T. G., *et al. Politics and economics in the Caribbean*, Río Piedras, Institute of Caribbean Studies, University of Puerto Rico, Special Study No. 3, 1966.

MATHIESON, WILLIAM LAW. *The sugar colonies and Governor Eyre, 1849–1866*, London, Longmans, Green, 1936.

MATLEY, CHARLES. *The geology and physiography of the Kingston District, Jamaica*, Kingston, Government Printing Office, 1951.

MAU, JAMES A. 'The threatening masses: myth or reality?' in ANDIC & MATHEWS, *op. cit.*, pp. 258–70.

— *Social change and images of the future: a study of the pursuit of progress in Jamaica*, Cambridge, Mass., Schenkmann, 1968.

MAUNDER, W. F. 'Kingston public passenger transport', *Social and Economic Studies*, vol. 2, no. 4, 1954, pp. 5–36.

— 'The significance of transport in the Jamaican economy', *Social and Economic Studies*, vol. 3, no. 1, 1954, pp. 39–63.

— 'The new Jamaican emigration', *Social and Economic Studies*, vol. 4, no. 1, 1955, pp. 38–63.

— *Employment in an underdeveloped area: a sample survey of Kingston, Jamaica*, New Haven, Yale University Press, 1960.

MILLER, ERROL L. 'Body image, physical beauty, and colour among Jamaican adolescents', *Social and Economic Studies*, vol. 18, 1969, pp. 72–89.

MILROY, DR. GAVIN. *Report on the cholera epidemic in Jamaica*, Kingston, 1852.

MINTZ, SIDNEY W. 'The Jamaican internal marketing pattern', *Social and Economic Studies*, vol. 4, no. 1, 1955, pp. 95–109.

— & HALL, DOUGLAS G. 'The origins of Jamaica's internal marketing system', *Yale University Publications in Anthropology*, no. 57, 1960, 58 p.

MOES, J. E. 'The creation of full employment in Jamaica', *Caribbean Quarterly*, vol. 12, 1966, pp. 8–21.

MOORE, JOSEPH G. & SIMPSON, GEORGE EATON. 'A comparative study of acculturation in Morant Bay and West Kingston, Jamaica', *Zaïre*, vols. 9–10, 1957, pp. 979–1019 and vol. 11, 1958, pp. 65–87.

MORDECAI, JOHN. *The West Indies: the federal negotiations*, London, George Allen & Unwin, 1968.

MORGAN, D. J. 'The growth of Jamaica', *Geographical Magazine*, vol. XL, 1967, pp. 588–98.

MORRISSEY, M. 'A spatial analysis of Jamaica's general elections in 1967 and 1972', Kingston, Department of Geography, University of the West Indies, 1972.

MOSER, C. A. *The measurement of levels of living (with special reference to Jamaica)*, Colonial Research Studies, no. 24, London, HMSO, 1957.

MULCHANSINGH, VERNON C. 'Some thoughts on the industrialization of Jamaica', in *Essays on Jamaica*, Kingston, Jamaican Geographical Society, Geology and Geography Department, University of the West Indies, 1970, pp. 45–53.

— 'Trends in the industrialization of Jamaica', Kingston, Department of Geography, University of the West Indies, 1970.

'Multinational Corporations', *Social and Economic Studies*, vol. 19, no. 4, 1970, special number.

MUNROE, TREVOR & LEWIS, RUPERT. *Readings in government and politics of the West Indies*, Department of Government, University of the West Indies, 1971.

MUNROE, TREVOR. *The politics of constitutional decolonization: Jamaica 1944–62*, Kingston, Institute of Social and Economic Research, University of the West Indies, 1972.

NAIPAUL, V. S. *The middle passage*, London, André Deutsch, 1962.

National plan for Jamaica 1957–1967, Kingston, Government Printing Office, 1957.

NETTLEFORD, REX. 'National identity and attitudes to Race in Jamaica', *Race*, vol. 7, 1965–6, pp. 59–72.

— 'Poverty at the root of race issue' in 'Jamaica: a special report', *The Times*, 14 September, 1970.

— *Mirror, mirror; identity, race and protest in Jamaica*, London and Jamaica, William Collins and Sangster's Book Store, 1971.

— (ed). *Manley and the new Jamaica: selected speeches and writings, 1938–1968*, London, Longmans, 1971.

— 'Manley and the politics of Jamaica', supplement to *Social and Economic Studies*, vol. 20, no. 3, 1971.

NORRIS, KATRIN. *Jamaica, the search for an identity*, London, Oxford University Press for the Institute of Race Relations, 1962.

NORTON, ANN V. 'The Kingston metropolitan area: a description of its land-use patterns' in *Essays on Jamaica*, Kingston, Jamaican Geographical Society and Geology and Geography Department, University of the West Indies, 1970, pp. 34–44.

— & CUMPER, G. E. ' "Peasant", "plantation" and "urban" communities', *Social and Economic Studies*, vol. 15, 1966, pp. 338–53.

NORVELL, DOUGLAS G. & THOMPSON, MARIAN K. 'Higglering in Jamaica and the mystique of pure competition', *Social and Economic Studies*, vol. 17, 1968, pp. 407–16.

NUGENT, MARIA. *Lady Nugent's Journal* (ed. Frank Cundall), London, West India Committee, 3rd edn., 1939.

OLIVIER, SIDNEY. *The myth of Governor Eyre*, London, Hogarth Press, 1933.

— *Jamaica, the blessed isle*, London, Faber & Faber, 1936.

O'LOUGHLIN, CARLEEN. 'Long-term growth of the economy of Jamaica', *Social and Economic Studies*, vol. 12, 1963, pp. 246–82.

ORDE BROWNE, G. ST J. *Labour conditions in the West Indies*, London, HMSO, 1939.

PAGET, ERNEST. 'Land use and settlement in Jamaica' in STEEL, ROBERT W. & FISHER, CHARLES A., *Geographical essays on British tropical lands*, London, George Philip, 1956, pp. 181–223.

— 'Value, valuation and the use of land in the West Indies', *Geographical Journal*, vol. CXXVII, 1961, pp. 493–8.

PAGET, HUGH. 'The free village system in Jamaica',

Jamaica Historical Review, vol. 1, 1945, reprinted in *Caribbean Quarterly*, vol. 10, 1964, pp. 38–51.

PALMER, RANSFORD W. 'Financing corporate investment in Jamaica', *Social and Economic Studies*, vol. 16, 1967, pp. 301–17.

— *The Jamaican Economy*, New York, Frederick A. Praeger, 1968.

PARRY, J. H. & SHERLOCK, P. M. *A short history of the West Indies*, London, Macmillan, 1956.

PATTERSON, H. ORLANDO. 'The social structure of a university hall of residence', *Pelican*, vol. IX, no. 3, March 1962, pp. 22–39.

— 'Slavery, acculturation and social change: the Jamaican case', *British Journal of Sociology*, vol. 17, 1966, pp. 151–64.

— *The sociology of slavery*, London, MacGibbon & Kee, 1967.

— 'West Indian migrants returning home: some observations', *Race*, vol. X, 1968–9, pp. 69–77.

PEACH, CERI. 'West Indian migration to Britain: the economic factors', *Race*, vol. 7, 1965, pp. 31–46.

— *West Indian migration to Britain: a social geography*, London, Oxford University Press for the Institute of Race Relations, 1968.

PECK, E. AUSTIN. 'Economic planning in Jamaica', *Social and Economic Studies*, vol. 7, 1958, pp. 141–69.

PHELPS, O. W. 'Rise of the Labour movement in Jamaica', *Social and Economic Studies*, vol. 9, 1960, pp. 417–68.

PHILLIPS, U. B. 'A Jamaica slave plantation', *Caribbean Quarterly*, vol. 1, no. 1, 1953, pp. 4–13.

PITMAN, FRANK W. *The development of the British West Indies, 1700–63*, New Haven, Yale University Press, 1917.

POST, K. W. J. 'The politics of protest in Jamaica, 1938: some problems of analysis and conceptualization', *Social and Economic Studies*, vol. 18, 1969, pp. 374–90.

PREISWERK, ROY. *Regionalism and the Commonwealth Caribbean*, Port of Spain, Institute of International Relations, University of the West Indies, 1969.

PREST, A. R. *A fiscal survey of the British Caribbean*, London, HMSO, 1957.

RAGATZ, LOWELL J. *The fall of the planter class in the British Caribbean*, New York, American Historical Association, 1928.

REGIONAL CONFERENCE ON DEVALUATION, Kingston, Institute of Social and Economic Research, University of the West Indies, 1968.

REPORT OF THE CHIEF ELECTORAL OFFICER, *Jamaica general election 1959*, Kingston, Government Printing Office, 1959.

— *Jamaica referendum*, Kingston, 1961.

— *Jamaica general election 1962*, Kingston, Government Printing Office, 1963.

— *Jamaica general election 1967*, Kingston, Government Printing Office, 1968.

— *Jamaica general election 1972*, Kingston, Government Printing Office, 1973.

Report of the commission of enquiry into the match industry, Kingston, Government Printing Office, 1955.

Report of the commission on unemployment, Kingston, Legislative Council Minutes, Appendix 41/1936, 1936.

Report of the commission upon the condition of the juvenile population of Jamaica, Kingston, Jamaica Gazette, Supplement, 1880.

Report of the factory inspectorate, 1960, Kingston, 1960, typescript.

Report of the factory inspectorate, 1970, Kingston, 1970, typescript.

REPORT OF THE MISSION OF U.K. INDUSTRIALISTS. *Industrial development in Jamaica, Trinidad, Barbados and British Guiana*, London, HMSO, 1953.

Report of the mission to Africa, Kingston, Government Printing Office, 1961.

Report of the Sugar Industry Enquiry Commission (1966), Kingston, Government Printing Office, 1967.

ROBERTS, GEORGE W. *The population of Jamaica*, Cambridge, University Press for the Conservation Foundation, 1957.

— 'Provisional assessment of growth of the Kingston–St Andrew area, 1960–70', *Social and Economic Studies*, vol. 12, 1963, pp. 432–41.

— 'Urbanization and the growth of small towns in Jamaica', *Jamaica Architect*, vol. 1, no. 3, 1967–8, pp. 69–71.

ROBERTS, GEORGE W. & MILLS, DONALD O. 'Study of external migration affecting Jamaica 1953–55', supplement to *Social and Economic Studies*, vol. 7, 1958.

ROBERTS, W. ADOLPHE. *Six great Jamaicans*, Kingston, The Pioneer Press, 1951.

— (ed). *The capitals of Jamaica*, Kingston, The Pioneer Press, 1955.

ROBERTSON, PAUL. 'Party "organisation" in Jamaica', *Social and Economic Studies*, vol. 21, 1972, pp. 30–43.

ROBINSON, E. 'The geology of Jamaica', in *Essays on Jamaica*, Kingston, Jamaican Geographical Society, Geology and Geography Department, University of the West Indies, 1970, pp. 1–9.

— VERSEY, H. R. & WILLIAMS, J. B. 'The Jamaica earthquake of March 1, 1957', *Transactions of the Second Caribbean Geological Conference*, Mayaguez, University of Puerto Rico, 1960, pp. 50–57.

RODNEY, WALTER. *The groundings with my brothers*, London, Bogle-L'Ouverture Publications, 1969.

ROTTENBERG, SIMON. 'Entrepreneurship and economic progress in Jamaica', *Inter-American Economic Affairs*, vol. 7, no. 2, 1953, pp. 74–9.

RUBIN, VERA, (ed). *Caribbean studies: a symposium*, Kingston, Institute of Social and Economic Research, University College of the West Indies, 1957.

— (ed). 'Social and cultural pluralism in the Caribbean', *Annals of the New York Academy of Sciences*, vol. 83, Article 5, 1960.

SEAGA, EDWARD P. G. 'Parent–teacher relationships in a Jamaican village', *Social and Economic Studies*, vol. 4, 1955, pp. 289–302.

— 'Revival cults in Jamaica', *Jamaica Journal*, vol. 3, no. 2, 1969, pp. 3–13.

SEGAL, AARON, with EARNHARDT, KENT C. *Politics and population in the Caribbean*, Río Piedras, Institute of Caribbean Studies, University of Puerto Rico, Special Study No. 7, 1969.

SEMMEL, BERNARD. *The Governor Eyre controversy*, London, MacGibbon & Kee, 1962.

SENIOR, CLARENCE & MANLEY, DOUGLAS. *Report on Jamaican emigration to Great Britain*, Kingston, Government Printing Office, 1955.

Sesqui-centennial anniversary of the granting of the charter to Kingston 1802–1952, Kingston, 1952.

SEWELL, WILLIAM GEORGE. *The ordeal of free labour in the West Indies*, New York, Harper and Bros., 1861.

SIBLEY, INEZ KNIBB. *The Baptists of Jamaica*, Kingston, Jamaica Baptist Union, 1965.

SILVERMAN, REV H. P. *A panorama of Jamaican Jewry*, Kingston, 1960.

SIMPSON, GEORGE EATON. 'Begging in Kingston and Montego Bay', *Social and Economic Studies*, vol. 3, no. 2, 1954, pp. 197–211.

— 'Political cultism in West Kingston, Jamaica', *Social and Economic Studies*, vol. 4, 1955, pp. 133–49.

— 'The Ras Tafari movement in Jamaica: a study of race and class conflict', *Social Forces*, vol. 34, 1955, pp. 167–70.

— 'Jamaican revivalist cults', *Social and Economic Studies*, vol. 5, no. 4, 1956.

SINGH, PAUL G. *Local democracy in the Commonwealth Caribbean*, London, Longmans, 1972.

SMITH, KARL A. 'Current research on family planning in Jamaica', *Milbank Memorial Fund Quarterly*, vol. XLVI, 1968, pp. 258–70.

SMITH, M. G. 'Some aspects of the social structure of the British Caribbean about 1820', *Social and Economic Studies*, vol. 2, no. 4, 1953, pp. 55–80.

— 'A framework for Caribbean studies' (1955), in his *The plural society in the British West Indies*, pp. 18–74.

— *A report on labour supply in rural Jamaica*, Kingston, Government Printing office, 1956.

— 'Community organization in rural Jamaica', *Social and Economic Studies*, vol. 5, 1956, pp. 295–314.

— 'Education and occupational choice in rural Jamaica', *Social and Economic Studies*, vol. 9, 1960, pp. 332–54.

— 'The plural framework of Jamaican society', *British Journal of Sociology*, vol. 12, 1961, pp. 249–62.

— *West Indian family structure*, Seattle, University of Washington Press, 1962.

— 'Introduction', to CLARKE, EDITH, *My mother who fathered me*, 2nd edn., pp. i-xliv.

— *The plural society in the British West Indies*, Berkeley, University of California Press, 1965.

— & KRUIJER, G. J. *A sociological manual for extension workers in the Caribbean*, Kingston, Department of Extra-Mural Studies, University College of the West Indies, 1957.

— AUGIER, ROY & NETTLEFORD, REX. *The Ras Tafari Movement in Kingston, Jamaica*, Kingston, Institute of Social and Economic Research, University College of the West Indies, 1960.

SMITH, RAYMOND T. 'Jamaican society since emancipation', *Times British Colonies Review*, no. 17, Spring 1955.

— 'A preliminary report on a study of selected East Indians in Jamaica', 1955, typescript.

SPACKMAN, ANNE. 'Electoral law and administration in Jamaica', *Social and Economic Studies*, vol. 18, 1969, pp. 1–53.

STEERS, J. A. 'The cays and palisadoes of Port Royal, Jamaica', *Geographical Journal*, vol. XXX, 1940, pp. 279–95.

STEWART, J. *A view of the past and present state of the island of Jamaica; with remarks on the physical and moral condition of the slaves, and on the abolition of slavery in the colonies*, Edinburgh, Oliver and Boyd, 1823.

STONE, CARL. 'Social class and partisan attitudes in Jamaica', *Social and Economic Studies*, vol. 21, 1972, pp. 1–30.

— *Class, race and political behaviour in urban Jamaica*, Kingston, Institute of Social and Economic Research, University of the West Indies, 1973.

STYCOS, J. MAYONE, & BLACK, KURT W. *The control of human fertility in Jamaica*, Ithaca, New York, Cornell University Press, 1964.

SWEETING, MARJORIE M. 'The Karstlands of Jamaica', *Geographical Journal*, vol. CXXIV, 1958, pp. 184–99.

SZULC, TAD, (ed). *The United States and the Caribbean*, Englewood Cliffs, New Jersey, Prentice-Hall, 1971.

TAYLOR, LEROY. *Consumers' expenditure in Jamaica*, Kings-ton, Institute of Social and Economic Research, University of the West Indies, no date.

TEKSE, KALMAN. *Internal migration in Jamaica*, Kingston, Department of Statistics, 1967.

— *A study of fertility in Jamaica*, Kingston, Department of Statistics, 1968.

THOMAS, C. Y. 'Coffee production in Jamaica', *Social and Economic Studies*, vol. 13, 1964, pp. 188–218.

THOMAS, ELIZABETH M. T. *The Jamaican tourist industry*, M A dissertation, University of Aberdeen, 1967.

THOMAS, R. D. 'Local government financing in Jamaica, 1944–59', *Social and Economic Studies*, vol. 12, 1963, pp. 141–59.

THOMPSON, R. 'The role of capitalism in Jamaica's development', *Caribbean Quarterly*, vol. 12, 1966, pp. 22–8.

THORNE, ALFRED P. 'The size structure and growth of the economy of Jamaica', Supplement to *Social and Economic Studies*, vol. 4, 1955.

— 'An economic phenomenon (study of an apparent psychological trait and its probable effect on regional economic development)', *Caribbean Quarterly*, vol. 6, 1960, pp. 270–8.

TIDRICK, GENE. 'Some aspects of Jamaican emigration to the United Kingdom, 1953–1962', *Social and Economic Studies*, vol. 15, 1966, pp. 22–39.

TIDRICK, K. 'The need for achievement, social class, and intention to emigrate in Jamaican students', *Social and Economic Studies*, vol. 20, 1971, pp. 52–60.

TIMPSON, GEORGE F. *Jamaican interlude*, London, Ed. J. Burrow, 1938.

The town and country planning (Kingston) development order, 1966, Kingston, Government Printing Office, 1966.

TROLLOPE, ANTHONY. *The West Indies and the Spanish Main*, London, Chapman & Hall, 1860.

'Unemployment', *New World Pamphlet*, Kingston, 1967.

VOEKLER, WALTER D. *Survey of industry in the West Indies*, Kingston, Institute of Social and Economic Research, University College of the West Indies, 1961.

West India Royal Commission Report, London, H M S O, 1945.

WHITBECK, R. H. 'The agricultural geography of Jamaica', *Annals of the Association of American Geographers*, vol. 22, 1932, pp. 13–27.

WILLIAMS, ERIC. *Capitalism and slavery*, Chapel Hill, University of North Carolina Press, 1944.

WILLIAMS, JOSEPH J. *Voodoos and obeahs: phases of West Indian witchcraft*, New York, Dial, 1932.

— *Psychic phenomena in Jamaica*, New York, Dial, 1934.

WILLIAMS, R. L. *Industrial Development in Jamaica*, Institute of Social and Economic Research, University of the West Indies, 1971.

WORTHINGTON, E. B. 'Ecology and conservation: Jamaica', *Nature and Resources*, vol. 7, no. 1, 1971, pp. 2–8.

YALLAHS VALLEY LAND AUTHORITY. 'Fifteenth anniversary brochure, 1951–1966', Kingston, 1966.

YIN LEE, T. (ed). *The Chinese in Jamaica*, Kingston, 1957.

YOUNG, BRUCE S. 'Jamaica's long-term development programme', *Social and Economic Studies*, vol. 13, 1964, pp. 370–77.

— 'Jamaica's bauxite and alumina industries', *Annals of the Association of American Geographers*, vol. 55, 1965, pp. 449–64.